# Remembering the "Forgotten War"

# A Study of the Maureen and Mike Mansfield Center

The Maureen and Mike Mansfield Foundation, established in 1983 as a 501(c)(3) nonprofit organization incorporated in Montana, was created to perpetuate the values embodied in Mike Mansfield's distinguished career and to enhance and carry forward the ideals of Maureen and Mike Mansfield by fostering United States-Asia relations, education in Asian studies, and ethics in public affairs.

The foundation supports the Maureen and Mike Mansfield Center at the University of Montana, an academic center focusing on Asian Studies and ethical questions that include Asian contexts and Asian ways of thinking, and the Mansfield Center for Pacific Affairs, designed to promote understanding and improved relations between the United States and the nations of the Asian-Pacific Rim.

**REMEMBERING THE "FORGOTTEN WAR"**
**The Korean War Through Literature and Art**
*Edited by Philip West and Suh Ji-moon*

**LANDSCAPES AND COMMUNITIES ON THE PACIFIC RIM**
**Cultural Perspectives from Asia to the Pacific Northwest**
*Edited by Karen K. Gaul and Jackie Hiltz*

**AMERICA'S WARS IN ASIA**
**A Cultural Approach to History and Memory**
*Edited by Philip West, Steven I. Levine, and Jackie Hiltz*

# Remembering the "Forgotten War"

The Korean War
Through
Literature and Art

Philip West and Suh Ji-moon
editors

AN EAST GATE BOOK

*M.E. Sharpe*

Armonk, New York
London, England·

An East Gate Book

Copyright © 2001 by the Maureen and Mike Mansfield Center

**Library of Congress Cataloging-in-Publication Data**

Remembering the "Forgotten War" : the Korean War through literature and art / edited
by Philip West and Suh Ji-moon.
    p.cm. — (Study of the Maureen and Mike Mansfield Center)
    "East gate book."
    Includes bibliographical references and index.
    ISBN 0-7656-0696-8 (alk. paper)
    1. Korean literature—20th century—History and criticism.  2. Korean War,
1950–1953—Literature and the war. 3. Korean War, 1950–1953–Art and the War.
4. Arts, Korean—20th century.  I. West, Philip, 1938–  II. Sŏ, Chi-mun.  III. Series.

PL957.5.K67 R46 2000
895.7′09358—dc21                                     00-047003

Printed in the United States of America

# Contents

# Foreword

## Looking Back at the Korean War

We Americans like to hang labels on past experiences, identifying them as "good" or "bad" or as a "win" or a "loss." We are often taken aback when a label that once seemed perfectly appropriate suddenly seems wrong, as in the case of our wars with Native Americans. The recent film *Dances With Wolves* completely turned the tables on dozens of Westerns I had seen as a boy in which the American Indians were mowed down, and the U.S. cavalry always came to the rescue.

This process of labeling is particularly difficult when it comes to major foreign wars. World War II continues to "hold still" for us, and we are in the process of virtually deifying those Americans who gallantly fought and won that global conflict.

Vietnam drives us crazy, because we have never been able to put it in clear enough perspective so that we can categorize it. Korea, to the extent that it is recalled at all, is generally considered to have been a noble sacrifice on our part. It contributed to the winning of the cold war, and the Korean people are appropriately grateful to us.

Imagine my surprise last summer when at the Missoula conference, which this book summarizes, I was brought face to face with an entirely new perspective. I found that the Korean artists (writers and poets) at the conference were not particularly grateful to us for our efforts to keep them free. War itself was the villain. And in a variety of ways the Koreans saw the war as having been our fault, either because we stupidly divided their country in 1945 (to accommodate the surrender of the Japanese occupation troops) or because we intervened in a civil war that, had we not intervened, would long since have been settled, with Korea reunited, one way or the other.

As I listened to these rather unexpected viewpoints being expressed I remember thinking, "We Americans think of ourselves as firefighters who bravely kept the Korean house from burning to the ground, and here are the Koreans complaining about water damage from our hoses."

The central problem in all of this is ethnocentrism. As long as we think of Korea, or Vietnam, in terms of what it means to us as Americans, we will never get either war in a clear perspective. The "answers" to Korea or Vietnam do not lie in responses to American questions. If there are ultimate answers, they need to be sought in an Asian context. We Americans were intruders in Asia, onto Asian soil and into Asian history in both Korea and Vietnam. It was mostly Asians who died in those wars, and it is Asians who have been faced with their aftermath. In the long run it is Asian reactions to those wars that will matter most.

Korean and American veterans of the war can still get together and find much to agree on in military terms. This was true in Missoula, where retired General Paik Sun-yup strongly expressed his satisfaction that South Korea had been preserved, although also eloquently voicing his deep regret at the continued tragic division of his country. General Paik's presentations were particularly stirring, embodying his courage as a soldier, his wisdom as a commander, and his gratitude to America for its intervention. Still, this was not the entire story. The conference brought together some of those who had ordered the attacks, fired the mortars, and driven the tanks and those upon whom violence and its aftershocks had been inflicted. Their perspective was entirely different.

What I heard in Missoula was deeply affecting and profoundly informative. It is my hope that readers of this book will be motivated, as I have been, to try to shed their ethnocentric skin and develop a vicarious sensibility.

Donald Gregg, President
The Korea Society

# Preface

In our pursuit of evenhandedness and objectivity, we historians and other scholars are mindful of the pitfalls of present-mindedness. Yet try as we might to prevent present concerns from overly influencing how we write about the past, we find it nearly impossible—and perhaps not desirable—to do so.

Separating the past from the present is particularly difficult in the case of the Korean War. Its impact on Korean life and on Korean-American relations nearly half a century later is still very powerful. The meanings and interpretations of its effect remain highly contested and will likely be so for years to come.

It is our hope that the cultural approach taken in this book highlights the human dimensions of war in innovative ways and nourishes a genuinely cross-disciplinary and cross-cultural dialogue. We are pleased if the book resonates with President Kim Dae Jung's "sunshine policy" and the momentous turn of events that we have seen on the Korean peninsula in recent months.

The winding road leading up to the Mansfield Center's project, "America's Wars in Asia: A Cultural Approach," began with my discovery, about fifteen years ago, of Suh Ji-moon's translation of Yun Heung-gil's short story, "The Rainy Spell." I was then teaching a unit on the Korean War in a course on American–East Asian relations and trying to convey to American college students the human dimensions of a war that was far removed from their personal lives and classroom learning. Yun's "Rainy Spell" did just that better than any other text or film available at the time and certainly better than any of my classroom lectures.

Since then, the road has taken many turns, culminating in the Korea-America Dialogue on the Korean War, held in June 1999. Much of the Dialogue's success must be credited to Ji-moon's commitment to the project, her excellent understanding of Korean sensibilities, and her high personal and professional standing among the Korean participants. In addition to co-organizing the Dialogue she prepared the English subtitles for Im Kwon-taek's film, *The Taebek Mountains*, for screening in the Dialogue. The magnitude of her contribution to the Dialogue is reflected in the three chapters she has written for the book.

Fifteen years ago I did not expect ever to have the chance to meet the author of "The Rainy Spell" and the other Korean writers, historians, artists, and military leaders who participated in the Dialogue—Pak Wan-sŏ, Kim Won-il, Hong Sŏng-won, Yi Mun-yŏl, Paik Sun-yup, Roe Jae-ryung, Ohn Chang-il, and Hong Hae-kyung. I deeply appreciate the warm support and encouragement of the American writers, diplomats, scholars, and journalists who participated in the week-long Dialogue—Max Desfor, Richard Kim, David McCann, Donald Gregg, Desaix Anderson, William Ehrhart, Rolando Hinojosa-Smith, Lary May, Elaine Tyler May, Don Oberdorfer, and Edward Baker.

The America's Wars project is inspired by the spirit of Mike Mansfield, whose decades of professional service are underscored by his uncommon appreciation of the historical and cultural underpinnings of American–East Asian relations. In the understated language of his Montana upbringing, "It never hurts to listen to the other side." Now ninety-seven years old, Mansfield is remembered for his eleven years as the American ambassador to Japan and his role in ending the war in Vietnam. But this is a good opportunity to recall that his first writing about Asia— nearly seven decades ago— was on Korea in a graduate thesis, "American Diplomatic Relations with Korea, 1866–1910" (1934). In keeping with Senator Mansfield's spirit, we plan for the day when the voices of North Korean people will be included in this cross-cultural dialogue.

We gratefully acknowledge Yu Ch'un-do for permission to use her poems in chapter 2; Keith Wilson and Rolando Hinojosa-Smith for permission to cite their poems in full in chapter 3; the artists and art museums in Seoul for permission to use their artwork in chapter 4, and Roe Jae-ryung for arranging those permissions; the Associated Press for permission to use Max Desfor's photography in chapter 5; the Academy of Motion Pictures Library for permission to reproduce the stills from American films, chapter 7; the Korean Film Arts Center in Seoul for permission to reproduce stills from Lee Kwang-mo's *Springtime in My Hometown,* chapter 7; and the National Archives for permission to reproduce photos of Chinese POWs, chapter 9.

Many thanks to the Maureen and Mike Mansfield Foundation and the National Endowment for the Humanities for core funding of the

America's Wars in Asia project and the Korea-America Dialogue on the Korean War of which it is a part. Our thanks too for the generous grants from the Korea Overseas Culture and Information Service and the Daesan Foundation in Seoul and those of the University of Montana Foundation in Missoula and the Korea Institute at Harvard University.

My thanks to Steven Levine for the rigor of his intellect and his cheerful collaboration on the project over the past seven years. Thanks too to Doug Merwin for his enthusiastic support for the project going back six years and to his colleagues at M.E. Sharpe, Patricia Loo and Angela Piliouras, for their help in preparing the manuscript. A final note of thanks to the staff of the Mansfield Center for their help with the Dialogue and to Amber Schwanke, a former student, for working closely with us in pulling the manuscript together.

Philip West
Missoula, September 2000

\* \* \*

When I translated "The Rainy Spell," I was happy to have discovered a short story that superbly captures the tragedy and the paradox of the Korean national division, but I never imagined how many friends the story would bring me and into what avenues it would lead me. Many were the gracious recognitions and compliments I received as the translator of the story, and each time I was deeply grateful. My pride and joy were boundless when, at the end of the Dialogue on the Korean War, Philip West told me that "The Rainy Spell" first inspired him with the idea of approaching America's wars in Asia through the "human dimension."

When Philip, whom I first met at the Association for Asian Studies Conference in 1997, asked me for help in organizing the Korea-America Dialogue on the Korean War, I consented readily and gladly. I worked on the preparations to the best of my ability, and I was gratified that the Dialogue was thought successful by observers and seemed to be profoundly meaningful to the participants. Personally, I found the Dialogue to be truly one of the greatest experiences of my life. I was a serious, committed student of Korean history and Korean fiction that probe into Korean's historical travails, but, if it hadn't been for the Dialogue, I would never have learned so much about my own nation's past nor felt so deeply my compatriots' tragedy. It was a profoundly saddening experience, but also tremendously enriching. I feel that I was only half a person before I came to study the Korean War comprehensively and purposefully. Additionally, the Dialogue led me to look for and translate poems on the Korean War. For me every translation project is a labor of love, but the deep pride and humility I felt while working on this one have been unique.

I felt that the Dialogue was truly a dialogue. There was some friction, perhaps a little offense given and taken, but almost everyone respected the candor of others and recognized that everyone was speaking from genuine feeling and from a need to give voice to his or her thoughts, not to score a point or show off acumen. And that was the objective of the Dialogue.

In a relationship between two countries, even two such friendly and mutually supportive countries as Korea and the United States, offenses are bound to occur and misunderstandings to arise. Owing to the great imbalance of power and wealth between Korea and America, Korea had too great an expectation of care and beneficence, while at the beginning America was profoundly ignorant about Korea and was unprepared to be the shaper of its destiny. There should have been a serious and thoughtful examination into the causes of mutual distrust and animosity (even though greatly overbalanced by goodwill and grateful appreciation) to prevent the relationship from degenerating and becoming distorted.

The Dialogue was an admirable start. When participants on each side unlocked their memories and revealed their true feelings about the other, one got a better sense of how one side's words and actions affected the other and how to address and perhaps redress the mistakes of the past. One six-day dialogue cannot solve the accumulated frictions and problems of more than half a century, but it was a great step toward that goal. A very small portion of the wisdom gained through the Dialogue is contained in this volume. The digital resource library being created by the Mansfield Center will make available, to anyone interested, the materials necessary for reliving the war from both points of view—Korean and American.

Going over the entire book once more for final copyediting, I was gratified by how well all the chapters read (although it is embarrassing for a contributing author to say this), how they not only inform us but speak to us as human beings. So, let me repeat that I felt honored to be part of the project.

I am grateful to all the contributors; to all those who participated in the Dialogue; to Mr. Park Young-gil, former director of Korea Overseas Culture and Information Service; Director Yun Sang-chul of Daesan Foundation; all the staff of the Mansfield Center; and Angela Piliouras and others at M.E. Sharpe. And I respectfully acknowledge the vision, the unwavering patience, and unremitting hard work of Philip West.

Suh Ji-moon
Seoul, September 2000

*Note:* In the matter of Romanization, the McCune-Reischauer system was used in principle. But we have followed slight deviations for cases of clear personal preference, for most widely known forms of Romanized names, or for names of fictional or cinematic characters appearing in the translated text or in subtitles. There are also instances of generally accepted usage, such as in "dong," an administrative unit.

# Remembering the "Forgotten War"

# 1
## Some Reflections on the Korean War

### *Steven I. Levine*

As Americans born in the middle third of the twentieth century, men and women of my generation have lived most of our lives in war or in the shadow of war. This is true even of those like myself who have never hefted a more serious weapon than a BB gun or worn a uniform other than that of the Boy Scouts or academic robes. Born on the cusp of World War II, we passed through childhood during the Korean War, graduated from college during the "long peace" of the cold war, and embarked upon our careers during the Vietnam War. For a student of international relations like myself, an abstract grasp of war as an element of international politics grates against a visceral understanding of the terrible intimacy of war. I realize that, consciously or not, we bear upon us and within us the scars of each one of the far too many wars our nation has fought within our lifetimes. At least, we *should* bear these scars. If we do not, we have failed the memories of everyone on all sides of each conflict.

Our memories of "good wars"—wars in whose justice we continue to believe—are more nearly alike than our memories of "bad wars"—wars that either at the time or in retrospect we acknowledge were mistaken, fought in error, or both. Of America's twentieth-century wars in Asia, the Pacific War, as part of the global antifascist crusade, retains for most Americans its aura of a good war even though the atomic bombings of Hiroshima and Nagasaki that marked its termination are bitterly contested. The Vietnam War, like the nasty counterrevolutionary war fought in the Philippines at the beginning of the twentieth century, has long since fallen into disrepute, becoming a matter for regret if not quite for apology. We like to think our motives in Vietnam were good, even if we acted in ignorance and arrogance. Whether this is true or not is another matter.

What of Korea? On this fiftieth anniversary of the outbreak of the Korean War, a war no longer forgotten, the jury is still out, perhaps because the war itself has not yet ended. When we engage in the sometimes unnerving exercise of confronting our own preconceptions with the memories, passions, and judgments of others, Koreans in particular, we are nonplussed. This is what happened during the Mansfield Center's Korea/America Dialogue in June 1999, which gave birth to the present book. On that occasion, some of South Korea's most distinguished writers repeatedly voiced bitter anti-American sentiments. Although I, too, have been quite critical of U.S. policy in South Korea, I was still surprised to hear these sentiments. After all, if not for U.S. intervention in Korea, these writers would likely be intellectual serfs in Kim Jong-il's dismal kingdom. The explanation for their bitterness, of course, lies in politics rather than ingratitude. When we as Americans consider the fate of Korea over the past half century, our memories and our judgments tend to be divided like Korea itself. When we contemplate the role that the United States has played in the politics of the Korean peninsula since the end of World War II, judgment is no easier. To get at the truth, we must hack our way through a thicket of thorny questions.

Even where to begin our interrogation of history is far from self-evident. Does the American share of responsibility for the tragedy of Korean history begin with the division of Korea in 1945? Or should it be pushed further back to supposed U.S. acceptance of Japan's domination of Korea in 1905 via the Taft-Katsura Agreement, an agreement the significance of which, incidentally, the newer scholarship has discounted? If we begin with 1945, we need to consider what role the division of Korea by the United States and the Soviet Union in July of that year played in the sequence of events leading to the Korean War. Had the United States not rescued South Korea in the summer of 1950, would a unified communist Korea over the past half century have exacted a toll in Korean lives and suffering similar to that of communist regimes in China and Vietnam? How can one measure such a hypothetical cost against the terrible loss of life and human suffering that the Korean War actually brought about?

After the Korean War, the United States supported South Korean authoritarian military rulers Park Chung Hee and Chun Doo Hwan, invoking the security threat from North Korea as grounds for overlooking the repressive character of the generals' regime. At the strategic level, the United States treated South Korea as just another pawn in the cold war. Throughout the postwar years, should the United States have intervened more effectively to support the forces for democratic change in South Korea?

Hanging over these and many more questions is the very status of a divided Korea with its painful separation of families, allocation of enormous resources to military security, hair-trigger confrontation between two garrison states, and periodic armed skirmishes along land and sea frontiers. Is this division a historical enormity so monstrous that it overshadows the emergence of a prosperous, democratic South Korea, home to two-thirds of Korea's people? It is difficult, if not impossible, for outsiders to empathize with, or even fully comprehend, the ache in the heart and the anger in the gut that the division of Korea engenders among Koreans, both north and south.

That the Korean War haunts very few Americans the way it haunts many Koreans, particularly from the older generations, is only natural. Nevertheless, wars have a way of taking hold of our memories. Among children, an awareness of war is part of a growing consciousness of the world outside of home, family, and local community. My own boyhood memories of growing up in Indiana and New York City during the Korean War are rather banal, but their very banality may shed a weak shaft of light on the political climate of the times. It was a paranoid time, dominated by fears of war and communism that percolated down from the national level into communities and families across the country.

The national emergency declared by President Truman in mid-December 1950 did not pass unnoticed in the Frances B. Slocum Elementary School I attended in Fort Wayne, an industrial city in northeast Indiana, where my family lived for two years. Sometime during that terrible first year of the war, my fourth-grade teacher informed her class of a wastepaper collection drive occasioned by the war in Korea. The little red wagon I had received for my ninth birthday was pressed into service as my personal contribution to the national mobilization for the Korean War. Thereafter, I regularly hauled down our driveway for collection at the curb neatly tied bundles of the *Fort Wayne News-Sentinel*. Even in retrospect, I admit to some difficulty in understanding the link between this act and the fighting going on in Korea, my first vague awareness of which came from the pages of that same newspaper. But it felt good to be doing one's bit for the war effort.

Several months later we moved from Fort Wayne to New York City. Just before Christmas 1951, at Public School 187 on Cabrini Boulevard in upper Manhattan, my homeroom schoolmates and I assembled Christmas stockings for hospitalized Korean War combatants from items we had each brought from home. On our grubby lists, we carefully checked off "comb, soap, pencil, pad of paper, hard candies, playing cards," and assorted other trinkets that were intended, I suppose, to help the wounded forget their amputated limbs and shattered bodies. It was many years later, reading Chinese-language accounts of the Korean War, that I learned Chinese schoolchildren had prepared very similar "comfort bags" (*weidai*) for delivery to the far greater number of Chinese wounded in Korea. (Given the primitive state of medical services in the Chinese People's Volunteers, and the devastating effects of UN weapons, including napalm and flamethrowers, only a fraction of Chinese troops with serious wounds survived.)

Around this time, my political consciousness took a great leap forward. I graduated from the *Fort Wayne News-Sentinel* to the *New York Times,* the *New York Post* (a liberal newspaper in the 1950s), the odd copy of the *Herald-Tribune*, and even an occasional issue of the *World-Telegram and Sun*. Precocious and indiscriminate reader that I was, a Korean geography of battles was drilled into my head by a daily drumbeat of datelines from that tortured peninsula, halfway around the world from New York. My parents were 1930s leftists who, I learned much later, had been hounded out of Fort Wayne following the publication of an article by the nationally syndicated columnist Victor Reisel viciously attacking them as Progressive Party (Henry Wallace) moles, Jewish Reds from New York, who had "infiltrated" a God-fearing midwestern community. Amidst the clutch of newspapers we received in our Manhattan apartment was the *National Guardian*, a "fellow traveling" newsweekly, which regularly carried dispatches from Korea by Wilfred Burchett, an Australian communist journalist. Burchett, who spent a long career reporting on the hot spots of the cold war from the other side of the lines, conveyed a quite different version of the Korean War from that transmitted by the mainstream American press. His telling reversed the heroes and villains, the triumphs and tragedies of the war. It was, I realize now, a very useful lesson on the complexities of politics and history.

This was also, of course, the era of the early cold war, when fear of a nuclear Armageddon was almost palpable. In 1953, the Boy Scout troop to which I briefly belonged was tasked by our scoutmaster with the job of establishing an alternative neighborhood communications network that could function after the expected Soviet nuclear attack had destroyed the telephone system. I instinctively balked at becoming a link in what I thought was a paranoid fantasy but, lacking the courage to tell the scoutmaster, I invented some pretext to drop out. It was around this time that New York schoolchildren were issued aluminum dog tags so that our charred and/or vaporized corpses could be easily identified after the nuclear holocaust. I'm unsure who was supposed to undertake this grim task—perhaps Boy Scouts on a field trip from suburban Westchester or Connecticut, which lay outside the prime impact area.

One other source of my early education about the Korean War may be mentioned briefly—Korean War comic books, which I and most of my friends read voraciously. The early 1950s were the twilight of the golden age of comics.[1] The genre of combat comic books, which had flourished during and after World War II, now turned to Korean War themes, depicting heroic GI's battling brownish-yellow hordes of North Korean and Chinese troops. Portrayed as unwitting pawns in the Kremlin's world conspiracy, communist forces were usually shown engaging in "human wave" attacks, proof positive of the Oriental disregard for human life. (That Kim Il-sung and Mao Zedong were doing Stalin's dirty work was a common theme in both low and high American discourse at the time. It was unfortunately true that Mao, and probably Kim as well, regarded his troops as a disposable commodity in plentiful supply.[2]) Oddly, a very few U.S. Korean War comics intimated the common humanity of the communist enemy. Their deaths in combat, it was suggested, were no cause for celebration because these poor innocents, too, left behind grieving mothers, wives, and children. But such humanistic comics were the exception. The standard comic book version of the Korean War, a morality tale of good versus evil, echoed the line of our national media and our national leaders. Needless to say, with three such disparate sources of information at my disposal—the mainstream press, the *National Guardian*, and Korean War comics— my childish understanding of the Korean War was confused and incomplete. It has remained so ever since. This, I now realize, is the proper condition for a teacher and historian like myself.

During the Korea/America Dialogue, Professor David McCann, a leading scholar of Korean literature, brought up Mikhail Bakhtin's notion of heteroglossia. The concept refers to a cacophony of disorderly and centrifugal voices that, by their very existence, implicitly challenge the tidiness of official narratives.[3] This idea, which subverts master narratives and monolithic truths in favor of multiple subjectivities, is very near in spirit to the Mansfield Center's America's Wars in Asia project. Our project seeks to make accessible a broad and disparate range of Asian, American, and other voices on the wars. We believe that listening to and engaging such a panoply of voices will help enrich our understanding of war in all of its complexity.

One of the first orders of business is what to call the Korean War, a problem that historians have wrestled with for several decades. William Stueck's chapter in this volume (see chapter 10) provides a critical discussion of the various labels that have been attached to the Korean War. Here, just a few words are in order. At various points in the Korea/America Dialogue, participants referred to the Korean War as a necessary war, a civil war, an international war, a tribal war, and an unfinished war.

Although I accept Stueck's labeling of the Korean War as an international war, I would like to highlight the notion of Korea as an unfinished war in three ways. First, and most obvious, the political and military conflict between North and South Korea is still unresolved, and the international ramifications arising from the conflict continue as well. Therefore, the Korean War, which may seem a mere interjection between the Pacific War and the Vietnam War, is actually the longest of the three wars. The Korean War is unfinished in another sense. There is not, and probably never will be, a consensus among historians as to its origins, its outcome, and its significance. If anything, the temperature of the scholarly discussions on the war has risen recently. A case in point is the contentious round table on the Korean War that took place at the January 2000 meeting of the American Historical Association, where leading scholars again failed to agree on how to categorize the Korean War. To be sure, this is the normal state of affairs, and it is what makes history a living discipline. One may suppose that even when the Korean War has achieved the antiquity of, say, the Peloponnesian War, historians will still debate its meaning. The Korean War is unfinished in yet a third sense. It has become a living part of our cultural as well as historical heritage in the realm of literature, the arts, film, music, and many other kinds of expression. Although much good literature and art have already been created on Korean War themes, the experiences and memories of the war will continue to inspire writers and artists for a very long time to come. Unfinished in these two realms of historical explanation and the humanities, the Korean War, like all wars, enriches the human experience, terrible as it may seem to say so.

Central to the historical question of the origins of the Korean War is the concept of responsibility, at the levels of both the nation-state and the individual decision maker. For students of the Korean War, one of the most exciting developments of the past decade or two has been the increasing availability of new research materials, including selective archival and memoir material from Soviet and Chinese sources as well as materials in English and Korean (see chapter 9). Access to these materials allows scholars to explore some of what had previously been forbidden zones, although we still await unfettered access to Chinese and Korean archives. The new sources shed considerable light on such critical questions as the role of the Soviet Union and China in the origins of the Korean War, the Chinese decision to intervene in the fall of 1950, the controversy concerning the UN's alleged use of biological weapons during the war, and the armistice negotiations. These new sources enrich the scholarly discussion of the Korean War.

Soviet and Chinese sources in particular enable scholars to achieve a better understanding of the role that individual leaders played in the decision for war in Korea. To focus on Stalin, Mao, and Kim Il-sung is not at all to deny that large-scale historical forces were at work on the Korean peninsula in the period 1945 to 1950. But the well-known centralization of foreign policy decision making in both the USSR and the PRC during this period requires that we focus on the motivations, calculations, thoughts, doubts, and actions of these men. To cite but two examples, we now know that Stalin refused Kim Il-sung's request for Soviet support of a North Korean invasion of South Korea on two occasions before finally agreeing early in 1950. We also know that Mao agonized over the question of whether to dispatch Chinese troops to Korea, pacing the floor for several nights.

A focus on elite-level decision making, however, need not preclude an interest in the activities of the "little people" who fight, suffer, and die in wars, and the civilians whose lives are uprooted, twisted, and often destroyed. Every one of the persons impacted by war has a story to tell, a colored pebble to add to the mosaic. Several of the Korean writers at the Korea/America Dialogue referred to the relative powerlessness of writers to influence history. The point should not be overstated. One remembers Aleksandr Solzhenitsyn's dictum that the writer is an alternate government. (Vaclav Havel proved that point in Czechoslovakia.)

The writer can be an alternate voice in the sense of being a teller of truths that subvert official lies, of being a moral conscience for a people, a repository of cultural traditions, the bearer of hope in apparently hopeless situations. Korean writers, who take as their mission the bearing of witness and the promotion of national reconciliation, have already made extraordinary contributions to history by participating in the struggles for democracy and social justice that took place in South Korea over the past generation and more.

Yet the role of writers, like that of other intellectuals, is shaped by the society in which they work. The differences between the functions of literature on the American and South Korean sides of the war, for example, reflect the very different experiences of the two countries in the war itself. Literature is produced within specific historical and political contexts, and it is the exceptional writer who speaks in universal terms. In all of the countries centrally involved in the Korean War, including the United States, there have been what are in effect forbidden zones, the boundaries of which writers and artists approach at their peril. As the boundaries shift over time, it becomes possible to speak the hitherto unspeakable, to question official shibboleths, to probe the painful heart of memory.

Writing about war is often a form of exorcising ghosts, of banishing Banquo from the feast of the living. Yet it is no less true, as Hong Sŏng-won noted at the Korea/America Dialogue, that "writers have the duty to be heartbroken on behalf of the dead." The most poignant of the Korean War poems (see chapters 2 and 3) give voice to those whom the war robbed of their lives and their tongues; restore them to us, both the named and the nameless; make room at the table for their ghostly presence; remind us again and again of the repetitive tragedy of war.

The impact of the Korean War on the nations that took part in it also varied greatly. The devastation that the war wreaked up and down the Korean peninsula far exceeded the effects of the war in China, to say nothing of the United States, which fights its wars abroad. Yet even in the United States, where the war was a sideshow, the influence of the Korean War was by no means superficial. Coming at a critical moment in the early cold war, it contributed to the militarization of what had hitherto been an ideological and political struggle, encouraged President Eisenhower's New Look nuclear weapons–based national security policy, and fed a national paranoia about communism that persisted well into the 1980s and, with respect to China and North Korea, right up to the present. Thinking about what might have happened in Korea absent the war is an interesting, if necessarily inconclusive, exercise. (See chapter 11). One wonders, too, how the early years of the People's Republic of China might have been different had national energies, resources, and manpower not been so heavily engaged in Korea.

Speaking about his own writing, but also, by implication, about the Korean War itself, the distinguished writer Richard Kim asked, "How will the story end?" If, in fact, the Korean War is an unfinished war in the ways I have suggested above, one might say that the story will never end. Kim offered us a metaphor. Each of us, he suggested, has a tin box of memories buried in the private reaches of our souls. Like Kim, we will be digging up those memories as long as we are able to do so.

## Notes

The author is grateful to Madeline G. Levine, Michael Mayer, and, above all, Martin Russ for critical readings of earlier versions of this chapter.

1. In 1954, Frederick Wertham's *The Seduction of the Innocents*—(New York: Rinehart, 1954) the title says it all—alleged that comics were poisoning the minds of young people, an honor later reserved for television and, more recently, the Internet. Widely echoed in the media, the allegation contributed to the subsequent decline of comic books.

2. When, in early 1951, Peng Dehuai, commander of the Chinese People's Volunteers, pleaded to postpone launching another major offensive on the grounds that Chinese troops were exhausted, Mao dismissed the plea out of hand. The ill-fed, underclad, and exhausted Chinese troops were defeated by UN forces, and the war soon stalemated.

3. See Gary Saul Morson and Caryl Emerson, *Mikhail Bakhtin: Creation of a Prosaics* (Stanford: Stanford University Press, 1990), 30.

# 2

# Whether Enemy or Brother: Patriotism in Conflict with Brotherhood in the Korean War Poems by Korean Poets

## *Suh Ji-moon\**

When I decided, as my contribution to the Dialogue on the Korean War, to look for poems on the Korean War written by Korean poets, I had no idea what I was going to find. Apart from one "patriotic" poem by a woman poet that I had read in a middle school textbook, I simply had never come across any poem dealing with the Korean War experience until 1998—that is, until I was fifty. Admittedly, I am not a Korean literature major, and I tend to read more fiction than poetry, but it seemed really odd that the only poem on the Korean War that I knew of was by a woman who never participated directly in the war.

This is in stark contrast to the fact that a majority of the really major fiction to come out after, say, 1980 deals in one way or another with the Korean War, what led up to it, and its aftermath. In fact, it seems that the Korean War is becoming more and more the central subject of contemporary Korean fiction. Of course, it is extremely hard to write poems on an experience after more than thirty years—although Yu Ch'un-do's poems, of which I have translated eleven and which I will discuss a little later, triumphantly show that as long as the experience remains vividly enough in the memory, the poet can turn it into powerful verse half a century later. In any case, I thought the fact that so few are read and

*I wish to thank my collaborator, James Perkins, a poet and professor of English at Westminster College in Pennsylvania, for his significant help in polishing the translation of the poems.

discussed today (as opposed to many still-cherished and much-discussed poems reflecting on the colonial experience under Japanese rule) must mean that there are few Korean War poems worth much notice. So I began the search fearful of negative results.

But when I discovered Yu Ch'i-hwan's and Cho Chi-hun's poems, I felt the elation of Keats when he came upon Chapman's Homer, or that of Edmond Dantes when he found the treasures of the isle of Monte Cristo. They were not really buried in such profound oblivion, and it was mostly my own ignorance, and my having come to literary awareness nearly two decades after the poems were published, that made me ignorant of their existence. Still, I felt as if I had been given an infinitely precious gift. That they were in a mode so very different not only from the poetry of the 1960s and after, but from other poems by the same poets, made them objects of special interest as well.

Because the poems employ very few of the techniques contemporary poets are fond of utilizing—deliberate ambiguity, savage irony, tortured syntax, and so on—and instead are stark and spare in the extreme, they read like poems from another era. At first glance they may look unsophisticated, but I felt the presence of major poets in the extreme simplicity and severity of Yu Ch'i-hwan's and Cho Chi-hun's poems. And many of the poems inspired in me the awe that only the most authentic emotion in the face of a great tragic experience can inspire.

One of my senior colleagues, himself a poet, directed me to the war poems of Yu Ch'i-hwan (1908-1967), Cho Chi-hun (1920–1968), and Ku Sang (1919– ). The poem by Mo Yun-suk (1910–1985) I remembered from my girlhood. The rest of the search was really laborious. I looked through all the crumbling volumes of poetry published in the 1950s that I could lay my hands on and asked friends to aid me in the search. A couple of friends sent me typed or photocopied poems and gave me the names of individual poems or anthologies. Although many of the poems gleaned from this later search lacked the sure touch of the major poets and were of uneven quality (not just from poet to poet, but also from one part to another within the same poem), they moved me in another way. Many of them were by actual combatants, and gave me a picture of what went on during the Korean War on the battlefield and in the soldiers' minds. About half the poets I thus found are poets of considerable note. But the rest of them are now almost totally forgotten, and because of the postwar social turmoil, even their biographical facts are not easy to ascertain. So I was doubly glad to discover them and bring them to light once more.

After I concluded this first round of translation, I heard about the publication of Yu Ch'un-do's (1927– ) *Unforgettable People* in the fall of 1999. Reading the slim volume of poems by this woman who was telling her story after fifty years of silence, I counted it a sign of heaven's blessing on my project that the book came out in time for me to include some of the poems in my collection—particularly as I happened to learn of its publication during my sabbatical abroad. The poems of this successful medical doctor and happy wife and mother, who has lived with her nightmare for half a century, forcibly brought home to me once again all the tragic paradoxes of the Korean War.

As a literary critic, I am aware that a number of the poems in my forthcoming collection are quite unsophisticated in terms of literary technique. Yet most of them gave me the kind of emotional experience only great literature can give—a sense of frail human beings rising to meet the tyrannies and cruelties of life with dignity and humility. It was a profoundly painful experience, yet it gave me at the same time a solemn and chastened kind of elation.

When the Korean War broke out, the South Korean Defense Ministry called in writers to broadcast morale-raising propaganda. But because the South Korean army suffered one shattering defeat after another in the beginning of the war and was pushed all the way down to the Naktong River, it was only after the North Korean advance was checked at the Pusan perimeter that the defense ministry could organize writers and poets into a kind of auxiliary unit, to make them write propaganda literature. However, since the defense ministry had many problems with running the war, the writers were not always properly regimented and cared for. Therefore, not only their material comfort but also their very lives were often exposed to danger. Cho Chi-hun provides a wry vignette of the conditions in which these noncombatants lived in "Romantic Army Life":

> Our camp, unguarded by any sentry,
> Is an old hut with a plank wall and a pomegranate tree
>     in the yard.
>
> We become more romantic
> The more precarious life becomes.

In the sweltering heat of August
We play chess sitting bare-chested,

And drink rice wine snacking on pickled apples
While bombs explode at night.

But at the command of the officer
We take up our arms—pen and paper—

And prepare for combat on table, desk, floor and
      verandah,
Vying to occupy the best strategic points.

This is our combat field, from where we fire paper
      bullets to slash the enemy's hearts.

Here we shed silent tears longing for our family
      and friends
And here we write them letters saying, "We'll be
      in Seoul soon."

Soldiers without weapons,
We carry cyanide in our bosom.

The pomegranate which was green when we first
      came
Has ripened and is popping open.

Yes, in the backyard of the army writers' camp
There's a self-exploded pomegranate screaming
      at the sky.

The self-mockery is more playful than resentful, and the patriotism is
genuine; but the level of frustration is extremely high. The writers, required to write propaganda literature without any security in their own
lives, must have stayed on partly because they dreaded the consequences
of escape or desertion. But I submit that they also stayed on from a
sense of duty, that is to say, from patriotic motives. Some radical critics
from the generation born a decade and more after the war, for whom

"patriotism" is a dirty word and for whom true courage is that channeled into opposing and trying to subvert one's own government, brand
these writers as "ŏyong," writers in the government's pay. This is not
only a great injustice to these writers but a calumny cast on the whole
nation that resisted the communist aggression and survived it. And the
poems these poets wrote are far from "patriotic" in the crude sense. In fact,
I am left wondering if the general tenor of their poems as well as a few of
their specific poems didn't get them in trouble with the military authorities.

   There is no knowing at this point what the literary and poetic output
of authors and poets in this unit was like in general, as most of them
have vanished out of print and out of memory. But, in the case of our
major poets, except for a handful of poems praising the valor of ROK
soldiers and denouncing the inhuman cruelty of the communists, most
poems are suffused with pain and sadness in the face of the devastation
wrought by the war and a sense of the futility of a war in which victory
only means death and injury for the other half of one's own nation. A
number of poems openly express compassion for and sorrow over the
enemy dead—enemies who might be one's own brothers. It must have
taken quite a bit of courage to write such poems while acting as the
"official" poets of the Republic of Korea.

Cho Chi-hun was the scion of a family of Confucian scholars, and he
was a poet and a professor of Korean literature at the time of the outbreak of the Korean War. Poetically, he was an aesthete tempered by
Confucian self-discipline and Buddhist spirituality, and his poems in
general are graceful meditations on objects that inspire a sense of spiritual beauty and nobility. His gentle, meditative quality is evident in many
of his Korean War poems, although not much of his aesthetic sensibility
is. The day after the Korean War broke out, when most people were
terrified but still clinging to the government's assurance that there would
be no difficulty in defending the capital, students came to class but
couldn't concentrate on the lecture. Cho, their professor, observes:

> Two o'clock in the afternoon
> I give a lecture on poetics in the third-story classroom
>      of  Korea University.
> I hear the noise of guns from the direction of Ŭijŏngbu.
>
> And the loudspeaker in the campus tremulously relays
>      news from the battlefront.

Youths seem to regard the language of poetry as
      irrelevant to the moment.
But it is at moments of crisis that poetry can be
      our support.

"Now you'll realize the meaning of your anxiety
      and being," I tell them.

. . . . . . . . . . . . . . . . . . . . . . . . . . . . . . . . . . . .

Coming out into the hallway,
I see poetry sucked away by the smoke of battle.
             ("Journal of Despair, Twenty-sixth of June, 1950")

"At Toriwon" describes the ruins of a village that was the site of one of the fiercest and most atrocious battles in the early stage of the war. It is written with a quiet sorrow that might look like detachment to a careless reader, but that really hides profound sorrow and even fury:

The war, which was so cruel,
Blew off like a rainstorm.

Leaving crumpled huts
And thatched houses with burnt roofs.

Today I pass this ruined and charred village
With casual steps.

The only thing that Heaven has spared whole
Is an old clay pot on a storage dais,

Reminding me that I, too, like the clay pot
Have been spared.

The villagers who have returned
Look up from the ruins toward the distant hills.

The sky is as blue as ever.
In the autumn sun of Toriwon

A fragile cosmos
Shivers in the breeze.

The near-total destruction of Toriwon and many other villages in the area and incalculable military and civilian casualties were the price the Republic of Korea paid for staying the communist forces along the Naktong River and preventing them from taking the whole of South Korea. The poet, far from congratulating himself for his luck in having survived, feels that he just happens to have been spared, "like the clay pot." The shivering fragile cosmos of the last stanza is a fitting emblem for all hapless and helpless Korean people.

"Here Lies a Communist Soldier" is a gentle and poignant expression of the sorrow of losing an "enemy":

> In the midst of hot pursuit
> Through Ŭisŏng, Andong, and the Chukryŏng Pass,
>
> I jump down from the truck to slake my thirst
> And touch the roadside daisies.
>
> A chalk inscription on a piece of wood
> Stuck in the grass catches my eye.
> "Here lies a communist soldier."
>
> The boy's body lying beside it
> Is still breathing faintly.
>
> His limbs, pickled in dark blood, are rotting,
> And his half-opened eyes cannot focus any more.
>
> You must have crept to this stream
> And drunk long draughts, to allay your thirst and pain.
>
> This is your country, too.
> Did you smell the earth of your hometown here?
>
> Whether enemy or brother,
> You are a human being,
> A sacred creature deserving love.
>
> Who dares add further injury
> To this bruised soul?

His dying face tells
His sorrow at leaving those he loves.
Death offers no transcendence.

A piece of wood
Inscribed with a tender and sad heart,

Tells of cruel battle
Under the clear blue autumn sky:

"Here lies a communist soldier."

In "At Tabuwon" and other poems as well, Cho takes sorrowful notice of the corpses of communist soldiers:

The corpse of a communist soldier
Prostrate in a weeping posture.

We were brothers under the same sky
Until a short while ago.

The "enemy" during the Korean War was not always an ideological foe. Many young men were conscripted into either the South or North Korean army simply by reason of their residence in the respective region, regardless of their ideological leanings. In addition, many South Korean youths (and mere lads) were "volunteered" to fight in North Korea's "Righteous and Valiant Army" from being unable to flee before the communists took over their region in the early months of the war. Similarly, North Korean youths were inducted into the South Korean army while South Korea occupied the North, in October 1950. Many such "volunteers" were pulled right out of paddies and fishing boats and were thrown onto battlefields with only a few days or even a few hours of military training. Therefore, instances of brothers, uncles and nephews, even fathers and sons fighting on opposite sides—some from conviction and many from compulsion—were not at all uncommon.

Cho's Confucian sense of loyalty to his country and his placement of public duty before private affection compelled him to report to the defense ministry's office immediately after Seoul was recaptured for the first time in September 1950, even though his heart was filled with the joy and pain of family reunion:

I hug and kiss my three-year-old who has oozing sores
From eating acorns.

My six-year-old says he loved the taste of crayfish
He fished from the stream and grilled on fire.

Poor things, you could have died,
Having a father powerless to protect you.

My heart ached with guilt thinking of you.
I had no other anxiety in the world.

My father must have loved me
As I do my little ones.

Father isn't back,
Though the son he worried about has come back alive.

Only his glasses and razor are back
Retrieved from the enemy.

There is no news of my mother gone to her hometown
Which the enemy occupied later.

Now, past thirty years of age, I realize in vain
How deep and strong one's love for his kin can be.

Without waiting to see my wife
I leave my house to return to duty.
This is wartime: how can I neglect my duty for the sake
        of private affection?

("On Returning to Seoul")

The ineffable sense of spirituality and refined perception of beauty that are the trademarks of Cho Chi-hun are not prominent features of the poems in his *Before the Tribunal of History* collection. But these quiet and spare poems are beautiful and moving in a unique way.

Yu Ch'i-hwan is a poet of more passionate and overtly romantic temperament, so his poems tend to work more directly on our emotions. But in most of the war poems published in his *With the Foot Soldier* collection, his expression is severely disciplined and restrained. "With the Simplicity of a Child" is saved from sentimentality and made poignant by its extreme simplicity:

> With boughs and leaves sticking out of helmet
> and uniform
> The soldier has fallen asleep, like an innocent
> baby,
> Curled up while waiting for a command.
>
> Hundreds of miles from home,
> The soldier expects no letters from kin.
> But he visits home in his dreams,
> So he has treasure in his heart.
>
> He can be so at peace
> Because he has set no price on his life
> And has let go of his attachment to life, like bad
> karma.
>
> The soldier sleeps like a flower,
> With the simplicity of a child.

Having paid tribute to the ROK soldier, Yu then voices his compassion for the communist soldier:

> Where the battle raged like a nightmare
> Last night,
> The corpse of a young enemy soldier remains
> Like a lone wild flower.
>
> Life's cruel tempest that drove you here
> Like a hunted animal
> Has dissipated,
> Leaving you this spot for your rest.
>
> Now your ears are opened,
> Your soul is awake.

> You'll hear the deep currents of the East Sea
> Merging with eternity.
>
> ("Like a Wild Flower")

The unpredictability of the fortunes of war and the futility of it all are admirably captured by Yu in this short eight-line poem, entitled "A Short Rest":

> Soldiers are shaking off the dust of battle
> By the shore of this lake in the quiet twilight.
>
> Anxiously exhaling cigarette smoke,
> Are you thinking of your family and hometown?
>
> Friendship and hostility
> Are transitory, like all human feelings.
>
> This morning the foe fled this wind and landscape
> You are unexpectedly savoring this evening.

The poet notes, not with heavy irony but simply as a fact of life, that even though ideological strife is devouring millions of lives and tearing the country to shreds, ideology means nothing to simple folk:

> In a backward seaside village
> On the shore of the vast East Sea,
>
> A flag flaps in the wind.
> Yesterday it was theirs, today it is ours.
>
> The wretched villagers do not care,
> The tides are their sole concern.
>
> They have always accepted
> What life gave them.
>
> ("The Meaning of Flags")

Few Koreans, however, were fortunate enough to be allowed to remain unconcerned about ideology. In many villages, half the population was wiped out when one side took over, and the other half when the other did, as accumulated resentments were played out in the name of lofty ideologies. Nonetheless, the fact that the number of people who fled, or tried to flee, from the communists outnumbered by many times the number of people who tried to flee ROK control can be taken as proof that many more people dreaded and hated communists than they did South Korean "democrats." Many people were grateful to the ROK soldiers who fought to repel the communists and gave their lives to guard the country. Compassion for the communist soldiers notwithstanding, such gratitude for the ROK soldiers, their valor and their dedication, finds many eloquent expressions. Antiwar sentiment was strong, but it did not result in the discrediting or maligning of the soldiers' valor. On the contrary, appreciation for the soldiers' sacrifices formed the core of antiwar sentiment. But, for Yu Ch'i-hwan, mixed with gratitude for the sacrifice and loyalty of the soldiers, is the concern that

> those may come. . .
> Who will exploit your sacrifice in the name of
>     our country,
> And you will come to regret
> The suffering and death you offered so nobly.
>
> ("To Comrades")

In spite of the perception that the Koreans were pawns in a war between superpowers, prevalent among the intellectuals of that period—and more widespread later—was genuine gratitude to the American and other UN forces who came halfway around the world to "save" South Korea from communist rule. Yu's "To a Deceased United Nations Soldier" and "To Major Den Audin" are sincere tributes to those soldiers who gave their lives to fight the communists, who were perceived as, and revealed themselves to be, enemies of freedom.

But in war, the greatest hardship may not be that suffered by soldiers: civilians suffered in other ways, but just as harshly. "Drifting" is a tribute to the tough resiliency of the Korean people. It enabled them to survive subhuman conditions in Pusan, where almost half the population of South Korea lived as refugees:

> Look at the crowd of people
> Thronging like tangled heaps of rubbish

> On this street almost touched by the cold waves
> of winter solstice.
> They have left behind pride and shame and
> attachment
> And are offering for sale anything that will fetch
> a few pennies:
> Their cherished furniture, clothes, shoes,
> Even their wives' underwear.

In "Port of Glory" Yu commemorates the energy generated by the refugees packing the city, living in the most miserable and squalid of conditions but united by the will to survive:

> Countless refugees carrying pots and pans
> Drift in the wake of the government which
> hopes to make you a springboard
> To vault over the thirty-eighth parallel.
> You were so overloaded your deck was leaning
> And waves were lapping into your stern.
> So precarious was this ship called Korea!
> But your fortitude restored its trim
> In nineteen hundred and fifty.
> You, the lever that lifted the country
> out of disaster!
> Pusan, Port of Glory.

"My Fatherland" is as fine a statement as any of love for one's country, not only in spite of all its defects, but also because of them. I hold that only the people of a country that has suffered one misfortune after another, and endured repeated threats to its very continuance (Ku Sang describes Korea as a country sustained by calamities) can understand that love. Nikolai Gogol expressed it in a startling but moving passage near the end of *Dead Souls*, his furious indictment of Russia as a hopelessly corrupt and sick country. Yu Ch'i-hwan declared his love for his woebegone and sore-infested fatherland after reading an interview story on Korea written by a foreign correspondent:

> You wrote that there's no other country in the world
> Whose land is so covered with festering sores

And where the stench of feces assails you
      everywhere you go.
And where every creature that ever plagued
      mankind thrives—
Fleas, bedbugs, mosquitoes, centipedes,
      venomous snakes, leeches.
And whose people are
Pickpockets, swindlers, beggars, corrupt
      officials or scoundrels.
You say this country's worse than New Guinea,
That it's a country you'd like to hand over
      to your enemy as a punishment.
Then you ask,
"What crimes have we committed that we have
      to fight for a country like this?"

I am a beggar child of that country.
I stay by its side
And weep over it all the time.

                                            ("My Fatherland")

In "At the Armistice Line," which is a poem not included in his *With the Foot Soldier* collection, Yu Ch'i-hwan makes a protest to God, who shows no sign of concern for a hapless nation continuing to exist in sheer hell for so long:

God!
What can we do to call your attention to our plight?

This must be a moment that calls for your intervention,
And which cannot end without your final judgment.
Are you holding back because it is still too early for
      you to step in?
Are you standing by to let humans commit these
      iniquities
So that they will repent the more starkly in the end?

God!
Are you staying aloof to make us grovel and supplicate?

> God, why are you nonchalantly swaying
>> on a blade of grass shaking in the breeze
>> of noon?
> God, how can you sit at ease at night
>> on the Big Bear constellation?

This poem voices the sense of utter loss many Koreans felt at the time about "heaven's intention." Throughout history, the absolute majority of Koreans, who were helpless as babes before the despotism of those in power, always clung to the belief that "heaven is not unfeeling": that, even though great injustices fall to the lot of many, they do not escape the notice of heaven, which will redress them in the course of time. That the heaven they had always relied on allowed such atrocious carnage and heartbreak to take place on such a massive scale and did nothing to put a stop to it, was a blow at the very root of the Koreans' belief in the existence of divine, or universal, justice.

Ku Sang is a poet of compassion. He has enjoyed popularity for many decades because his poetry is accessible to most readers. He looks at the experiences of ordinary people with deep compassion tinged with a bit of irony—just the right combination for the majority of Korean readers. His poetry is not difficult or complicated, but its insight and emotional depth satisfy the serious reader. His "Poetry on Burnt Ground" sequence, which was written following rather than during the war, is a meditation on the sad and absurd state of his war-devastated country. On his "burnt ground"—Korea during and after the war—young women have to sell their flesh to keep alive, and children mock and persecute such young women (sarcastically dubbed "Western princesses") while in their next breath trying to lure American soldiers to patronize those very women.

In the famous section two of the sequence, the poet happens to be sitting opposite a tired prostitute and her mixed-blood boy on a night train. The boy frets, and the mother tries to pacify him. The poet offers the boy caramels out of his pocket, and the boy climbs into the poet's lap. The boy's mother, exhausted from her unequal battle with life and the taxing role of a mixed-blood child's mother, falls asleep, and the boy also falls asleep, so that to all appearances the poet has become the father of the boy, who is completely black.

The poet's predicament can be appreciated only if one is aware of the extreme prejudice Koreans have against mixed-blood children. To look as if he had fathered a child with a black woman is an indignity a man of his class and temperament could hardly support. But the poet, imagining the few paper notes that must have brought the boy into being, shudders at the cheap rate of human life and hugs the innocent child breathing peacefully in his lap. He sees the face of all Koreans in the tired and abandoned face of the woman who has to raise her child amidst prejudice and discrimination—if not downright persecution—in expiation of a sin born of desperate necessity, a sin in which all Koreans are implicated. The poet thus suggests that all Korean men recognize their paternal obligation to mixed-blood children.

Beyond having to cope with the aftermath of the war, the poet also recognizes the need to heal the basic rupture of the country. In section seven, subtitled "At the Cemetery of Enemy Soldiers," Ku, who is a devout Catholic, muses:

> We were bound to you in life
> By ties of hate.
> But now, your lingering resentments
> Are my tasks
> And are incorporated in my prayers.

In section nine, subtitled "At the Time of the Armistice Negotiations," he likens his fatherland to Sim Ch'ŏng, the legendary daughter who sold herself to seamen as a human sacrifice, an offering to appease the wrath of the sea god: a helpless victim at the mercy of the superpowers:

> My fatherland! You are pitiful as Sim Ch'ŏng, sold
>     as sacrifice to redeem her blind father's pledge.
> The poet grows tearful whenever he calls your name.
> There, all the butchers of the century
> Are going to carve you, like a piece of meat
>     on a chopping block.
> But Heaven seems to be just looking on.

> My fatherland! On your streets people are going mad
> Unable to hope or even despair.
> Your enemy and the enemy's patrons
> Are trying to cut you in half again.
> Are you a reed that thinks merely to be cut?

Min Chae-shik (1930– ) also likened Korea, in his "Scapegoat," to "a bargain on the sale table of superpowers." This perception of the utter inability of Korea to determine its own fate evokes both self-pity and self-derision in many poets and intellectuals, who also shared a violent hatred of the corrupt politicians and entrepreneurs who exploit their sick country and compound its maladies. But Ku Sang concludes his sequence with an exhortation to all his compatriots to sow seeds of life on the ruin that is his fatherland, "so that they will bloom on [our] graves / And testify to [our] resurrection."

Yu Ch'un-do, the only poet in this collection to have sympathized with the communists and worked for and with them, has different identifications for friend and enemy, but the war reflected in her eyes is just as absolute an evil. This successful medical doctor turned poet in her seventies was a fifth-year medical student when the Korean War broke out. She was forced to function as a medical doctor in the absence of enough trained personnel, first for the South Korean wounded and then for the North Korean soldiers after Seoul was taken over by the communists.

In sharing the pains and agonies of the wounded North Koreans in a field hospital with insufficient equipment and medical supplies, she came to feel a close human bond with them and a deep respect for their ideology. When the North Koreans were pushed back, she tried to follow them to the North, but was prevented from doing so by the American bombing, a scene she describes in "The Girl Soldier and the Moon." Afterward, while trying to find her way to her hometown, she was captured by a South Korean soldier. Rescued from a summary execution by the ROK soldier, thanks to the timely intervention of a passing American officer (as described in "Kŭmgang River Ghost"), she was sent to prison as a prisoner of war, undergoing a long and terrifying march delineated in "Let's Take Our Own Lives." In the prison for communists she witnessed horrors that remained indelible, and describes them in the poem "In Ch'ŏngju Prison." Released from the prison with the help of an acquaintance, she was able to join her family in her hometown but was forced to suffer several imprisonments and torture as a communist "collaborator." She describes this experience in "Crickets Chirping in My Ears."

After the war Yu was able to hide that portion of her life history, going on to become a successful gynecologist and the wife of an eminent scholar—an enviable woman to all in outward appearance. But a half century later, she says she still suffers nightmares and wakes up crying. After her husband died and she retired from active practice, she decided to bear witness to the nation's history as she saw and experienced it, hoping to gain relief from her tormenting memories by making them public. Although her prosody lacks sophistication, her guileless verses present with photographic clarity the most dramatic and terrifying experiences a human being can undergo.

Yu records the beginning of her affiliation with the communists, in which she had no choice, with fine irony: the setting and the figures are the same as the day before, when she was surrounded by South Korean soldiers, with only minute differences in the insignia on the soldiers' caps and the stronger odor of sweat. But it marks the first day of heartache, torment, and bitterness that will last many decades:

> I go to the outpatients' room with my assignment slip.
> Yesterday's wounded ROK soldiers are nowhere
>         to be seen
> And only the doctor and the nurse are pacing
>         the empty room.
> Jeeps carrying wounded soldiers arrive
> In the hospital yard.
>
> Some are carried in on stretchers, some hobble
>         in leaning on others,
> And some hop in on one leg.
> From beyond the window the sight is the same
>         as yesterday's.
> The only difference is they have red stars on their
>         caps and a stronger odor of sweat.
> The doctor and the nurse do the same things they
>         did yesterday.
> Is that the spirit of the Red Cross?
>
> Our destiny began that day
> Of partings, death, and imprisonment.
> The bitterness of many decades lay in wait.
>
> ("Destiny")

Yu's bond with the communists was cemented by shared suffering, as she looked after a boy soldier whose leg was cut off without anesthesia and cleaned another's maggot-infested wound, and so on. When the communists began fleeing to the North in September 1950, the North Korean soldiers told her to go to the rear before they stepped into the Namgang River to begin their retreat of death:

> In the pitch darkness, the crossing to death begins.
> The first batch. Then the second batch. Then the
> > third batch.
> The soldiers begin
> Their crossing of no return.
> Holding their guns straight up to heaven.
> . . . . . . . . . . . . . . . . . . . . . . . . . . . . . . . . . . . .
> "You must live.
> Return to the rear.
> There will be no more wounded for you to treat,"
> The young commander says to me solemnly,
> Telling me to hold life sacred before stepping
> > into his own death.
>
> ("Namgang River")

Yu nevertheless tried to follow them, drawing three oxcarts loaded with wounded North Korean soldiers. But she was met by bombing and had to flee alone, with many backward glances at the wounded soldiers spilled out of the oxcarts and dyeing the street red with their blood. as they Then she was captured by a South Korean soldier, narrowly escaped summary execution, and was sent to prison. On the way to prison she and other captured female communists had to resolutely resist the aggression of sex-hungry American soldiers. In the prison, she witnessed prisoners suffering unspeakable miseries, which became sharply etched in her memory:

> Tetanus spreads among the prisoners.
> The flustered Americans create an infirmary
> And let DPRK army doctors and women prisoners
> > treat the patients.
>
> There is no vaccine and no medicine.
> All we can do is to sterilize the wound
> And sprinkle antibiotic powder.
> The infirmary stinks with the stench of rotting flesh.

> Unable to shut their mouths, the tetanus patients
>     keep drooling,
> Their jaw joints have locked.
> They can neither talk nor eat.
> They can only wait for death.
>
> My professor at the medical school
> Said that once you see the face of a tetanus patient
> It remains printed in your memory.
>
> Yes, this is what happens in a war,
> And this is a wrong war, I thought.
>
> American trucks
> Bring in prisoners
> Day and night.
> More prisoners die of tetanus.
>
>                                             ("In Ch'ŏngju Prison")

But again she was rescued from death by a stroke of luck, reminding her once more that in war sheer luck and chance divide the living from the dead:

> One day I met a friend of my brother
> In the prison.
> "Why are you here?" he asks in amazement.
> He fetches an American officer
> With whose help I was released
> And escaped death once more,
> Incredibly.
>
> In those days
> You lived if you were lucky
> And died if you were not.
>
>                                             ("In Ch'ŏngju Prison")

Yu Ch'un-do's poems remind us that war was not easier on women. Admittedly, she was a special case, and she was in a sense an active participant rather than a passive sufferer, but her womanly sensibilities made her suffer more deeply and longer. For the majority of women who could do nothing but suffer, the agonies, anxiety, and heartbreak of war were excruciating.

Mo Yun-suk in her other poems portrays the agonies of newlywed brides waiting for their husbands who went to war and were not heard of again, and other predicaments of women in the rear. But in the poem translated in my collection, which is her best-known, though not her best, poem, she makes—through the mouth of a dead soldier of the Republic of Korea—ringing assertions about guarding the country not just until the end of one's life, but until the end of time:

> I gladly forego a grave for my body
> Or even a small coffin to shield me from
>     wind and rain.
> Soon rough winds will whip my body
> And worms will feast on my flesh.
> But I will gladly be their companion.
> My ardent wish is to become a handful
>     of earth
> In this valley in my fatherland
> Waiting for better times in my country.

The soldier in Mo's poem exhorts his compatriots to defy even fate itself:

> You mustn't stand by, calling it Fate.
> What if it is Fate?
> We are stronger than Fate.
> Friends! Shatter this Fate imposed by our enemy.
> With your strong arms and legs,
> Your red blood, and the dauntless spirit of Tan'gun,
> You must fight your battles and die your deaths
> To breathe life into our expiring country.
>                          ("What the Dead Soldier Said")

Poetry written by men who actually participated in the war expresses as resolute a determination to fight, but is less rhetorical and more anchored to concrete battle situations. In Pak Il-song's "The Eye of the Sentry," the sentry's eyes are so piercing that "Not even an ant / Would dare risk entering / Your vigilant ken." Chang Ho-gang (1925– ), a career soldier who attained the rank of a general before retirement, dug trenches without number to repulse the enemy's approach:

> We dig, build, install, and bury,
> Firing trenches, shelter trenches, wire fences,
>     and mines
> In a tight network
> So that even a swarm of enemies skilled in
>     night maneuvers
> Couldn't penetrate our defense system
> Even by burrowing underground like a mole.
>
> ("Kansas Line")

Chang was willing to carry the whole weight of the country on his back:

> We must carry our Fatherland on our back.
> Because I have your support
> And your love,
> My veins throb with fire
> Even in the trench noisy with exploding shells
> And I am ready for a million communists.
>
> ("A Hymn to a Comrade")

Chang Ho-gang's wish to vanquish the enemy so that the country would be unified is so intense that he wishes his body to lie exposed to the weather if he falls in battle so that his bones will crumble to dust, be blown by the wind, and fall in Ch'ŏnji Lake, the crater lake on top of Mt. Paekdu on the northern border of Korea.

Yi Yun-su, in "The Foot Soldier Marches," declares his resolution to march to the end of the earth and until the end of his life in defense of the country:

> We march everywhere,
> We march in silence.

We march, bathed in sweat,
Our bodies sizzling in the sun.
We march along endless dusty country roads.
We wade through rivers if bridges are exploded.
We push through like tanks on roads tanks can't
     run.
We march with iron will and high spirit.
We march through rain, clasping the guns whose
     straps dig into our shoulders.
We march through mud,
We march over felled trees,
And navigate through forests.
. . . . . . . . . . . . . . . . . . . . . . . . . . . . . . . . . .
We march until the soles of our boots feel like
     red-hot iron.
We can go everywhere, we go everywhere.
When we can't walk, we crawl.
Now, nothing can stop us.

Chang Su-ch'ŏl (1916– ), standing "In the Freezing Trench," affirms his resolve to fight and vanquish all communists:

Though the enemy may rush at us
Like a pack of wolves,
Our iron will and eager young blood
Will vanquish all communists.

My body and the gun in my hands
Throb with the pride
Of the times I smashed the enemy
And made victory songs resound.

Many of the poems express hatred of the enemy and the determination to exterminate them, but in what seems to me an impersonal way. Often, expressions of hatred and contempt for the enemy are tinged with regret, as in Mun Sang-myŏng's "Light-Limit Line":

The red enemies
Are those whose souls

Live in darkness.
They think and act without light.
If only they had the conscience
To love light,
I would be driving a golden carriage
Brimming with happy songs
Over this hill clad in autumn foliage
And speeding towards the Diamond Mountains
Scattering laughter in the wind.

It is remarkable that even the combatants, whose lives were constantly endangered by the enemy and who saw so many of their comrades killed and wounded by them, also regarded the enemy with sorrow and compassion once the enemy were dead or captured. This is owing to the peculiar paradox and tragedy of the Korean War noted earlier: that Koreans regarded the whole nation as "blood kin descended from the same original forefather, Tan'gun," and the enemy one killed could turn out to be one's own neighbor, or brother. Yu Ch'un-do, contemplating the North Korean boy soldier who had his leg amputated without anesthesia, shudders at the thought that her brother, who was about the same age as the boy soldier, "might be aiming his gun at us as a soldier of the Republic" ("The Emergency Field Hospital"). And Yu Chong has a hallucinatory sense that "Those emaciated shoulders heaving in pitch darkness / [He] glimpsed while peering beyond the frozen thirty-eighth parallel" are without a doubt those of his brother, who had run away from home with the family bull ("Brother").

To be sure, fratricide is a horror and a trauma for all mankind. For Koreans it is a horror they cannot bear to contemplate, as traditionally their lives revolved around kinship ties. The requirements of the family always took precedence over individual needs. Therefore, many imagined reconciliations have been suggested. Kim Kyu-dong's "A Grave" is a rhapsody on the imagined brotherhood of a North Korean soldier and a South Korean soldier, achieved after death through being buried in one grave. Pak Pong-u (1924–1990), in "Blooming on the Wasteland," also dreams of the day when North and South Koreans can cross the boundary as freely as butterflies.

The soldier-poets exhibit staunch determination and courage, but nowhere in their poetry is war glorified. War itself, more than the enemy, is condemned for causing all the tragedy and suffering. Yi Tŏk-jin (1923– ) shudders at the carnage of war, which not only alters the landscape but seems to make the earth a gigantic maw of death:

> Flesh bursts and blood spurts,
> And streams of crimson blood dye the surrounding
> valleys red.
> As the landscape alters, corpses pile up,
> And the ridge becomes a bloodthirsty devil.

Mun Sang-myŏng also mourns the innumerable lives given without any discernible effect, to all appearances simply consumed:

> Over four hundred thousand shells and bullets
> were fired
> On this hill where the death agonies of
> innumerable soldiers
> Consumed the mystery of aeons
> And lives fell like grass and twigs.
> Ah, the blood that ran down the hill
> In a flood!
>
> ("The White Horse Hill")

At the National Cemetery, the same poet muses on the futility of lives sacrificed in war:

> In the space where thought is on fire
> The sun which has lost heat
> Is driving the pigeons home.
> But the silent witnesses
> Of the wounds
> Which nothing can compensate
> Keep their silences
> Till the end of time.
>
> ("Lost Time and Effaced Language")

In Korea, it is never counted a weakness in brave soldiers to harbor nostalgia. Nor have I encountered in the literature of any country any blame that redounded on a soldier for yearning for his home, family, and sweetheart. Chang Ho-gang, in spite of his stout soldier's heart, cannot help yearning for his hometown:

> Another meteor glides in the silence.
> When the chirping of insects evokes memories
>     of home,
> The soldier recalls the face of his beloved.
> The Dipper, which had been sitting on the bead
>     of his northward-aiming rifle,
> Has disappeared.
>
> ("The Armistice Line at Night")

> Tonight, after pillars of napalm fire have subsided
> And the moon and stars are weeping together,
> The soldier's heart flies to his hometown in the North
> Which abound in legends.
> Ah, who drew this Kansas Line
> That hinders the manly spirits of soldiers
> From ranging unfettered?
>
> ("Kansas Line")

Chang Su-ch'ŏl, even while "aiming sharply at the enemy," standing in a dark trench feeling his very marrow freeze, cannot help thinking of home.

Love for one's particular home notwithstanding, one's patriotism often comes into conflict with one's concern for oneself and one's kinfolk in times of war, although in principle one's love for one's country and one's family should reinforce each other. This conflict is noted by Yi Hyo-sang as an astonishing and painful discovery. First, the sense of his long-suffering fatherland in imminent danger inspires in him boundless loyalty and love:

> I never loved my fatherland as dearly as now.
> I didn't know that one's fatherland was something
>     so precious.
> I realize for the first time that my life is a mere feather
>     weighed against my fatherland.
> I realize belatedly that your fatherland is something
> You embrace with death looking over your shoulder.
>
> ("Fatherland")

But giving up a son in defense of a country, even a country one loves so dearly, is far from easy:

> The day I sent my servants, nephews, cousins on
>     Mother's side
> Cousins on Father's side, and a hundred youths from
>     the village to the war
> I made a moving speech with words welling up from
>     my heart.
> But the day I sent my son, the thought that I had been
>     a hypocrite
> Smote my conscience.
>
> The day I sent my beloved son to the war
> I wished I could fight in the war myself.
>
> ("War")

Fighting a war for a country like Korea requires true loyalty and a spirit of sacrifice, because the country is so weakened that it cannot compensate its citizens' sacrifices and losses in its defense:

> Your meritorious service in the war
> Should bring you glory and rewards.
>
> But our hungry and threadbare country
> Can give you nothing.
>
> Even if you leave the perilous armed forces
> A troubled society awaits you.
>
> The destroyed cities and ruined villages
> Are still standing on denuded hills and parched
>     valleys.
>
> (Chang Ho-gang, "Dedicating a Flower")

Therefore, those who fatten themselves by exploiting their weakened and ailing country are objects of special opprobrium and hatred. Such "irreverent snakes" are to be extirpated by keeping alive the spirit of the brave warriors who gave their lives to the country:

If an irreverent snake
Brought in by the confusion of life and death
Lurks on this land purified by your sacrifice,
Let the torch of your spirit,
Oh nameless warrior,
Be lit up on all the hills your breath has touched.
 (Kim Chong-mun, "The Legacy of an Unknown Soldier")

At the time of the Korean War, the country was so torn apart and people were so battered by emotional, physical, and material suffering that there was little hope for comfort, to say nothing of prosperity, and despair was all too pervasive. Hope for a better future was something as fragile as a roadside plant looked after by nobody, but also as definite as the will of the plant to bloom:

At whose request have you bloomed on this wasteland where men slaughtered men, you nameless flower which confronts the sky with your fragile sweetness? How can you, a delicate plant standing on a sunny road under the blue heavens, try to efface, with your ineffable smile upon your frail stalk, the deafening din of cannon roars and bomb explosions and yells and bloodbaths that shook the earth to its axis?

(Park Yang-kyun, "Flower")

Korea's survival owes itself entirely to its people having held onto that fragile hope.

# 3
# Above All, the Waste: American Soldier-Poets and the Korean War

## William D. Ehrhart

One fact of war is that wars produce literature. From Homer's *Iliad* to Walt Whitman's Civil War poems to Tim O'Brien's *The Things They Carried,* war and literature are each a subset of the other. And as soldiers have increasingly become more literate, the twentieth century has seen a marked increase in the body of literature written by soldiers and veterans themselves. No longer does war await a Homer or a Tennyson or a Kipling to be translated into literature, but rather the Siegfried Sassoons and James Joneses and Robert Butlers speak for themselves, making use of creative imagination to be sure, but fueling it with the raw stuff of experience.

The war I fought in Vietnam has produced a huge body of literature written by those who fought in it, including dozens of first-rate poems.[1] Early on in my life as poet and veteran, I discovered the vast body of poetry to have come out of the British trenches of the Great War, a body that extends far beyond Wilfred Owen's much-anthologized "Dulce et Decorum Est." And American veterans of World War II have produced such classic novels as Norman Mailer's *The Naked and the Dead* and Joseph Heller's *Catch-22*, along with poems like Randall Jarrell's "The Death of the Ball Turret Gunner," James Dickey's "The Firebombing," and Richard Eberhart's "The Fury of Aerial Bombardment."

Only recently, however, have I begun to realize that there is a significant if rather smaller body of literature by Americans about the Korean War, including novels such as Pat Frank's *Hold Back the Night* and Richard Kim's *The Martyred*; memoirs like James Brady's *The Coldest*

*War* and Martin Russ's *The Last Parallel*; Rod Serling's play *The Rack*; Keith Wilson's *Graves Registry and Other Poems*; and short stories such as Donald Depew's "Indigenous Girls" and John Deck's "Sailors at Their Mourning: A Memory." Yet for much of the last fifty years, this literature has been all but ignored.[2]

It is not my purpose here to explore in depth the differences between Korean War literature and the literatures of the two American wars on either side of it, the Second World War and the Vietnam War. But without going into great detail, a few observations are appropriate. The Second World War was the kind of experience that literally transformed an entire generation of Americans. One need only read Studs Terkel's *The Good War* or Tom Brokaw's *The Greatest Generation* to get a sense of that. And in its own way, though for very different reasons, the Vietnam War did that to another generation, as is readily apparent in Gloria Emerson's *Winners and Losers* or Myra MacPherson's *Long Time Passing*. The Korean War simply did not have that kind of impact. It was not the central event of the fifties, and most Americans remained untouched by it from start to finish. "People had other things to do and unless your son was there, nobody seemed to care much about Korea," writes Korean War veteran Charles F. Cole in *Korea Remembered: Enough of a War!* And when it ended, he adds, "the Korean War vanished from view like a lost football game."[3]

The reasons are multiple and complex, but like the war itself, I would suggest that the literature of the Korean War has never been recognized or widely read precisely because that experience was not the kind of transformative experience that the other two wars were. Put briefly, as Philip K. Jason and I write in *Retrieving Bones: Stories and Poems of the Korean War*, "The Korean War did not capture the American popular imagination."[4] Why? The soldier-poets themselves offer some possible answers.

"Korea was a 'non-war,'" says William Childress, "being alternately a 'police action' and 'Harry Ass Truman's war.' Korea was no war to inspire poetry or fiction. It lacked all nobility and didn't settle a damn thing." Keith Wilson calls the war "a very dirty and murderous joke." Reg Saner's answers take the form of questions: "Is it because Korea wasn't officially a war, just bloody murder on both sides, while being officially termed 'a police action'? Is it because for a long time people referred to it as 'the Phony War'? . . . Or, finally, and perhaps most likely, had World War II made us small potatoes by inevitable comparison—among even ourselves?" In spite of "all the ink spilt about poor public support for Vietnam veterans," Saner believes that "we Korean veterans got neither respect nor disrespect. Except amid our immediate families, there was no reaction." Unlike the Vietnam War, which "split the U.S., creating in the process a vast readership for anti-war writing," Saner observes, the reason "major U.S. publishers were slow to print the [Korean War] stuff" was not relevant to "anything but fiscal caution."[5]

Beyond the level of popular culture, however, even within the highly specialized world of those who actually study war and the literature of war—a world which has given at least some attention to much of the literature from the Korean War—the poetry from that war remains virtually invisible. Paul Fussell's *The Norton Book of Modern War*, for instance, includes no poetry on the Korean War, nor does Jon Stallworthy's *The Oxford Book of War Poetry*, although both books include poems dealing with the Second World War and the Vietnam War. Colonel James R. Kerin's 1994 doctoral dissertation from the University of Pennsylvania, "The Korean War and American Memory," states that aside from Rolando Hinojosa-Smith's novel-in-verse *Korean Love Songs* and a poem called "Heartbreak Ridge" by Edith Lovejoy Pierce, "verse inspired by the Korean experience seems to be limited to the doggerel of contemporaneous figures writing for service journals or sincere but unpolished tributes written by veterans."[6]

Ignored and unrecognized even by these specialists on war literature are such poems as Thomas McGrath's "Ode for the American Dead in Asia," Hayden Carruth's "On a Certain Engagement South of Seoul," and Howard Fast's "Korean Litany," along with the work of half a dozen veterans who fought in Korea and later went on to become prolific and serious poets.[7]

The human dimensions of war—the theme of the Korea/America Dialogue—are amply reflected in the poetry of the Korean War and are far too many even to begin to be enumerated in the course of this brief introduction. I want to begin, therefore, by focusing on one particular aspect that shows up in American veterans' poetry, and that is the way in which, at least in memory and in retrospect, these soldier-poets seem to recognize, empathize, and sympathize with the suffering of the Korean people. A number of the poems display remarkable compassion, given that they were written by combat veterans who undoubtedly endured their own share of suffering, and this compassion is often accompanied by powerful undercurrents of guilt and shame for what they have witnessed and done and been a part of.

In "They Said," for instance, former army infantry lieutenant Reg Saner first details the kind of lock-step cultural conditioning Americans go through while growing up, then concludes:

> They said, "Democracy is at the crossroads everyone
> will be given a gun and a map in cases like this
> there is no need to vote." Our group scored quite
> well getting each of its villages right except
> one but was allowed to try again on a fresh village
> we colored it black and then wore our brass
> stars of unit citation almost all the way home.

The closing two lines of the poem, especially Saner's choice of the word "almost," make it clear that he takes neither pride nor pleasure in what he and his "group" (i.e., the American Army) have done.

In "The Korean," ex-marine sergeant William Wantling coldly details the summary execution of a Korean civilian who

> stood stiffly pressed against
>         the wall
> arms folded
>            staring
> . . . flinched
> when the bullet sang
>            fell
> outward into the cobblestoned
>       court
> one too many holes in his head
> for stealing from Americans[,]

but the very fact of the poem belies the apparent detachment of the narrator. And in "Without Laying Claim," Wantling recounts American soldiers hurling grenades into a crowd while "mumbling an explanation / even we didn't believe." In "Pusan Liberty," Wantling also writes sympathetically about his Chinese adversaries, describing himself and "2 Chinese agents" he encounters in Pusan as "just / three angry boys lost in the immense / absurdity of War & State[.]"

Even more remarkably, former infantry sergeant James Magner, Jr., who was wounded so severely that he had to be evacuated and eventually medically discharged from the army, also writes with compassion and even tenderness about those who machine-gunned him. In a poem called "To a Chinaman, in a Hole, Long Ago," Magner seems literally to apologize to a dead Chinese soldier he has killed:

> I, your ordered searcher
> with a killer on my sling,
> do bequeath my life to you
> that you might fly the Yellow Sea
> to your startled matron's arms[,]

wishing the dead man were instead at home asleep among the children Magner imagines him to have. In another of Magner's poems, "The Man Without a Face," one cannot tell if the dead man "sprawled like a broken crab" on the barbed wire in front of Magner's position is Chinese or North Korean, but although the man is "dead and alone in his body," he is also "entombed in the heart of our mind." In the poem, and in his own thoughts, Magner gives his dead enemy the burial—and the respect—that battlefield circumstances have denied him.

Two poets in particular seem to be especially sensitive to the suffering brought upon others, and several of their poems require reproduction in full. The first two are by William Childress, a demolitions expert during the war. His parents were sharecroppers and migrant farm workers, a life he also lived until he joined the army in 1951. Indeed, he joined the army not to fight for freedom or democracy, but because the army promised him the chance for the first time in his life to have a bed of his very own and three meals a day with meat.

### Letter Home

> Mother, they line the roads
> like broken stalks,
> children with bellies swollen,
> and O, the flowers
> of their faces, petals all torn,
> and the flags
> of their threadbare garments.

Mother, we give
them everything in our packs
and still they moan
so sadly. More with eyes
like stone.
These kids will never sing
again.
O, Mother, wish me home!
With just one field of Kansas grain,
what I can do for them.


## The Long March

North from Pusan,
trailing nooses of dust,
we dumbly followed
leaders whose careers
hung on victory.

The road might
have been the Appian Way
except for the
starved children lining it.
We gave what we could

to hold back the grave,
but in Pusan the dead-truck
snuffled through frozen dawns
retrieving bones in thin sacks,
kids who would never beg again.

When we bivouacked
near Pyongtaek, a soldier
fished a bent brown stick
from a puddle. It was
the arm of someone's child.

Not far away, the General
camps with his press corp.

Any victory will be his.
For us, there is only
the long march to Viet Nam.

Although "Letter Home" seems to be the straightforward expression of an innocent farm boy newly arrived in the war zone, the voice in "The Long March" is that of a battle-weary soldier, old before his time. The latter poem is more thematically complex than the former, including, as it does, reflections on the brute endurance of soldiers and the vanity of leadership, and making an overt association between the Korean and Vietnam Wars. Yet even the hardened soldier—in the second, third, and fourth stanzas—focuses not on himself or his buddies or on matters American, but on Korean civilians, on children.

Here are two more poems by Keith Wilson, author of *Graves Registry*, who served three tours in Korean waters as a naval officer.

### Guerilla Camp

We arrived at Sok To
before dawn, caught the last
of the tide & slipped the LST's bow
high on the beach.

       he was waiting, bent
       slightly over, hiding
       his hand. He didn't
       wave.

Later, after a good breakfast
aboard, an Army captain took
us on a tour of the guerilla
camp:

       & he followed, tagged
       along like somebody's
       dog, a tall Korean,
       patient.

We were shown the kitchens, & the
tent barracks, the specially built
junks with their concealed engines

& he watched, never
leaving us with his
eyes

Through the hospital, saw 4
sheetcovered bodies from the
raid the night before, didn't
ask whose men they were, spoke
kindly to the wounded & gave
them cigarettes

until he strode up,
stuck his shattered hand
in my face, anger & hatred
flaming in his eyes &
shouted & shouted & shouted

waving that hand, the
bones crumpled by a rifle slug & pushed
almost through the skin,
hardened into a glistening
knot

He was one of ours, a retired fighter,
about my age, my height. They told me
he wanted to know how a man
could farm
with a hand like that.

**Commentary**

After the raid, the bodies
are lined on the beach. We can
see them across the way, the living
standing beside them in their white
robes, the wind hitting in gusts
across the separating bay
that these men died
that our guerillas shot them

down in a darkness
is perhaps not so important.

God kills, they say
justifying man's ways
to those patterns they
see surround them

deaths. lists of victims
in a language the uncle
back home couldn't read
if he saw it, whose enemies
are always faceless, numbers
in a paper blowing in the
Stateside wind.

How many bodies would
fill a room
living room with TV, soft
chairs & the hiss
of opened beer?

We have killed more.
The children's bodies alone
would suffice.

The women, their admittedly
brown faces frozen in the agony
of steel buried in their stomachs,
they too would be enough

but aren't, are
finally not piled high enough
the cost of war must be paid, bullets
made for firing, fired. O,
do not dream of peace while such bodies
line the beaches & dead men float
the seas, waving, their hands
beckoning
        rot, white bones
      settle on yellow bottom mud.

A graduate of the United States Naval Academy at Annapolis whose great-granduncle had been an admiral, Wilson had fully anticipated making the navy his career. Poems like these help to explain why he resigned his commission and spent his life instead as a teacher.

A similar empathy and sympathy are trained on the pain, trauma, and despair of the American soldier in combat in the poetry of Rolando Hinojosa-Smith, whose *Korean Love Songs* comprises the single largest group of poems about the Korean War published by a single author. Writing mostly in Spanish, Hinojosa-Smith is not well known among English-speaking readers, but in the Spanish-speaking community in the United States, throughout Latin America, and even in Europe, he has been widely published and widely read ever since winning the Premio Casa de las Americas in 1976 with his second novel, *Klail City y sus alrededores*. Although Hinojosa-Smith is best known as a writer of prose and does not fancy himself a poet, his *Korean Love Songs*, composed in English, is in fact a novel in verse. The poems selected here show the human side of American combat.

**Friendly Fire**

Light travels faster than sound,
But sound travels fast enough for some.

The burnt hand caught the shrap direct and sailed off
As the abandoned arm shot upward
Looking for its partner
Now partly buried in the mud.

The hip, too, felt the smoking clumps
Which now don't have to be surgically removed:
That wire-laying signalman is as good as dead.

The spent shell
Bounces and clangs with the others,
As the hangman's lanyard sways and waits to reactivate the howitzer.

Sometimes, however, sound doesn't travel fast enough:
    "Raise those signs, Sergeant Kell,
    The forward ob. says you're still short."

Still, sound travels fast enough for some
As it did for them
Who heard the first scream
In time to hug the sodden field.


## Above All, the Waste

Lt. Phil Brodkey up and shot himself two days ago;
We found his helmet, the binocs,
    The paper, the pencil,
Two packs of cigarettes and a Japanese lighter,
All in a row; We found him face down.
Half in half out of his forward ob. hole.

He used to say he was a Philadelphia Jew
Doing time; for once he was wrong.
He was a friend; he was resourceful and kind, calm, precise,
And something that most of us here are not:
He was very good at his job.
And yet, he cracked,
As I imagine many of us will,
In time.

My God, but I'd hate to see
The letter Bracken will send off to his family.
Maybe, just once, Bracken'll do the right thing:
He'll personally recommend him for the Purple Heart and the Bronze
And then leave the writing to one of the other firing officers.


## One Solution

Early this morning, Louie Dodge jumped into the latrine,
Sat down, and refused to come out.
Threats and direct orders couldn't budge him,
And he stayed there all morning and well into the afternoon until
Bracken drove in to check up on us.
Hatalski reported to the Captain, and,

Straight face and all,
Directed him to the latrine where
Louie Dodge has made plans to sit out the war.

Hook says Louie jumped up and saluted when he saw the Captain.
Hatalski, without a word,
Ordered everyone else away; leaving him,
Hook, Bracken, and the firing officers looking at poor Louie Dodge.

>  "What's the meaning of this?"
>  No answer.
>  "Just what the hell do you think you're doing?"
>  Still no answer.
>  "Get up here right now!"

Saluting once more,
Louie Dodge walked the length of the latrine,
Clambered up the side, and
Reported to Bracken:

>  "E-5 Louis Dodge reporting as ordered, sah."

Bracken could have delivered twins then and there;
He pointed to the jeep and said:

>  "Take off your boots and that uniform,
>  and wait for me over there."

By this time, Hatalski had a blanket which he handed to Hook;
Give this to him he says,
Until he goes and stands with the firing officers where
Bracken wheels and asks:

>  "Who threw him in there?"

It's explained that this was Dodge's own doing;
That we tried to get him out,
That he had refused to come out,
That he had been behaving in a peculiar manner,

And that he was probably suffering from fatigue.
The officers were explaining away with Hatalski and Hook
Standing there at parade rest.

> "All right, I've heard enough . . . Hatalski, radio
> that I'm coming in with a casualty."

Hatalski almost chokes, but off he goes to the phone and says,

> "Rafe, get Potter on the line; tell him Dodge's coming
> in with Bracken on casualty status. And, Rafe,
> tell Potter to prepare transfer papers
> on the son-of-a-bitch."

Somebody got Louie a wool cap and
Wearing that and Frank's blanket,
He climbed into the jeep. Sitting there, looking straight ahead,
With his right hand shaking,
He begins to cry as the jeep
Makes its way down the hill,
And away from the war.

There can be no doubt that a great many American soldiers contributed a great deal to the misery and suffering of Korea and its people. That is the nature of war. But for these poets at least, the human dimension of the Korean War transcends their own suffering to encompass the suffering of their comrades, their erstwhile enemies, and the Korean people. These former American soldiers and veterans of the Korean War seem very much mindful, at times painfully so, of the defenseless and the innocent who always, when armies clash, get caught in the middle. It is a small testament to the humanity of these poets and a powerful reminder of the frightful cost of war.

## Notes

1. See "Soldier-Poets of the Vietnam War," *The Virginia Quarterly Review* 63, no. 2 (spring 1987).

2. Depew's and Deck's stories are included in *Retrieving Bones: Stories and Poems of the Korean War*, along with stories by ten other authors and forty poems by seven poets. The anthology, which I coedited with Philip K. Jason, also includes an annotated bibliography of novels, memoirs, and histories from the Korean War.

3. Cole, *Korea Remembered*, 212, 273.
4. Ehrhart and Jason, eds., *Retrieving Bones*, xix.
5. See my "I Remember: Soldier-Poets of the Korean War," introduction to *War, Literature and the Arts* 9, no. 1 (spring/summer 1997): 33, 39–41.
6. Kerin, "The Korean War and American Memory," 183–84.
7. Most of this soldier poetry is included in *War, Literature and the Arts*. The poems reproduced in whole or in part in this essay, along with biographical and bibliographical information about the poets, can be found there.

## Works Cited

Brady, James. *The Coldest War: A Memoir of Korea*. New York: Orion Books, 1990.
Brokaw, Tom. *The Greatest Generation*. New York: Random House, 1998.
Carruth, Hayden. "On a Certain Engagement South of Seoul." In *The Crow and the Heart*. New York: MacMillan, 1959.
Cole, Charles F. *Korea Remembered: Enough of a War!* Las Cruces, NM: Yucca Tree Press, 1995.
Deck, John. "Sailors at Their Mourning: A Memory." In *Greased Samba and Other Stories*. New York: Harcourt Brace, 1970.
Depew, Donald R. "Indigenous Girls." *Harper's,* March 1953.
Dickey, James. "The Firebombing." In *Poems 1957–1967*. New York: Collier Books, 1968.
Eberhart, Richard. "The Fury of Aerial Bombardment." In *Collected Poems 1930–1986*. Oxford: Oxford University Press, 1988.
Ehrhart, W.D., ed. "I Remember: Soldier-Poets of the Korean War." *War, Literature and the Arts* 9, no. 2 (fall/winter 1997).
Ehrhart, W.D., and Philip K. Jason, eds. *Retrieving Bones: Stories and Poems of the Korean War*. New Brunswick: Rutgers University Press, 1999.
Emerson, Gloria. *Winners and Losers: Battles, Retreats, Gains, Losses, and Ruins from the Vietnam War*. New York: Random House, 1976.
Fast, Howard. "Korean Litany." In *Korean Lullaby*. New York: American Peace Crusade, undated (but undoubtedly published between 1950 and 1953).
Frank, Pat. *Hold Back the Night*. Philadelphia: Lippincott, 1952.
Fussell, Paul, ed. *The Norton Book of Modern War*. New York: Norton, 1991.
Heller, Joseph. *Catch-22*. New York: Simon & Schuster, 1961.
Hinojosa-Smith, Rolando. *Korean Love Songs*. Berkeley, CA: Justa Publications, 1978.
Kerin, Col. James R. "The Korean War and American Memory." Ph.D., University of Pennsylvania, 1994.
Kim, Richard E. *The Martyred*. New York: George Braziller, 1964.
MacPherson, Myra. *Long Time Passing: Vietnam and the Haunted Generation*. New York: Doubleday, 1984.
Mailer, Norman. *The Naked and the Dead*. New York: Holt, Rinehart & Winston, 1948.
McGrath, Thomas. "Ode for the American Dead in Asia." In *Selected Poems 1938–1988*. Port Townsend: Copper Canyon Press, 1988.
Owen, Wilfred. "Dulce et Decorum Est." In *Collected Poems*. New York: New Directions, 1964.

Pierce, Edith Lovejoy. "Heartbreak Ridge." In *Where Steel Winds Blow*, Robert Cromie, ed. New York: McKay, 1968.

Russ, Martin. *The Last Parallel: A Marine's War Journal*. New York: Rinehart, 1957.

Serling, Rod. *The Rack*. In *Patterns: Four Television Plays with the Authors' Personal Commentaries*. New York: Simon, 1957.

Stallworthy, Jon, ed. *The Oxford Book of War Poetry*. Oxford: Oxford University Press, 1984.

Terkel, Studs. *The Good War: An Oral History of World War Two*. New York: Pantheon, 1984.

Wilson, Keith. *Graves Registry and Other Poems*. New York: Grove Press, 1969.

# 4
## The Korean War and the Visual Arts

*Roe Jae-ryung*

### Representations of the War Experience

With the outbreak of the Korean War, most artists evacuated Seoul and fled to the southern port city of Pusan or to their hometowns. Whereas the full extent of artistic activity in Pusan or elsewhere during the war is unverified and undocumented, there are surviving records of exhibition catalogs, reviews, articles, and memoirs of artists and writers. There are also records of military history compiled by the defense ministry that can be used to study and review the relationship between the Korean War and the visual arts.

In the war paintings that do survive and that have been published, the war is represented in images of battle, of massacre, of people fleeing their homes, of refugee camps, and of cities and villages in ruins. The paintings are limited in subject matter, and although a small number of them are descriptive and figurative, most are semiabstract, allegorical, and suggestive.

Two paintings by Yi Su-ŏk, *The Korean War* (1987, figure 1) and *Seoul in Ruins* (1953, figure 2), are important examples of artistic representations of the Korean War. The differences in the styles of the two paintings might be somewhat puzzling, but note that *The Korean War* is a repainted version (dated 1987) and therefore differs stylistically from the much earlier *Seoul in Ruins*. In the latter, there is a greater sense of immediacy and fresh visual memory, and of the artist's impressions as witness to the city's ruin as seen in the photograph in figure 3.

Figure 1. Yi Su-ŏk, The Korean War, 1987, oil on canvas

Figure 2. Yi Su-ŏk, Seoul in Ruins, 1953, oil on canvas

Yi Ch'ŏl-ŭi's painting *Massacre* (1951, figure 4) is a recording from memory of an actual scene of the brutal killings that often took place before and during the war. The massacre takes place in the dark, and the murderers are painted as dark silhouettes, their figures forming an ominous presence against the dim and hazy moonlight. The picture is ren-

Figure 3. Photo, City Hall and vicinity. October 1953

Figure 4. Yi Ch'ŏl-ŭi, Massacre, 1951, oil on hardboard

dered with very coarse brushwork and emphatic contrast of lights and darks. Sim Suk-ja's *Mother and Two Children* (figure 5) reveals another theme that recurs in representations of the war, namely the absence of

Figure 5. Sim Suk-ja, Mother and Two Children, 1953, oil on canvas

the father figure. Painted with a degree of abstraction, it is nevertheless powerful in its symbolic implications. The loving mother gently embraces one of the fighting boys in order to separate them. The boy on the left holds a sharp toy/weapon and is about to strike his brother. The artist has explained that this picture of siblings fighting is symbolic of the warring between the North and the South.

Pak Ko-sŏk painted *Scene of Pŏmil-Dong* (figure 6) in 1953 as a depiction of the neighborhood around the refugee camp in Pusan where he lived. The well-composed village scene and the motif of a woman with a child on her back were common features in early modern period paintings, as well as part of the conventions of academic painting. But here, such familiar features have been incorporated into a somber picture made up of rough outlines, simplified and distorted forms, and a dark palette—befitting the grim nature of the subject matter.

## Absence of the Korean War from Art History

The war drastically altered people's lives and uprooted homes and families, and artistic activities and official exhibitions—most notably the

Figure 6. Pak Ko-sŏk, Scene of Pŏmil-Dong, 1953, oil on canvas

Kukjŏn* exhibition—came to a temporary halt during the war years. But it is important to note that creative work did continue in the midst of the war and that art events and the art community did not completely dissolve and disappear. In Pusan, a temporary ad hoc art community staged artists' gatherings and small-scale exhibitions throughout the war years. Art critic Yi Kyŏng-sŏng recalls that small exhibitions would be held in teahouses, which also served as casual daily gathering places for artists, writers, and critics. These events served as a much-welcome outlet, and Yi himself would spend most of his afternoons visiting the shows and artists at these teahouses.

The teahouse exhibitions consisted of paintings produced by an official group of artists who were hired to document the war. This artists' group was formed in 1951 under the supervision of the defense ministry's Department of Information and Education, and eventually employed

*Kukjŏn (National Art Exhibition) was an annual juried art exhibition inaugurated by the Korean government in 1949 and continued until 1979. It was the longest-surviving art institution in modern Korea and was the central exhibition venue for aspiring artists as well as a conservative institution that was controlled by establishment artists.

seventy artists, most of them in their thirties and forties. These artists were not the equivalent of war correspondents, who report live from the scenes of battles, but were more like an inspection party that went to the battlegrounds afterward to draw sketches. A former member recalls that membership in this troupe was desirable for practical reasons, especially for refugee artists who had fled from the North, because the artists were issued official identification and provided with room and board. Another important privilege was that the defense ministry provided the artists with painting materials imported from Japan, which would have been difficult for most artists to obtain otherwise. In return, the artists were required to submit one painting each.

Members of the official artists' group did not show much zeal for producing war paintings. They rarely went on trips to the battlefront, and most memories are of scores of artists huddled together in one room. A glance at the exhibition records reveals a recurrence in the painting titles of such words as "still life," "family," "spring," and "stars," suggesting that many of the paintings that were produced and exhibited in Pusan during the war years were irrelevant to the nature of the artists' mission or to the war experience. Instead, artists would exhibit samples of old artwork produced prior to the war.

From this general overview of the art community and artistic output during the war years, one may receive the impression that there was an overall disinterestedness and apathy toward representing the war experience. Or one might think that the artists were simply inept at visualizing the realities of war, which were surely too vivid and horrific to ignore. The sluggish appearance of the art scene of the 1950s, coupled with the extensive loss of documentation and original artworks, has been part of the reason for a lack of interest among Korean art historians and critics in writing about and studying the art of the war years. As the war must have been the most traumatic and disruptive of experiences for the artists, it is surprising that there is so little visual testimony from the 1950s. In view of this disappointing impression, the most compelling discussion surrounding the impact of the war on the visual arts no longer concerns how disruptive the war situation was for art production, or how the war was represented in works of art. Instead the question is, Why do we see so little evidence of the war in the visual arts? Several explanations are possible.

The paintings themselves do not represent the extent of the war experience, and the war did not have the direct impact of transforming the nature of the artists' work in terms of either content or style. This is not because the war did not have a great impact on individual artists or the art community. Rather, the absence of the war in the art of the 1950s occurs in tandem with the general absence of realism in modern Korean painting—a phenomenon that has historical and institutional roots. During the colonial period, the Japanese governor-general exercised repression and institutionalized censorship on all forms of social critique and realism in art. Even innuendoes and allegories that referred to social realities were prohibited. Although there had been earlier attempts at social and historical commentary in a mode of realism painting during the 1920s, this never developed into mainstream art. The exercise of colonial cultural policy was later followed by the repression of the political left in the art community, through arrests, imprisonments, confiscations, and the forced breakup of artists' groups. The repression of the political left was therefore also an effective repression of artistic realism. Thus, in retrospect, we read that significant developments in the history of modern Korean art tended to center around abstraction.

On the other hand, the absence of the war experience in art is also due to the fact that artists lacked a working visual vocabulary with which to represent such vivid and real experiences. The war was an experience altogether too disruptive of family life and artistic production, and all too immediate, to be translated contemporaneously into visual language. In the case of literary representations of the Korean War and its aftermath, a lapse of time was necessary to acquire perspective on historical events. It was only decades after the war that writers began publishing serious and important fiction on the basis of personal memories and research on the war experience. This was to be the case with representations of the war in the visual arts as well.

## The Artists' Experiences

It seems rather difficult to reconstruct the Korean War through surviving artwork, since the war was not fully represented or illustrated, and much of the art that did visualize the war experience has not survived. Rather, in rethinking the impact of the war on the visual arts, it seems that the lives of the artists themselves serve as the most powerful testimonies to the war experience. Through their individual histories, we see how the war completely uprooted families and homes, permanently scarring lives and impoverishing everyday existence—not only during the war years, but in the postwar years as well.

Art history in Korea has focused primarily on the pursuit of modernism. In light of this, the decade of the 1950s has been reviewed mostly as the period that shaped the emergence of the early masters of modern Korean painting, among them Pak Su-gŭn, Yi Chung-sŏp, and Kim Hwan-gi. The following section is an introduction to the personal histories of these three master painters and a summary of how the war affected their lives. The painter Yi Kwae-dae, whose biography is also presented, is not considered part of this art history triad, but was himself an influential artist prior to the war. His life and art had been silenced and forgotten in Korea until he was rediscovered quite recently.

## Pak Su-kŭn (1914–1965)

Pak Su-gŭn (figure 7) was born in 1914 in Kangwon Province. When his family went bankrupt, Pak was not able to continue his education beyond elementary school. It is said that he came across a reproduction of one of Jean François Millet's paintings as a child and determined to become a great artist himself. He would later paint scenes of rural agrarian life and simple folk that reflected the deep impact that Millet had on him as a young artist. Pak has earned national recognition and enduring public affection as an artist who has been able to synthesize the Western mode of oil painting with native subject matter, executed in a unique personal painting style. The hardship of his destitute existence on earth has been somewhat compensated by posthumous honors.

Pak had neither a formal education nor professional art training, but was a self-taught painter. In 1932, when he was eighteen, his watercolor was accepted at the Sŏnjŏn* exhibition. His work continued to be accepted regularly at the Sŏnjŏn, although he never became an establishment figure.

A memoir written by Pak's wife describes in detail the family's experience of the war. The family moved to Pyongyang before the war. After the outbreak of the war, their house was subject to constant surveil-

---

*Sŏnjŏn (Chosŏn Art Exhibition) was an annual juried art exhibition that was organized by the governor-general in 1922 and continued for twenty-three years up to 1944. It consisted of the categories of Oriental painting, Western painting, and calligraphy, and was the first comprehensive art exhibition in Korea and the only public art exhibition venue during the colonial period. The Sŏnjŏn exhibition forced Korean artists to conform to Japanese artistic conventions and aesthetics, and was also politically efficient in curtailing nationalist activities among Korean artists.

Figure 7. Photo, Pak Su-gŭn, with his family in Seoul, 1959

lance, and Pak was frequently arrested and subjected to overnight questioning by communist forces. He would hide in the mountains during the day and sneak back home after dark. Finally the family decided to flee to the South. Pak fled in advance, leaving his family behind. Because of his flight, the family was branded as reactionary and subjected to confiscation of all household goods, including their tableware. Pak was reunited with his family in Seoul two years later and survived the war years by painting portraits for American soldiers at a U.S. military base (figure 8). Even after the war, when the postwar art community was getting back on its feet, Pak—a man of quiet, restrained character and passive nature—remained a marginal figure. Pak the artist is featured as one of the key figures in Pak Wan-sŏ's celebrated novel, translated into English as *The Naked Tree*.

Pak Su-gŭn's wife recalls that immediately after the war the family lived on rations of corn and barley, wore secondhand clothing handed down from their landlords, and saved the money that Pak made painting portraits. Once in a while American soldiers would visit their home to look at the paintings and would sometimes buy Pak's work. An officer offered him help, bringing a load of painting material from Japan. This prompted him to quit the military base and devote himself to painting

Figure 8. Photo, Pak Su-gŭn painting portraits at a U.S. military base, 1952 (Pak is third from right)

full time. It was through the sales of paintings to American acquaintances that Pak's family survived. His difficult life was cut short at the age of fifty-one.

Although he remained poor, Pak never abandoned his affection for honest, hard-working simple folk. The painting *Grandfather and Grandson*, 1960, is representative of his mature style of painting. Pak painted scenes of farmers working the fields, women washing clothes by the river, people going to the local market, children at play, and village elders gathering to chat and smoke. There is a sense of timelessness, an absolute pastoral utopia that is visual poetry. The humble humanity and dignity of this painter's images explain why he has been so much revered and loved by the Korean people.

### Yi Chung-sŏp (Lee Joong Sub, 1916–1956)

Born near Pyongyang into a wealthy farming family, Yi Chung-sŏp (figure 9) received a formal education and was able to study abroad in Japan. He has become almost a national myth as an artist whose tragic personal life reflected the hardships of the nation, and his life's story has been widely made known to the general public through the publication of his biography, which was later produced as a dramatic play.

After the outbreak of the war, Yi left everything behind as he fled his home, including his mother, whom he left with his elder brother. As he bade her farewell, Yi handed his mother a bundle of his paintings to keep by her side. Then he grabbed and tore the paper flooring in his mother's room, which she had herself glued, pasted, and varnished.

Figure 9. Yi Chung-sŏp, photo, n.d.

One of his artist friends recalled that Yi would later carry this roll of floor paper on his person with great care.

Yi and his family fled to Pusan, but he did not settle there. Instead, they led a vagabond existence from one city to the next. This partly explains why the bulk of his work consists of small-scale drawings and paintings rather than large-scale masterpieces. In 1952 the family could no longer bear the hunger and poverty, and Yi sent his wife and two children to her parents' home in Japan. They remained separated, and although Yi did visit Japan on a seaman's pass, he would remain alone for the rest of his life. The difficulty of the prolonged separation and the mutual affection of Yi and his wife are revealed through their many letters that have been published.

Despite his destitute life, Yi remained committed to painting full time. Most of his surviving paintings and pictures date from the five years after 1951, and a comprehensive overview of his art was made possible prior to his death during a one-man exhibition in 1955, which showed some forty paintings. But this occasion was also a traumatic experience that broke the artist: the authorities banned fifty of his drawings on cigarette wrapping paper as obscene material.

Yi suffered from malnutrition and mental illness, and was hospitalized in 1955. He died the following year at the age of forty, leaving

Figure 10. Yi Chung-sŏp, Children with Fish, 1952, oil on paper

behind only unpaid hospital bills. His body remained at the hospital for several days because there was no immediate family member to claim him.

Yi Chung-sŏp met his wife, who was Japanese, at school in Japan. She recalls that he would often recite poems by Rilke, Baudelaire, and other poets. Yi was an artist deeply immersed in Western aesthetics; however, he was also a resolute nationalist. He was against the Sŏnjŏn exhibition during the colonial period, and after liberation did not participate in the Kukjŏn exhibitions. In his art, he developed a repertoire of imagery suggestive of his affection for ethnic and traditionally Korean elements; for instance, the recurring images of small children in his paintings allude to the child motifs in Koryo celadonite and in folk paintings from the Chosŏn Dynasty (figure 10). The cow or bull is also representative of pastoral life and of the agrarian Korean nation and the rural landscape, and was a symbol of resistance and nationalism during colonialism (figure 11). Whereas renditions of cows in Yi's paintings during the colonial period were of a rustic nature, this changes to images of feisty bulls charging at each other during the war years. After his separation from his family, Yi's bulls are shown increasingly tormented and despairing. The one shown here was painted in 1954 after the armistice and shows progressive emaciation from earlier white bull paintings in 1952 and 1953.

Yi's painting style has been identified as personally unique and is praised for being different from Western examples. His pictures are basically linear, more suggestive of calligraphy than of the painterly brush-

Figure 11. Yi Chung-sŏp, White Bull, 1954, oil on board

work of Western oil painting. The makeup of his pictures, with their panoramic display of imagery in nonillusionary space, also rejects logical composition and illusionary spatial representation.

Yi Chung-sŏp is especially noted for his charming miniature pictures on cigarette wrapping paper. He would etch the soft metallic surface, then paint over the etching with a layer of color wash and wipe the surface clean to produce a linear drawing with incised colored lines. The cigarette wrapping paper was a readily available painting medium at a time when materials were scarce and expensive. Yi produced many of these paper pictures during long idle hours sitting at teahouses and bars in Pusan during the war years.

### Kim Hwan-gi (1913–1974)

Kim Hwan-gi (figure 12) was born in Chŏlla province and is regarded as one of the most important pioneers of abstraction. He went to Japan to study art, and on the eve of the war he was living in Seoul, an active and celebrated artist and faculty member of a prestigious art college. Like Yi Chung-sŏp, Kim Hwan-gi took refuge in Pusan, where he was appointed

Figure 12. Kim Hwan-gi, photo portrait, n.d.

to the faculty of Hongik University. He did not produce any major work during the war years. An artist friend who lived with Kim's family in Pusan recalls that Kim always wore blue work clothes, and when it was time for laundry, he would not come out of the house. The friend assumed that Kim had nothing else to wear. The two families nonetheless had happy memories, and Kim Hwan-gi survived the war years by writing essays and drawing illustrations for various publications.

Kim's painting *Shanty House* (figure 13) was painted in 1951 during his stay in Pusan and is an abstraction of an actual seaside café in a nearby port city where artists and writers would frequently gather. In this charming picture, although the artist employed only minimal elements with great restraint in shapes and colors, he produced an image of a small temporary shack built at the water's edge, packed with people inside. The shabby reality is translated into rhythmic variations in line, color, and shape.

Kim Hwan-gi was the image of an accomplished, successful member of the Korean art community, a suave and well-liked individual who was very much aware of how to position his art between Western influence and native identity. He was also ambitious and looked westward for international recognition. In 1956 he went to Paris, and he stayed in France for three years. The paintings he produced in Paris were to some extent influenced by his exposure to and interest in the thick paint textures used by Rouault and Dubuffet, whom he admired.

Upon returning to Korea, Kim continued teaching and held important art administrative positions. On his way to São Paolo in 1963 as commissioner, he detoured to New York City, where he stayed for the next eleven years until his death, never returning to Korea. He wrote in a letter to his friend that he had left Korea because it was too stifling, but, being away, he could not help but long for Seoul.

In his mature paintings from New York Kim began to replace his earlier suggestive and lyrical titles with numbers indicating the date of completion of each work. The surfaces of his paintings are covered with dots and lines that seem to stretch into infinite space. Despite the large-

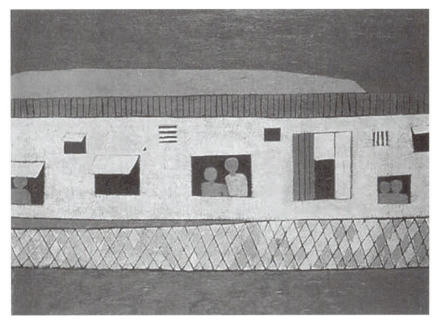

Figure 13. Kim Hwan-gi, Shanty House, 1951, oil on canvas

scale size of these paintings, they retain a delicate sensibility and intricate details. Kim wrote to a friend in Korea that he was confident that his large-scale dot paintings would succeed. He also wrote that in painting each of these dots he was thinking and longing for Seoul and his friends back home.

## Yi Kwae-dae (1913–1987)

Yi Kwae-dae (figure 14) was born into a very wealthy family in Taegu and enjoyed an exclusive upbringing, seemingly untouched by the realities of colonialism. Yi had the privilege of receiving his art education in Tokyo. After his return to Korea he did not participate in the colonial Sŏnjŏn exhibitions, but instead was an active member of an alternative artists' group. He had earlier studied figure painting, and during the years following independence he became increasingly interested in representing a nationalist ethos. His earlier work has been interpreted in terms of local color. Following independence he became a member of the Artists' Federation, which was composed mostly of artists affiliated with left-wing politics. The artists of the left wing professed that art must reflect reality,

Figure 14. Yi Kwae-dae, Self-Portrait, n.d.

but despite their rhetoric there was no in-depth theoretical or critical discourse to pursue this line of thought, nor were there substantial artistic examples to support such politics. It is Yi Kwae-dae's surviving paintings that provide superb material evidence of the artistic program of the political left. He opened a private art academy and seemed settled in his teaching, but a series of events tossed him into the center of the political and ideological mayhem of the war years.

Yi's elder brother defected to the North because he was a high official in the Communist Party at a time when rampant anticommunist and left-wing persecution began in the South. In 1949, Yi was forced to join the National Guidance Federation, which rounded up ideologically suspect artists and forced them to join in weekly workshop sessions to produce political posters designed to pacify the "rebels." With the outbreak of the war, Yi remained in Seoul because of his bedridden mother, and when the northern troops occupied Seoul he was forced to renew allegiance to the communists. Despite his former membership in the National Guidance Federation, he was readmitted into the leftist Artists' Federation to paint portraits of Stalin and Kim Il-sung. Many artists who remained in Seoul when the capital was occupied by North Korean troops either willingly or reluctantly pledged alliance to the Artists' Federation. Personal survival meant adapting to the radical shifts in ideology and politics.

When Seoul was recaptured, the members of the Artists' Federation all fled to the North in fear of persecution. It has not been verified whether their defection was of their own free will or whether they were kidnapped. Yi Kwae-dae fled Seoul on foot a week before the city was recaptured, but was arrested only five days later by the Republic of Korea Army and sent to a prisoner-of-war camp in Pusan. His exact whereabouts and activities thereafter remain largely unknown. We know that he sent a letter to his wife from the POW camp dated November 11, 1950, and that when the armistice was signed in 1953 he chose to go to the North. It seems that the artist presumed that the separation from his family would only be temporary, that peace would be reached and that he would be able to rejoin his wife.

There is only scattered information on Yi's years in North Korea. He participated in an art exhibition in Moscow in 1957, and it seems he continued to produce art but did not become an important artist in the North. He later remarried, and died in 1987.

Yi Kwae-dae produced a series of large group paintings of which four canvases survive (1948, figures 15 and 16). The elaborate group scene that was painted in 1948 after the nation's independence is un-precedented in the history of Korean art. It is a picture of extraordinary composition and drama, a pictorial allegory of historical realities. The viewer's eyes are swept through the intricate web of nude and seminude figures from the bottom left corner—sunken, destitute, and famished—into a crescendo that culminates in the standing figures on the right, who gaze into the distance toward hope and a better future for the people.

These were the artists born and raised during the period of Japanese colonialism. They experienced the war in their thirties and lived through the postwar years with great difficulty, personal loss, hunger, and poverty. They are not exceptional in their experiences alone; many other individuals and families suffered in the same way. It is probably not their personal suffering itself that merits recognition, but the manner in which they remained committed and uncompromising in their work. They produced artwork of such excellence *in spite of* the war and the times—not necessarily as a result of, or as a reflection on, the war experience.

**The Postwar Generation**

The young generation of artists that emerged as the new avant-garde in the postwar Korean art community identified themselves with artists in post–World War II Europe. These artists believed that postwar Korea had close affinities with postwar Europe. The members of the so-called informel movement were part of the generation that fought in the Korean War, or that experienced the aftermath of the war during their formative years and in college. These Korean artists marked a pivotal point in the history of modern art. They were the first generation trained in

Figure 15. Yi Kwae-dae, Group Painting, 1948, oil on canvas

Figure 16. Yi Kwae-dae, Group Painting (detail), 1948

Korean, rather than Japanese, art schools. This generation also marked the beginning of exposure to, and exchange with, the international art world as a few artists began to participate in overseas exhibitions.

The so-called informel artists professed a new mode of expression that rejected painterly finesse and correct composition and aimed at capturing the emotions of personal experiences of the Korean War. Their philosophy manifested itself in mural-scale paintings encrusted with thick layers of paint in vivid and clashing colors or a somber dark palette applied in vigorous brushstrokes and gestures. It was a mode of painting that was nonrepresentational and unbound by any strictures—thus, nonformal, or *informel* in French. It was influenced by the informel art in France as well as American abstract expressionism.

Pak Sŏ-bo is one of the most important artists of the informel group and has been the spokesperson for the artists of his generation, of which he says the following:

> Although [we] survived the war, poverty and hunger disillusioned the dreams and visions of the young . . . young men were burning with undaunted energy for life. With the experiences of war, the current art establishment was uniformly preoccupied with figurative representation. The anachronistic Kukjŏn (National Art Exhibition) was the center of it all, and we rebelled against it.

## Revision of Korean History in Art

In the 1980s, a widespread grassroots movement called Minjung generated political consciousness within the Korean art community. The critical basis for Minjung art was the belief that Korean modernism was a result of misguided attempts to mimic the West, a by-product of neocolonialism and cultural imperialism that was neither native to Korea nor pertinent to the experiences of the Korean people. The Minjung artists sought to retrain themselves, to unlearn what they had been taught at art school, to develop a pictorial style that was pertinent to the reality of Korean society. These artists dismissed the earlier art forms as products of the art establishment and of a hierarchical culture dominated by specialists and intellectuals and separated from any real-life experiences of the people (*minjung*). Because they saw art as a consciousness-raising medium, Minjung artists nationwide worked together on collaborative projects and held workshops on location at factories and farms, on college campuses, and on city streets. Among the staples of subject matter in Minjung art were the Korean War itself and the postwar nation, military buildup and military dictatorship, division between North and South, and the separation of families.

One of the most impressive Minjung artists, Shin Hak-chŏl, incorporates photographic images into his composite paintings. In his series of paintings titled *History of Modern Korea* (figures 17, 1993, and 18, 1985), Shin deals with historical events as illustrated by photographic documentation to create powerful, soaring images depicting the way in which chaos and upheaval from the past ultimately feed the current state of society.

Im Ok-sang has also been a versatile artist in the Minjung movement.

Figure 17. Shin Hak-ch'ŏl, History of Modern Korea: Division of the Nation, 1993, oil on canvas

Figure 18. Shin Hak-ch'ŏl, History of Modern Korea: Military Dictatorship, 1985, photo collage

He used a wide range of different media, producing paintings, collages, and sculptures. In his painting, *The Kim Family After the Korean War* (figure 19), the artist uses papier-mâché to produce a unique raised surface and coarse texture. Although rendered in a rather cartoonlike simplistic style, this painting effectively communicates the extent of the loss of human lives through the simple portrayal of a family portrait in which several members and loved ones are missing.

## Some Reflections

The early modern era, which roughly corresponds to the colonial period (from the turn of the century to the years immediately following independence in 1945), is one of the most highly concentrated periods of study among Korean art historians. This critical period involves numerous problematic yet significant issues, such as the assimilation of modernism and Western art practices and Western institutions; the consequent changes in traditional art forms; the impact of colonialism and

Figure 19. Lim Ok Sang, The Kim Family After the Korean War, n.d.

Japanization on artistic production; and the quest for national art, for "local color," and for nationalist sentiments in the art community. The time frame of early modern art terminates in 1950 with the Korean War, and the war years are something of a vacuum. The period has been written off as a temporary standstill in artistic activities, and art representing the war has been generally disregarded as lacking artistic merit or critical interest. Whereas prewar early modernism is exemplified by the works of master painters such as Pak Su-gǔn, Yi Chung-sǒp, and others, the postwar Korean art scene may be very differently defined. It was the war and the aftermath of the war that became the crucial contexts for shaping an avant-garde spirit in the Korean art scene—equipped with a rebellious agenda and experimental art practices.

As a member of the postwar generation writing on Korean art, I have the leisure to review the significance of the relationship between the Korean War and the visual arts with some detachment. But such a dry and academic evaluation is not meant to erase or belittle the horrors of the war as experienced by the older generation. The war as an immediate reality was represented through different means by artists during the war years and continued to be a compelling concern for Minjung artists decades later. These works of art are visual translations of history and memories and therefore reach the viewer visually, emotionally, and intellectually. But most inspiring and moving are the very biographies of the artists' lives—the raw facts of which seem quite incredible to the postwar generation of readers. It is for their heroic artistic spirit in producing commendable artwork in the face of such adversity that Korean art historians and the general public bestow so much praise and affection on the early master artists—praise and affection which might seem unwarranted in the eyes of foreign viewers. Nevertheless, the artists' stories may be equally appreciated by non-Koreans, since their personal experiences have been translated into a pictorial language that helps to overcome the barriers of language and culture.

# 5

# The Korean War Through the Camera of an American War Correspondent

## *Max Desfor**

I made two inauspicious entries into Seoul in 1950 and 1951. On both occasions, I jeeped or walked in with American troops as they slowly fought their way in to oust the enemy forces and recapture the capital city. Some twenty-seven years later, and again twenty-two years after that, I reentered Seoul, but comfortably by air and limo. On both of these occasions, I found that much had happened and much had changed in the intervening years.

I was a staff photographer for the Associated Press. I had left my post in Rome, Italy, to start my scheduled home leave, and arrived in New York with my family the first week in June 1950. I was told I was to be transferred to the domestic service after years in the foreign service. I was assigned to the Miami bureau and was to make my arrangements accordingly.

On the twenty-fifth of the month, North Korean troops crossed the thirty-eighth parallel into South Korea and the war was under way. I immediately volunteered to go as a war correspondent, but was told I wasn't needed. According to my boss, and I quote, "The war will be over within two weeks." I'm not denigrating my boss; everyone had the same opinion. However, within a few days my boss called me and asked if I was still willing to go. My reply was affirmative, and I rushed to the office. Within fifteen minutes, my passport was on its way to Washing-

*All photos appearing in this chapter were taken by Max Desfor, Associated Press correspondent.

ton for visas, my trip to Florida was canceled, and I had a ticket to fly to Tokyo, with a stopover in Seattle where my passport would catch up with me in time for the rest of the journey. I stopped long enough in Tokyo to get the necessary military accreditation and clearances and some more suitable clothing. Within two weeks of the beginning of the war, I was in Korea.

I have listened to the dissertations of a number of scholars who labeled and categorized various types of national and international conflicts. They provide thoughtful, interesting, and profound discussions on the causes and effects of the Korean War in particular. They write and talk of the effects as shown in the art, literature, and poetry that was created and produced after the war. They also provide the impressions of individuals and families, the effects on them personally and socially.

I am not an academician, nor am I a historian, a philosopher, a scholar, a poet, or a high-ranking military or government official. I was a professional news photographer who went where the news was. I did not differentiate or give specific names to the types of wars that I was involved in professionally. I was a war correspondent, and covered many conflicts. Whether a war was called an "international war," like World War II; a "police action," like the conflict between the Dutch and Indonesians in 1946; or a "limited war," like the Kashmir War in India in 1947, I always believed that my camera spoke for itself as objectively as possible from my vantage point. I never had an ax to grind, and I did not shoot my pictures for any purpose other than to record and show what was actually happening, what I was witnessing. Any philosophy I may have acquired came long after these wars and conflicts, when I could take another look at the pictures I made and the circumstances that prevailed at the time.

I caught up with the American troops after the military defenders had evacuated Seoul. My first contact was with the Twenty-fourth Division south of the city. The first action I saw was the army fighting its way through the back streets of a small town. There, I ran into engineers laying land mines on the roads to protect the retreating American and Korean soldiers. The engineers also had to take up defensive positions with their rifles, trying to slow down the rush of North Korean troops whose forward elements were on their heels. The rout continued until the retreating troops were driven to the southern port city of Pusan. There, they gathered to regroup and form a perimeter.

The breakout from the Pusan perimeter came shortly after the United

Marching a line of naked prisoners off in Pusan area

Aid to a wounded Marine in the Inchon area

States Marines arrived to reinforce the beleaguered troops. The advance gained momentum with General Douglas MacArthur's brilliant stroke: flanking the enemy with an amphibious landing operation at Inchon, the port city west of Seoul. The combined troops formed a pincer movement that caught the North Koreans between the Inchon force and the troops pushing them from the Pusan breakout. Now it was the North Koreans who fled, with the UN troops in hot pursuit. Gaining a strong foothold around Inchon put the American forces solidly on the road toward Seoul,

Three soldiers firing over top of sandbagged barricade in Seoul

their immediate objective. The enemy was still able to inflict damage on the landing force, but many of them were also captured as the American force spread out and moved inland.

Every mile of the way toward the capital was a struggle. But the most intense fighting came upon entry into the city. It was street-by-street, house-to-house fighting, every inch of the way gained by close-range combat. In the heart of the city, the troops got protection from sandbag barricades that had been abandoned by the North Koreans in the earlier stages of the war. At one such barricade, the portraits of Kim Il-sung and Stalin were still hanging on the side of a nearby building, looking down at the American troops firing at the retreating soldiers from behind the protection of the tall, stacked sandbags.

The U.S. troops had to go slowly through the rubble, fighting their way through the demolished city. They had to blast their way into tunnels and even into trenches dug in the sidewalks. Although supported by tanks, the men had to carefully walk through the debris, as many of the enemy soldiers were well concealed and able to inflict deadly fire. On one street, the advance was held up by a sniper who would fire off a

Marines catch North Korean sniper popping out of hole in sidewalk in Seoul

round, then disappear as quickly as he had fired. The marines were pinned down for a long time until they got a fix on the sniper. In a quick flash, they got a glimpse of the head and shoulders of a soldier materializing out of a hole in a paving block on the sidewalk. He would pop up, fire off a round, and immediately duck down into the hole in the sidewalk again. Once they got a fix on him, the marines zeroed in on his location and waited for him to pop up again. They caught him on the rise, finished him off, and were able to move on to the next spot of danger.

The tragedy of conflicts is that it is not only the combatants who pay with their lives. It is not uncommon for civilians to pay the price of being caught in the path of war, and it is not uncommon for the camera to capture such tragic sights. In a street in the heart of the city, after the immediate shooting passed through the area, I caught sight of the aftermath of the battle. Lying in the street were a man and wife, she cradling a young man in her lap, helplessly sprawled in the midst of their household possessions, which were strewn on the ground. They apparently had been caught in crossfire as they tried to flee the area.

On another occasion, I photographed another heart-rending scene. A mother was awkwardly sprawled in death on the side of a road. Alongside were her two children, crying and bewildered, left there to an un-

Old man, wife, and son, lying in a street of Seoul

Dead mother sprawled on side of road with two children crying

known fate. They, too, appeared to be innocent victims, caught in the crossfire as the soldiers battled for that piece of territory.

After Seoul was regained and effectively secured, the troops continued to push on northward. The terrain outside the city was more rugged, making

Waves of paratroopers dropping out of planes

the going more difficult physically. In hilly and mountainous areas, it is a matter of capturing the heights, one hill after another. The soldiers had to trudge slowly up in long lines to gain the peaks for commanding positions. It is on the heights that troops can set up their heavy mortars and observation posts to direct their fire at the enemy, who may be on the next peak, only as far away as three thousand yards.

Sometimes the going was a little easier. Sometimes the troops were able to move forward speedily in trucks and other vehicles. And, sometimes, the South Korean inhabitants were able to come out to welcome the onrushing troops and cheer them on.

I was with the British contingent when I got word of an operation plan for a paratroop jump. I managed to get back to Kimpo Airport and reported to the commanding officer of the 187th Regimental Combat Team, a regiment of the famed 101st Airborne Division. I arrived at about 7:00 P.M., and a sergeant was immediately assigned to rig up a pack for me that would securely hold my camera gear so it would not get damaged or lost in the jump. I then attended a briefing session, where I learned what the operation was about. It was a full-scale combat assault jump behind enemy lines. Its mission was twofold. One objective was to cut off a concentration of North Korean troops as they were fleeing northward. The other was to cut off a train that was also moving north. According to military intelligence, the train was carrying American POWs who were being taken to prison camps in the north.

Our takeoff time was 5:30 A.M., but rain and fog delayed us until noon. Once I was in place in the plane, I started to interview the men around me. The young paratroopers, most of them at least ten years younger than I, were eager to get into the action and accomplish their mission. I wrapped up my interview notes and gave them to the pilot, who would contact my colleagues on his return to the airport and hand the notes over to them.

Settling back, waiting for whatever came next, I learned two things. The first was that in having chosen to follow the jumpers out of the plane (my plan was to shoot pictures as they went out), I was what they called "last man on the stick." A stick is formed when the men line up, tightly packed together, ready to step up to the open door and move out into space. I found out that no experienced paratrooper liked that position. One main reason was that enemy troops on the ground had time to aim and fire at the paratroopers who came out later. However, I declined to change positions with those who offered to switch with me. I was thinking of my photo strategy as well as the fact that I was such a complete novice in this matter that I didn't think it would make any difference.

The second thing I learned was how to jump out and land. These were my first-ever and only instructions on the subject.

We reached the drop zone flying at an altitude of seven hundred feet. From that height, it takes only thirty seconds to hit the ground. I heard only sporadic, scattered firing as the waves of parachutists came down. After landing, the troops quickly spread out, searched the area, and cleared out and mopped up any pockets of resistance that they found. The second aim of the mission was not fulfilled because no train came through then or at any time during the next few days. The paratroopers were relieved a week later by a column of tanks and infantry. The reality or reliability of the intelligence information about the train is still a mystery to me.

As the UN forces continued to advance, I was with a leading column in pursuit of the fleeing troops. We stopped for a brief rest, and I got out of the jeep to stretch my legs. There was a layer of snow blanketing the ground. As I wandered in the field, I suddenly noticed an odd break in the snow. I saw a pair of blackened, stiffened hands sticking up through the snow, the fingers protruding as if in supplication. They were the

only things visible in the daz-
zling whiteness around them. I
told the ranking officer of my
discovery, and he sent his men
to clear away the snow and see
what lay below. Those hands
were bound at the wrists. As the
men continued to remove the
snow, they uncovered many
other bodies, all civilians, men
and women, scattered over a

Frozen hands sticking through snow

large area. The officers surmised that what most likely happened was
that the civilians had been forced to flee with the retreating troops. Their
speculation was that the civilians must have slowed the troops down, so
the fleeing soldiers had decided to get rid of their burden. The civilians
were shot and left there. Snow then fell and covered the bodies, except
for that one pair of hands sticking up to mark the spot. I had noted a
small round hole in the snow very close to the fingers, which indicated
to me that the man must still have been alive after he was bound and
shot. He breathed his last after the snow fell and covered him.

The troops I was with continued their onward push and went on to take
Pyongyang. They thrust through the North Korean capital and advanced
almost to the northernmost border on the western side. It was at that time
that the Chinese "volunteers" swarmed across the Yalu River and struck at
the American forces in the central sector. When the central sector was over-
whelmed and forced to flee, the flanks also became untenable, and we in
the western sector also had to flee. In the confusion, I liberated a jeep from
someone and joined the retreat. With me were two other correspondents
and an army signal corpsman. We fled back through Pyongyang and drove
to the Taedong River. We crossed it on a pontoon bridge that had just been
hastily erected by the army engineers, enabling tanks and trucks to ride
across the river. On the south side of the river, I stopped to make pictures of
the civilians trying to cross. They were walking across where the ice was
solid and clogged the river. A little farther upstream, where the water was
still open, they were crossing in small boats.

As we jeeped farther southward, we noted some activity and stopped
to see what was happening. It was an incredible sight. I saw what had
been a sturdy span across the river, obviously recently destroyed by
aerial bombs. Only the remains of the steel supports and girders were

Civilians in boat crossing ice-clogged Taedong River

sticking high out of the water. Crawling in and through the broken, bent, and twisted remains were thousands of civilians, inching their way across to reach the south side of the river. They were carrying small bundles of what must have been their only remaining possessions. And on the shore on the far side of the river were thousands more civilians, waiting to follow their compatriots across the destroyed bridge.

I got as close to the edge as I could on what had been the solid ground side, where the bridge had been anchored. It was a sheer drop of about fifty feet down to the ice in the river. It was freezing cold and, in spite of my gloves, my fingers were so cold that I had great difficulty operating my bulky camera. With that problem, plus the realization that we had to move away from there quickly and continue our push southward, I was able to shoot only about eight exposures of that tragic, memorable sight. In those moments, I could only fleetingly imagine the incredible determination of these people, going through awesome physical hardships as well as the trauma of having to abandon their homes and land to escape the onrushing Chinese troops.

Almost a year later, the same impression must have been made on the judges who selected this scene as the Pulitzer Prize–winning news photo of 1951.

Resuming our retreat, we encountered other memorable sights of civilians and soldiers squeezed into tiny spaces on top of boxcars and

Civilians crawling through girders of destroyed bridge over the Taedong River

between the couplings of trains. They were bundled up in coats or blankets, but nothing could keep them from the bitter cold and wind.

At some point farther south, where we thought it was safe enough, we headed our jeep eastward and made our way to the port city of Hungnam. There we caught up with the flotilla of ships that would evacuate all the troops retreating from the northeast, including the marines who escaped from the Chosin Reservoir debacle. It was an orderly withdrawal involving an estimated sixty thousand troops from various UN units. They had eluded an estimated one hundred thousand Chinese troops. The ragged UN troops lined up and marched onto the civilian freighters and military vessels awaiting them. One outfit still retained a sense of humor, even in the tension and grimness of the situation. At the edge of the boarding ramp of an LST, one of the men had placed a poster-sized sign that read "We didn't want the damn place anyway." When all the men were aboard the ships and the vessels were steaming out, those on deck could see the results of the work of the U.S. Navy Seals as they finished the job, blowing up and demolishing the installations in and around the harbor.

Landing at a port below the thirty-eighth parallel was like starting all over again: back up to the outposts on top of high hills; more fighting for strategic positions; more battles that added to the casualty lists but didn't have any convincing outcome. However, a movement was afoot to start negotiations for an agreement to stop the fighting, and the first meetings took place in a small building in Kaesong. Serious negotiations got under way from there, and the neutral area for the talks was set up at Panmunjom.

As the talks dragged on and Christmas of 1952 approached, a skeleton staff was left in Korea while the rest of the Associated Press staff was brought to Tokyo to enjoy the Christmas and New Year holidays. As is usual at such R&R times, a gang of us got together at the Foreign Correspondents Club, the press club that was our home away from home in Tokyo. Four AP correspondents—Bureau Chief Bob Eunson, reporter Bob Tuckman, photographer Bob Schutz, and myself—proceeded to wash down the war and the haggling at the peace talks and temporarily forget the harsh living in Korea.

While pontificating at the club, we recalled that our colleague Frank "Pappy" Noel was languishing as a POW in a North Korean prison camp. Photographer Noel, a Pulitzer Prize winner for Associated Press in 1943, was with the First Marine Division, Seventh Regiment, which was one of the first American units to engage the Chinese near Hamhung. During the night of November 29, 1950, Noel accompanied a convoy that was to carry supplies and reinforcements. The column was attacked, and the surviving marines and Frank Noel were taken as prisoners of war.

As we continued to guzzle, our conversation turned a bit maudlin as we talked of Frank and how we wanted to send him some Christmas presents. We turned to dreaming up appropriate gifts, with cigarettes, food, and whiskey quickly proposed. Jokingly, I said that as long as we were dreaming, how about a camera? The more we drank and the more we digested my offhand suggestion, the more serious it became. We determined that after the holiday respite, Tuckman and Schutz would return to Korea and would check out feasibility and means during their daily coverage at the peace talk site.

Tuckman and Schutz discreetly approached Wilfred Burchett, an Australian journalist who was attached to and covering the communist side at the talks for *Paris Ce Soir*. He consulted with Chu Chi-ping, of *Ta Kung Pao*, a Peiping [Peking] paper. A short time later, Burchett told Schutz that he had found some authorities to cooperate with him on the plan. Schutz packed and readied a camera case filled with equipment. Schutz hid it until Burchett gave the cue, whereupon he and Tuckman sneaked the case over the fence. Burchett picked it up with the help of Chu. At that point of positive progress, I dubbed the project "Operation Father Christmas." Frank Noel was always known as "Pappy," hence *Father*; and *Christmas* was for his surname as well as to mark the time of the idea's inception.

In 1953, I left Korea to head the AP photo staff in Tokyo. In mid-January, Bob Schutz said there might be something in the works from Father Christmas. It was time for my next big task. I went to General William Nuckols, Chief Public Information Officer, and told him what we were trying to do. As I expected, the reaction was a lot of shouting and accusations, claims that we were aiding and abetting and trafficking with the enemy. He threatened to pull our accreditations and have us kicked out of the theater. I countered with a list of benefits the military would gain. I pointed out that I knew Frank very well, as a friend and professionally as a colleague. I knew he would do a masterful job of providing names and hometowns for his subjects. That information would be the first and best source of verification of captives' identities, and the military could check it against their lists, which we knew were incomplete or inadequate. I was also certain that Frank would include as much background as possible, which would be of value to the intelligence branch of the military. In addition to the benefits to the military, I stressed the great morale boost it would give the families of POWs, who would be able to see their loved ones alive. I also thought that Frank could not be forced to shoot only pictures that would be propaganda for his captors. I got grudging permission to go ahead with our arrangements.

Having cleared that hurdle, it was time to inform AP headquarters in New York. I phoned and gave them a complete fill-in of the entire project, the status at that time, and what could be expected. About three weeks later, I got a coded message that Operation Father Christmas was in progress. On a signal from Chu Chi-ping, Schutz surreptitiously managed to pick up the film. He hand-carried the precious material to Tokyo as we had arranged, and I immediately had sets of prints made. One set was given to General Nuckols, and another was taken to the censor's office for the formality of having it stamped "Passed by Censors." Our New York office had been alerted to what was coming their way. Within a few hours, seven pictures made by Frank Noel in the prison camp in North Korea ran continuously via radiophoto transmission to the United States and were relayed onward around the world. The pictures showed groups of Americans in their prison garb, each one carefully identified by name and hometown. As his internment dragged on, Noel made several hundred pictures, which we continued to receive and send on. On August 9, 1953, after thirty-two months of incarceration, Noel was freed at Panmunjom in Operation Big Switch.

It was a joyous time for us when Frank "Pappy" Noel and all the other prisoners were exchanged in operations Big and Little Switch. In 1954 I was ordered to return to AP New York headquarters. I tried to resist the move, but was convinced by my chief of bureau to accept being kicked upstairs because, he said, it was the first time Associated Press had promoted a photographer to an executive position. Before leaving, I went to Seoul for a "last look around," as well as to say my farewells. I took away with me many warm spots in my heart for my Korean friends and colleagues and many indelible memories of the ruined city.

I returned to Seoul in 1977 to participate in the dedication of a memorial established at Munsan to honor the eighteen war correspondents who were killed in the war. I went again in 1999, and could hardly believe my eyes. Seoul was a city reborn—literally risen from the ashes. People were well dressed and bustling about. The stores and shops were filled with plentiful consumer goods of every sort. There were new restaurants as cosmopolitan as any you could find anywhere in the world. Transportation of every kind, public and private, was jamming the streets. Observing the monstrous gridlock, I was reminded of the worst of the traffic in the Washington, D.C., metropolitan area. I was tremendously awed by the growth, size, dimensions, and designs of the buildings in

the heart of the business area and in the enormous housing developments surrounding the city on both sides of the Han River. The river
itself now had seventeen bridges spanning it, and three more under construction, instead of the one it had had when I arrived in Seoul in 1950.

I can't help but think that the spirit and principles that compelled the
Koreans to flee from the North to the free world in the South are very
much alive. There are the lingering, sad situations of individuals still
uprooted, families separated, and children orphaned. But I can't help
but believe that the Koreans have proved the point of their flight and
have somewhat overcome the trauma of the hardships they endured.

# 6

# The Korean War in the Lives and Thoughts of Several Major Korean Writers

## *Compiled by Suh Ji-moon*

War does not come to writers in a different shape than it does to "ordinary" people. It does not go especially hard on them, nor does it spare them. But writers, even when young, tend to feel more intensely about extraordinary happenings, and they retain their impressions in a more vivid form. Even many of those writers who were not personally affected by the events of the war (in terms of loss of family members or major changes in the family's material fortune) are motivated to become writers by the desire to sort out, for themselves and their contemporaries, the cause and meaning of the great social and historical upheavals that have changed the destiny of their nation.

This chapter will be an exploration of how the Korean War, the ideological conflict that led to the war, and the devastation wrought by the war affected and shaped the lives and writings of six major Korean novelists, as told largely in their own words.* The six writers are Pak Wan-sŏ, Hong Sŏng-won, Yun Heung-gil, Kim Won-il, Yi Mun-yŏl, and Richard Kim. In sketching a profile of their lives and examining their writing and opinions concerning the effects and legacies of the Korean War, I have addressed six broad questions: How did the war affect them

---

*All six writers participated in the Korea/America Dialogue on the Korean War, organized by the Mansfield Center, June 19–25, 1999, in Missoula, Montana. Much of the material used in writing the chapter is based on videotaped interviews with each of the writers during the Dialogue, excerpts of which will be entered into the Digital Resource Library, which is one of the major activities of the Center's larger project, "America's Wars in Asia: A Cultural Approach."

personally? How did the experience of the war affect their work as writers? What were the main factors that influenced the way people felt about the war? What was the most important social change wrought by the war? What in their minds are the important lessons of the war that we should teach the next generation? And do they think the personal memories of those who experienced the war are important for the Korean-American relationship today? Before offering a synopsis of their answers to these questions, it would be useful to say a few words about each of their personal histories.

Pak Wan-sŏ is the oldest of the six writers. When the Korean War broke out she was just nineteen, a time in a young woman's life when her hopes and dreams are at their zenith. As a freshman in Korean literature at Seoul National University, she had every reason to be proud of herself and have the highest expectations of life. But the Korean War wreaked havoc on her hopes and dreams, as it did on those of most young Korean men and women of the day. Soon after the war broke out, her uncle and her brother died. Pak had lost her father when she was just two years old, and her uncle, true to the Confucian tradition in which the nearest male relative takes the responsibility for fatherless children in the family, had supported her widowed mother, her brother, and herself and sponsored the education of her brother and herself. Her uncle was therefore virtually a father to her. And her brother, having grown into fine young manhood, was to be a rock of support for her mother and herself. But the twin male pillars of her family were mercilessly felled in the tempest of the Korean War. Whereas most women of her age in more fortunate parts of the world would have been nurturing romantic dreams, she was thrust into the role of surrogate head of the family, responsible for earning a living for herself, her aged and grieving mother, and the young children of her brother.

What made that tragedy so hard to bear was that neither her uncle nor her brother had been "guilty" of the crimes that had led to their deaths. Her uncle had died because a malicious neighbor had falsely accused him of being a communist, even though he had never participated in any communist movement or activity. Her brother, around the time of Korea's liberation from Japanese colonialism, had been a mild sympathizer with the communist movement, but after a long internal struggle had changed his allegiance and declared himself openly in support of liberal democracy. Her uncle died in prison, summarily executed by the South Korean police just prior to the second evacuation of Seoul in January 1951, following the Chinese entry into the war. Her brother died in the aftermath of torture inflicted by South Korean authorities who distrusted his conversion. (His was a fate shared by many avowed "converts" from communism.) Pak gave a fictionalized account of her brother's death and her own activities and mental reactions during the two three-months-long occupations of Seoul by the communists in her second novel, *A Season of Thirst* (Mok Marŭn Kyejŏl, 1972).

Pak's experiences as the breadwinner during wartime and her bitter, cynical frame of mind in the face of these catastrophic happenings are told in her first novel, *The Naked Tree* (Namok, 1970, translated into English by Yu Young-nan and published by the Asian Studies Series, Cornell University, 1995). Perhaps the mortifying deaths of her kinsmen paradoxically gave her a kind of strength and steeled her to numerous humiliations and frustrations that would have been overwhelming to a young woman of her upbringing. The girl heroine of *The Naked Tree*, who gets a job as an assistant in a portrait-painting studio at a U.S. Military Post Exchange, is curt and domineering to the painters who hold onto the low-paying job as their lifeline. Most of them are more than twice her age. She also keeps the boss from becoming too familiar or overbearing to her. The heroine, Kyung, also has to handle the impertinence of American soldiers. A Korean girl of her background and education would normally find such circumstances beyond her capacity to handle and unbearably humiliating. Kyung recovers a measure of humanity when she discovers that one of the portrait painters—whom she has tended to despise wholesale as artists *manqué*—is a true artist.

Nearly twenty years after her marriage and when her sixth and last child started to go to school, Pak decided to become a writer. But she was not so much seeking a romantic fulfillment of her youthful dream. She was rather motivated by a compelling desire to bear testimony to the experience that wreaked such havoc on the lives of so many of her compatriots. Pak says that she wanted to prevent the Korean War and its aftermath from becoming a mere historical record of territories lost and gained, and the death of a family member from becoming just a number in the wartime casualty toll. She wanted to record the personal meanings and consequences created by the war.

None of Hong Sŏng-won's family members died or suffered serious bodily injury because of the war, but like every other Korean, Hong and his family suffered great psychological shock and pain. It is Hong's belief that because the shock of what they saw and experienced during the war was so great, most Koreans suppressed and denied those shocks so that they could get on with their lives. Such a reaction is a defense mechanism common to all human beings. To break down that defense mechanism and check that evasion, Hong wrote the first major work of fiction to examine the Korean War closely and rigorously. He began writing the six-volume *North and South* (Nam Kwa Puk, 1987) in the 1960s and concluded it in the seventies. He significantly revised it in the nineties, to explore matters he could not in the politically sensitive climate of the sixties and seventies. Many of his other works treat, or touch on, the Korean War directly or indirectly. In writing his magnum opus he examined a vast number of documents and historical records.

A strong motivation in writing his great saga of the Korean War was his desire to combat the view, prevalent among many intellectuals, that the Korean War was a war by proxy. According to this view, the Korean people became involved in the war because the superpowers happened unluckily to clash on the Korean peninsula. Such a view enables Koreans to evade their share of responsibility in the outbreak of the war and avoid squarely facing the consequences of the war. Hong Sŏng-won wanted to show that even though the superpowers did clash in the Korean War, the war itself was primarily a civil war, and that Koreans have to accept that fact and cope with the social disintegration and psychological wounds caused by the war. To persuade readers of his conviction, Hong put into his novel thirty-four major characters from all strata and walks of Korean society—soldiers, intellectuals, shopkeepers, students, children, housewives, and so on. He takes each of these characters all the way through the Korean War, from shortly before its outbreak to shortly after the formal signing of the armistice agreement. Through what happens to these characters and how they act in and react to the war, readers are forced to encounter head-on why the war broke out, what it did to us, and what its consequences are that we have to deal with.

Yun Heung-gil is the author of "The Rainy Spell" (Changma, 1974), one of the best-known Korean short stories in the English-speaking world. Yun was eight years old, just like the child protagonist of his famous story, when the Korean War broke out. The war had a profound effect on young Yun because it destroyed the family line on his mother's side. His maternal uncle, who served as an officer in the South Korean army, died in combat. This tragedy and its effect on his maternal grandmother are vividly recreated in "The Rainy Spell." The grief of that loss and the "guilt" of failing to ensure the continuation of the family line were the cause of his maternal grandparents' deaths soon after. This maternal uncle was also a young man of great promise, the author's hero and idol in his childhood.

The family tragedy was intensified by the abduction to the North of his maternal aunt's husband. His maternal aunt was a beautiful, tender-hearted, and artistic woman whom the author passionately adored in his childhood and who instilled in him the aspiration to become a writer early in life. He adored this aunt so much that as a child he used to declare that he would marry her when he grew up. Sadly, the aunt contracted tuberculosis, which grew worse after the forced separation from her husband, and she died of the disease. So, the tragedy that struck his mother's maiden family in Yun's childhood was to remain an irreparable loss and a source of profound grief to him long into his adulthood.

Another tragedy that happened during the Korean War left a scar on Yun for many years. Like many unemployed men who were too old to fight, his father was drafted to the battle front to do auxiliary work (such as burying dead soldiers, carrying supplies, helping set up barracks or build trenches, and so on) for combat forces. Before his father left for the front, where many men similarly drafted lost their lives, his mother would go every day to the place where such draftees were waiting to be transported to assignments, to see him and bring food to him. While she was gone, the duty of taking care of his ailing youngest brother fell to Yun, the eldest son. Himself a mere child with all the desire for play and freedom, Yun could not but regard his fretting little sibling as a hateful burden, and looked after him half-heartedly. His pitiful little brother died one day while strapped on the back of the author, who did not even realize that the baby had died until his mother came home that night. The shock of that death and the feelings of guilt that he had for his younger brother's hapless young life made him feel as if he had been the murderer. These feelings were to torture and haunt him into adulthood and form the core of the short story "A Sheep" (or "Scapegoat," Yang, 1980).

Kim Won-il is also one of those people who encountered history and national destiny very early in life, in an intensely personal form. It was an encounter that could hardly be more dramatic. Kim's father was an active communist in the South who defected to the North, leaving the family to struggle in poverty. His father was a highly educated young man during the period of Japanese colonial occupation. Like many other intellectual young men of his generation, he became a socialist. As the Japanese authorities suppressed socialism severely, Kim's father also suffered persecution, meeting the day of national liberation from Japanese colonial rule while sitting in prison in Pusan. It seems that his father was convinced that the way for Korea to survive as a country was to adopt communism as the state ideology.

During the years of Japanese occupation, Kim's father had engaged in a "night school movement," to instruct and enlighten the children and youths of Korea in social and political ideals. Kim's grandfather had been a firefighter in his youth and later became a legal scribe. In those days, when illiteracy was the norm for common people, a legal scribe served also as a legal counselor, sometimes performing the role of a solicitor. With the money he made, the grandfather bought land and gave his son a good education. Unlike his father, Kim's mother was not educated, although she came from a traditional Confucian-literati family—education for girls being traditionally neglected and/or frowned upon. Her lack of education was one of the factors that made his parents' marriage incompatible. Even though they were married for nearly a decade and a half, they lived together in the same house for only about three years in all. Much of the time his father stayed away from the house, engaging in socialist movements and having affairs with other women. As a consequence, Kim's mother had strong resentments against his father and never mentioned her husband to her children after his defection.

In contrast to Thomas Mann, who had a very artistic mother and a business-minded father, Kim inherited his literary and bohemian temperament from his father and acquired the habits of practical industry from the example of his mother, whose unremitting hard work enabled her to support herself and her four children through taking in sewing after her husband left them. Kim's father had not meant to desert them, even though he had had a series of affairs with other women. In fact, the period of 1949–1950 was the happiest time for the family, when Kim's father relocated the family to Seoul and lived with them. He had served as vice chairman of the South Kyŏngsang Provincial Committee of the Southern Labor Party, but as his communist affiliation became more and more known it became dangerous for him to continue working in his native province. The party also felt the need to have its future leaders work in the capital, so he was transferred to Seoul, to work there in the headquarters of the Southern Labor Party. During the three-month period from late June to September 1950, while the North Korean army occupied Seoul, his father served as vice chairman of the finance committee of the party's Seoul city headquarters, a position comparable to that of the vice minister of finance. When the communists were forced to abandon Seoul and flee north, pushed back by the combined Republic of Korea–United Nations forces, his family waited for him, but gave up and fled south, returning to their native town. They were later to learn from their neighbors that Kim's father had come with a car to take his family north, exactly one hour after they had fled the capital. This incident is told in Kim's seven-volume magnum opus, *Festival of Fire* (Purŭi Chejŏn, 1997).

The family was never to meet the father again, but Kim learned much later that his father had returned to the South once more, as the leader of a communist guerrilla force in the Taebaek Mountains during 1952 and 1953. He also learned that his father was one of the delegates representing North Korea at the Geneva Conference in 1954 and later suffered politically in North Korea, as had most Southern Labor Party members who had defected to the North. His father, who trained secret agents to be dispatched to the South, had married again and had a son and a daughter before dying of tuberculosis in a sanatorium in 1976. Kim obtained this last information only in the winter of 1997.

Because his mother harbored resentment against his father and because he himself felt deserted, Kim grew up feeling estranged from his father. But after growing up, his thoughts about his father changed. He now regards his father as a man who gave higher priority to ideology than to family, living the life he wanted to live but ending up as a failed revolutionary.

The tribulations that Yi Mun-yŏl's family suffered because of his father's defection to the North during the Korean War can only be suggested in this brief sketch. His mother, who had no professional training or skill, had to survive the penurious fifties and sixties with five children. The sufferings of his family, both on account of poverty and on account of being the family of a defector, were a decisive factor in his becoming a writer. Yi wrote a two-volume imaginative biography of his father, entitled *The Age of Heroes* (Yŏng-ung Sidae, 1984), tracing his father's career as a socialist revolutionary from a Confucian family to his defection more or less factually, and afterward imagining him as an ideologue caught up in the power struggle in North Korea. Yi wrote in the preface to the novel that he became a writer to write that book. After the great success of the book, he received a letter from his father, informing him of his survival and remarriage in North Korea. (His father almost certainly wrote to him with the permission or at the order of the North Korean government.)

Over the years Yi sought ways of corresponding with, and meeting, his father, but to no avail. In 1996 he wrote the short story "An Appointment with His Brother" (Au waŭi Mannam) in which he delineates an imagined meeting with his stepbrother, his father's son from his second marriage in North Korea. This short story eloquently testifies to the cost of the Korean War for people on both sides of the divide. Perhaps in response to this story and his open letter of appeal to Kim Jong-il, Yi received offers to arrange a meeting for him with his father, and for a while it looked as though it was with the sanction of the North Korean authorities. So in the summer of 1999 Yi made two trips to Yenji, the central city in the Korean autonomous district in China. Yi came back sorely disappointed and grief-stricken from his first trip, after being told that his father had passed away. Then someone offered to arrange for him to meet his stepbrother, so he made another trip, but came back confused and unhappy, because the man who was presented to him as his stepbrother failed to offer convincing proof of kinship. The Korean War has yet to come to an end, as far as Yi Mun-yŏl is concerned.

Although he was born and grew up in the North under the Japanese occupation, Richard Kim, who has retired in Shutesbury, Massachusetts, as a professor of English at the University of Massachusetts, identifies himself as an American writer. In a recent interview published in *Education About Asia* (Fall 1999), Kim said he doesn't feel he belongs either to Korea or to the United States. The uncertain feeling about his Korean nationality arises, not from his wish to deny his Korean origins or to pass as an American, but rather from his having fled North Korea and finding successive South Korean regimes to be equally hateful. His voice as a writer is that of a witness to the Korean War, often drawing on his experience as a soldier in the South Korean army. Two of his internationally acclaimed novels, *Lost Names* (1970; republished, University of California Press, 1998) and *The Martyred* (1964; republished, University of California Press, 1998), both written in English, give a good picture of how things were in North Korea during the last years of Japanese colonial rule and under communist domination. It therefore seems highly appropriate to include him in this profile of Korean writers.

When the Korean War broke out, there was no question in Kim's mind that he ought to serve in the military to fight against and repel the communists, because his family had fled from North Korea to escape the communist persecution. His family had been middle-class, landowning Christians, which was reason enough for the communists to persecute them. During his training at Chinhae (a port city on the southern coast of Korea and the site of the Korean Naval Academy) as an officer candidate in the Korean Marine Corps, he came down with pneumonia and was honorably discharged. He was released and told to go home, but couldn't because he didn't know where his parents had fled. In wandering around, he eventually found his parents and went to live with them for a while. Recovered from his illness, and bored with life for lack of meaningful work, he joined the military once again, this time serving in the army from March 1951 to December 1954, first as a language liaison officer with the U.S. Army Seventh Division and then, until late in 1954, as a general's aid in the South Korean army. In 1954 he was chosen as a recipient of a special four-year scholarship to study in the United States. He was reluctant to accept, but was "ordered" by the army to go. He wound up making the United States his permanent home.

When asked to share some of his memories during the army years, he said he had no ludicrous, surreal stories to entertain his listeners with. Being in the army, he observed, doesn't mean risking one's life in battle every day. On the contrary, boredom, more than danger, was hard to bear. His unit, which was stationed near Turkish and Ethiopian troops who were regarded as rough soldiers, didn't engage in combat with North Korean troops, but fought Chinese soldiers. His life as a soldier in the Korean War turned out to be a cosmopolitan experience.

Moving from these brief profiles of the six Korean writers to their views on the Korean War, we find a powerful common voice that is rarely heard in the American discussion of the war. But we also find striking differences. Pak Wan-sŏ observes that the Korean War was traumatic to the Korean people in ways that previous national calamities were not. Over and above the fact that three million soldiers and civilians died in the Korean War and that much of the country was laid waste by merciless bombing, all kinds of pent-up emotions created over many generations in the rigidly structured Korean society exploded during the war. Pak is struck by the extent to which Korean people ignored or denied what they had in common and accused each other of "leftist" and "right-wing" sympathies, knowing that such accusations would lead to the shattering of communities and the deaths of the persons concerned. Pak therefore dates the end of solidarity in Korean society and the beginning of its division and fracturing to the Korean War.

It was not only death and poverty and privation that were responsible for the disintegration of social bonds and traditional order. Korean people suffered almost the same degree of privation toward the end of World War II, when the Japanese requisitioned almost all the grain and all the metal in every household, even bowls and spoons. Nonetheless, all through the three and a half decades of Japanese colonial rule and the harsh years of the Pacific War, Koreans retained a strong sense of national solidarity. Korean society, in spite of Japan's colonial exploitation, was a close-knit and mutually supportive agrarian society. But, because of the fratricidal nature of the ideological confrontation that followed liberation from Japan, and the Korean War that grew out of that confrontation, family and kinship ties were destroyed. It was not uncommon for brothers born of the same parents to fight on opposite sides of the ideological line. Relatives also refused to help other relatives in distress, for fear of being implicated in the latter's ideological "guilt," the cost of which could be high indeed, frequently as high as death. What had sustained the Korean people through repeated historical trials was the fact that they could fall back on family and relatives for help and support. Pak believes that the breakup, or weakening, of kinship ties, aggravated by the influx of the idea of individualism from the West, has made the Korean people self-centered.

Like Pak Wan-sŏ, Yun Heung-gil thinks that the direst consequence of the Korean War is that people have come to distrust each other. Not only was the war one in which one-half of the Korean people tried to kill as many of the other half of their brethren as possible, but many civilians died as a result of mutual accusations and finger pointing. It became impossible, Yun observes, for a Korean to trust even his closest neighbor or next of kin, and when people cannot trust their fellow human beings, they become diminished in their stature as human beings. Not being able to tell whether someone is a clandestine communist or safe to associate with had the effect of severing family and friendly ties. It was not only that a Korean could not trust another Korean. The distrust extended to include all foreigners as well. One of the lines in a popular song after the war ran: "Beware of American cheaters/Beware of Russian swindlers." The traditional community built on mutual support and trust was disrupted and destroyed. This became a prominent theme in both Pak's and Yun's writing.

Kim Won-il likewise thinks that Korean society, which had been agrarian and communal up to the time of the war, has become divided and fractured. He too believes that mutual distrust and enmity have come to replace the mutual care and support that previously held society together. Because so many Koreans died in a vicious cycle of grudges and vengeance, the bad karma continues today.

In his evaluation of the impact of the war on Korean society, Hong Sŏng-won emphasizes the drastic change in class relations caused by the Korean War. Hong argues that even though Korea has undergone rapid and tremendous social changes almost continuously since the country was forced to open its doors to foreign powers at the end of the nineteenth century, the Korean War was the decisive factor in the breakdown of social cohesion within the traditional class structure. Although much weakened during Japanese colonial rule, classes continued to exist, exercising practical and psychological influence on social and individual life. But the Korean War made everyone paupers, placing everyone back at the same starting line. Social ethics also changed as a consequence of the war. American materialism and pragmatism supplanted the Confucian respect for propriety and decorum. The war, which generated a sense of life having to be lived in the present moment and of the meaninglessness of regard for convention, also destroyed a great number of sexual inhibitions, creating a sea-change not only in patterns of human relations but in human psychology and values as well.

Yi Mun-yŏl speculates that the typical Korean reaction to the war was bewilderment and self-abandon. Koreans had a sense that the war was neither caused by them nor fought for them. Rather, the war originated as an ideological clash that did not begin in Korea. But the attitude of Koreans toward the war has changed greatly in the course of the half-century since the war. In the fifties, of course, all literature was strongly anticommunist. In the sixties, such a simple, black-and-white viewpoint was no longer convincing, so a kind of neutral outlook began to emerge, the most prominent example of which is *The Square* (Kwangjang, 1960) by Ch'oe In-hun. In this landmark novel, the hero leaves his hometown in the North and escapes to the South, fleeing the repressive climate of North Korea. But he becomes disgusted with the materialism and corruption of South Korea. When the Korean War breaks out, he joins the army, eventually becoming a POW. Given the choice between North Korea, South Korea, and a neutral country for repatriation, the hero chooses the last option. But while sailing to the third country—which appears to be India—he jumps overboard and commits suicide.

The seventies saw the beginnings of cautious exploration into the issue of ideology and the causes of the ideological split, often through "borrowing" the eyes of children. Yun Heung-gil's "The Rainy Spell" may be the best example. In the eighties, the reaction of the younger generation against the legacies of the fifties became an irresistible tide, and literature began to glorify the leftists and their cause. The general public, however, were put off by the radicals' infatuation with communism. Yi Mun-yŏl believes that most people nowadays reject both extremes and choose a point somewhere in-between, according to their own judgment and temperament.

In Richard Kim's opinion, people felt differently about the war based on the regions they lived in, their ideological bias, their class background, and their religious affiliation. In his own case, being a refugee from the North, he believed he had to see the war through, because his family couldn't flee forever and didn't want to flee to Japan or any other foreign country. When the war broke out, the Syngman Rhee government promised to defend the people, but then fled, leaving people stranded and at the mercy of the invaders. Moreover, they exploded the bridge on the Han River, which not only cut off the refugee route for the citizens of Seoul, but also produced enormous casualties for the retreating army. Kim, therefore, felt betrayed, abandoned, and sold out—feelings that linger fifty years later and affect the way he views Korea today.

When the writers were asked if they thought that everything that needs to be known about the Korean War has become known, Pak Wan-sŏ's response was largely positive. She said that thanks to the sufficient lapse of years and the diminution in fact and in Korean minds of the threat of another major aggression from the North, the causes and consequences of the Korean War have been examined from many angles and with relative openness. To be sure, there are still tales that remain untold. But people who have been nursing their wounds in secret all their lives are "coming out" with their stories. We have, for example, a multivolume diary by a woman, who published it at her own expense, and a personal record entitled "Before the Eye of History" by a former Seoul National University professor, both published recently. There were many nonfiction accounts of the Korean War experience printed in various media shortly after the Korean War, in the brief hiatus before the firm enforcement of government control, and Pak trusts that some of them will be excavated and reprinted for posterity.

Yun Heung-gil agrees that most of the salient facts of the war have been uncovered, but speculates that different interpretations may emerge with the perspective gained as more time elapses. It is true that there are still some allegations that haven't been verified, including the extent of Korean civilians killed and wounded by "friendly fire" from the UN forces, and the use of biological weapons against the communist guerrillas in the South. And even those facts that seemed incomprehensible at the time and that gave rise to misunderstanding can be understood and more persuasively interpreted now. For example, when American troops recaptured Seoul on September 28, 1950, and drove the communists out of the city, the North Korean army, in their hurry to flee, left behind huge supplies of food, explosives, and fuel. When Yun saw American troops setting fire to these supplies he was dumbfounded because so many Koreans were starving from lack of food and freezing in the winter for want of fuel. At the time it seemed insane as well as inhumane, but now he understands. Yun holds that the cultural gap has to be bridged or narrowed and fuller information made available in order for misunderstandings on the part of Koreans concerning the actions of foreign troops to be cleared. His opinion is echoed by Yi Mun-yŏl, who also believes that most of the facts concerning the Korean War have come out, but that some issues and facts will have to be further debated and examined from more diverse angles in order for their significance to be properly understood.

Even though most of the facts about the Korean War have come out, Hong Sŏng-won believes that much examination remains to be done of the impact of the war on women, both in fiction and in scholarship. War is traditionally conceived of as a male affair, and most war literature focuses on the death and injury men suffer in the war and the effect it has on their lives. But women are equally the victims of war. Korean women and children suffered starvation, illness, and other excruciating hardships while trying to take refuge, and a great many of them were killed and injured as they were caught in crossfire while fleeing. Hong's hope is that the experiences of women during the war will be illuminated by more writers.

As for the lessons that should be taught to younger generations, the writers are in general agreement that young people should be made to realize that war is a terrible thing and should be avoided at all costs. Even Korean young people, to say nothing of the world outside, need to develop a greater appreciation for the terrible disruption of Korean life and culture and the destruction of the Korean peninsula caused by the Korean War. Pak Wan-sŏ believes that the task of today's generation with regard to the legacy of the Korean War and the future of Korea is to recognize and admit that, even though North Korea bears the primary responsibility as the one that started the aggression, there were reasons for hostility on both sides and South Korea is not exempt from the responsibility of causing the war. Remembering that the world is a place where imperfect people must live together, she urges us to make allowances for human shortcomings and fallibility and seek ways of attaining unification without expecting the other side to kneel down to us.

Yun Heung-gil expressed the hope that children and youths will be made to understand the atrocity of war and clearly realize that wars have to be prevented at all costs. All wars are evil because they are destructive, and starting a war is a great evil. However, that does not make fighting an aggressor good—only a necessary evil. Kim Won-il also emphasized the horrendous cost of the war, pointing out that one-third of the Korean people died, were wounded, or became separated from their families. The next generation should be made to understand the great price Koreans paid for the war that erupted as a consequence of the confrontation between the East and the West.

Hong Sŏng-won likewise stressed that we should make clear to the next generation that war, being the greatest brutality people can perpetrate upon others, should be prevented at all costs. He thinks that traditionally people have tried to prevent war through increased capability for violence—that is, through increased armament. But that is neither the wisest nor the most effective way of preventing war. Hong's conviction is that war should be prevented by showing the next generation the cruelties and pains of war through literature and visual arts. That is by far the more economical as well as the more effective way of preventing war.

To Yi Mun-yŏl, it seems that the Korean War could stand as an eloquent negative object lesson in what happens when people sacrifice human lives at the altar of ideology, and when a nation tries to solve its problems with the help of foreign powers. As for what the Korean War might teach the young generation of Americans, Yi replied cryptically that that would depend on whether America fought the war to consolidate its hold on the world or to defend the freedom and well-being of the people living on that land.

In contrast to the other five authors, Richard Kim admitted to not knowing what we might teach the younger generation about the Korean War, other than that it was a necessary war, even though no war is desirable.

Last, writers were invited to give their thoughts on the current status of the Korean–American relationship, and asked if they thought personal memories were important to that relationship today. Most agreed that personal memories can promote friendly relations and cement the bonds between the two countries, whereas a couple of them drew attention to the distorting, unbalancing effects of memory. Pak Wan-sŏ's feeling is that even though there are unjust elements in the anti-American sentiments of radical Korean youths of today, she is at times inclined to sympathize with them when she sees how excessively dependent Korea is on the United States and how unequal Korea is vis-à-vis the United States. Koreans and Americans, therefore, must work together to rectify this state of affairs so that they can associate as equals and truly cooperate for their common goals and interests.

Yun Heung-gil is convinced that personal memories are important to U.S.–Korea relations. Yun thinks that the best resolution for the division of Korea would have been to be united without having fought a war. The next-best solution would have been for either side to have won the war. The best solution after that would have been to have concluded the war honorably. Because none of these three possibilities were the result of the war, we must find a way of achieving peaceful reunification of the country even at this late date. To achieve this objective, Korea and the United States must cooperate. So Koreans and Americans should listen to each other's living voices and come to a true understanding of each other. Then, with their trust based on mutual understanding, Korea and America can work together in true partnership. Yun hopes that the Dialogue served as a good occasion for advancing mutual understanding between Koreans and Americans.

To Kim Won-il, the Korean War demonstrated how easily small and weak nations can become victims of the clash between superpowers. He quotes Kim Nak-chung, a South Korean who made his way to the North five years after the end of the war and then fled the North to return to the South, as saying that on his first night in Pyongyang he heard the sound of old people, children, and women working to rebuild the ruined country. To him it was a reminder of the horrendous damage North Korea suffered from the bombing by the UN forces. Kim suggests, therefore, that the United States realize that the violent enmity of the North Koreans toward them is not the result solely of North Korean propaganda and indoctrination, but is founded on the reality of the almost total destruction of their physical and economic livelihood.

To the question of whether the experience of the war is important for understanding the present-day Korean-American relationship, Kim Won-il submitted that even though America firmly established itself as Korea's blood ally by coming to the aid of South Korea during the war, it is not without reason that the young generation thinks that America exercises excessive political leverage on South Korea, and that its presence hinders the autonomous development of South Korea. What Kim recommends especially for America is a careful self-examination of the mode in which it conducts warfare. During the Korean War, too many civilians died from "friendly fire." The United States dropped too many bombs in a small and densely populated country—far exceeding the volume of explosives used during World War II—so that inevitably the country was greatly devastated. That is a merciless, inconsiderate act, and America as a superpower should be more careful and responsible in exercising its military capabilities. On the other hand, Kim strongly disapproves of young people who try to incite anti-American sentiments by calling attention to isolated misbehaviors of Americans, especially GIs in U.S. army campside towns, because such things are simply part of human nature, and Koreans are not exempt from such human vices and shortcomings. On balance, Kim is grateful to the United States for the decisive help Korea has received throughout the period of the Korea-America relationship.

Hong Sŏng-won acknowledged that during the Dialogue he pointed out mainly the negative aspects of the American influence on Korea and Koreans' contact with America. He explained that this was because he thought that everybody knows what benefits Korea has received from America, and that the negative aspects needed to be examined. However, America and Korea, having been involved in the great maelstrom of the Korean War, are knit together inseparably. One side benefit of the

Korean War, he believes, is that Koreans have met the country called the United States and entered into an enduring and close-knit relationship, which makes it important that the two parties understand each other. Hong is certain that if understanding is achieved, then small conflicts and resentments can be easily overcome. He was greatly heartened to find people on the other side of the Pacific who try to sort out and grapple with the meanings of the Korean War and its impact on the relationship of the two countries. He hopes to see more such dialogues, and to be invited to participate again.

Yi Mun-yŏl and Richard Kim expressed concern that personal experiences, which cannot but be narrow and particular, could lead to wrong inferences and misconceptions. Yi Mun-yol cited, by way of an example, the recollection by one of the participants of how gentle and courteous the Chinese soldiers were to Korean civilians during the time they occupied Seoul in early 1951. Yi believed that such individual memories could distort the whole picture of the war and the picture of Korean-American and Korean-Chinese relations. Korean contact with Chinese soldiers was limited to the two-month period when they occupied Seoul as a victorious army, which made it easy for them to show generosity. On the other hand, Koreans' contact with Americans, especially American soldiers, lasted half a century, and all kinds of incidents can happen over half a century. Moreover, Americans come from a widely different cultural background, whereas the Chinese come from a similar cultural background. Yi therefore believes that to generalize on the basis of personal and emotional experiences can be dangerous and unfair. The negative aspects of the Korean contact with America should be balanced by the positive aspects, such as the aid Korean orphans received from American soldiers at nearby American camps and bases. He himself spent a few months in an orphanage in his childhood, and experienced firsthand the happiness that American soldiers gave the poor orphans through their visits and their gifts.

Richard Kim surprised himself by responding "yes and no" to the question of whether personal memories are important to U.S.–Korea relations today. Kim acknowledged that memories are obviously important because they affect one's sense of who one is, what one's place is in the world, and so on. But memories are also very tricky. If individual memories are not correctly recalled, or digested, or understood, Kim pointed out, they can have a terribly disastrous impact. They can distort one's view of the present, of oneself, and of the world. For example,

Kim imagined someone who suffered terribly in childhood during the war, or whose family suffered persecution and displacement because of the war, through the father's defection or through becoming victims of bombing. If such a person becomes obsessed with those memories, it could prevent his objective assessment of history and society, interfere with his coming to grips with himself and the world, and inhibit his sense of accountability. One should evaluate one's personal memory in the larger context, Kim admonished. Otherwise, memory can be misleading and dangerous.

Of the six authors, two were children of communist fathers who defected to the North, and one was a refugee from North Korea who fled the persecution of the communists but who had no love for South Korea or for the United States, whose intelligence agency suspected his father of being a communist spy and tortured him during the American military occupation of South Korea. Two had family members and close kin who were killed in the maelstrom of the war, and only one lived through the war without the loss of close kin. It is true that the writers invited to the Korea-America Dialogue at the Mansfield Center are writers who treated the Korean War as important subject matter in their works, but as a group they are not unrepresentative of the Korean population at large.

It is significant that it was Hong Sŏng-won, the only one of the six authors who did not suffer loss of blood kin during the war, who wrote the first major novel on the Korean War. The ideological causes of the war were too delicate a subject in the 1960s, when Hong began writing the novel, for writers with communist connections to confront. Hong, of course, had to be very careful and had to pass over many things he would have liked to discuss. But writers did push at the wall of censorship, tacit and proclaimed, cautiously at first (but at enormous risk), and wore down that wall little by little, until, by the 1980s, the origins, courses, and aftermath of the Korean War had been illuminated from many angles and vigorously debated not only in a literary context, but also from historical and social perspectives. Korean writers accomplished their historical and social mission as writers honorably and bravely, and the writers represented in the Dialogue are some of the finest examples, in honesty, courage, and artistic achievement.

# 7

# Reluctant Crusaders: Korean War Films and the Lost Audience

## *Lary May*

*This is one picture that every showman should play (figuring from the patriotic point of view), although you will probably lose your shirt, like we did. . . . Had the first walkouts we've seen in our theater.*

—J. R. Snavely, Leith Opera House, Leith, North Dakota, on the failure of the Korean War film *My Son John* at his movie theater.[1]

The impact of the Korean "police action" on the American home front presents students of the cold war with a central dilemma. On the one hand, President Truman committed troops to the defense of South Korea by harking back to the lessons of World War II. Writing in his private diary, the president noted, "It occurred to me, that if the Russian totalitarian state was intending to follow the path of the dictatorships of Hitler and Mussolini, they should be met head on in Korea." The commitment to military intervention in Korea "established to the Kremlin, the determination of free peoples to defend themselves." Applying the lessons of the last war to the Korean conflict, the Truman administration reinstituted the military draft and started a system of global commitments to contain communism. One of Truman's advisers recalled that ideological earthquake by noting that it was "the Korean war, and not World War II that made us into a world military-political power."[2]

Yet as President Truman evoked the ethos of the World War II victory culture—which Tom Engelhardt describes as the nation's sacred mission to win the battle against evil and expand democracy around the globe—the tragic events of the United Nations' police action eroded that ethos. In World War II, the conquest of fascism had been unconditional. American troops landed at Inchon and marched to the Yalu River expecting that the past would repeat itself. That was before the Chinese army entered the war, followed by the American military forces' retreat to the thirty-eighth parallel, which ensured that unconditional surrender was out of the question. Meanwhile, President Truman fired the famed World War II commander Douglas MacArthur for seeking to expand the war into Manchuria, and the combat stagnated at the thirty-eighth parallel. By the second year of the conflict, over 50 percent of American people told pollsters that Korea was a major "mistake"; President Truman lost the battle to win public opinion and public support, and Dwight D. Eisenhower became president with a pledge to end "Truman's war."[3]

Over the next few decades scholars agreed on the importance of these events in the history of foreign relations. Revisionist historians led by Bruce Cumings have not liked the results, but observe that it was "the Korean War, not Greece or Turkey or the Marshall Plan or Vietnam that inaugurated big defense budgets and the national security state, that transformed a limited engagement doctrine into a global crusade . . . that gave the Cold War its long run." Even though conservatives disagree on the negative effects of that "long run," they concur that Korea stood for a turning point in postwar history. A former adviser to President Ronald Reagan, Richard Stillwell, noted that in the construction of the Korean War memorial in Washington, D.C., the public could see that the war was the "cornerstone for defense and foreign policy" and demonstrated the "last victory in stark geopolitical terms—we won and they lost." Yet given the far-reaching impact of the conflict, it is disconcerting to find that scholars have ignored the implications of public disenchantment in their assessment of the domestic cold war.[4]

In fact, nothing is more common than for political historians to assert that anticommunism struck a populist chord with the population.[5] They point to the Federal Bureau of Investigation (FBI)'s and the House Un-American Activities Committee's pursuit of subversives whose spying, as the judge at the visible Rosenberg Trial proclaimed, led to the Russians' attainment of the atomic bomb, and to the Korean War. Yet it appears that domestic cold war militancy never gained uniform public backing. Amid the eroding support for the war on the home front, pollsters asked respondents to name the three tasks that the government should pursue. Those in professional and business groups rated as number two, after taxes, the elimination of communists from the state and business. But among the majority—the middle class, small property owners, and workers—the pursuit of the "Reds" did not appear as a priority for government action, suggesting that anticommunism had far less support than we have been led to believe by current scholars.

What is most evident is that a split existed between foreign policy and the domestic cold war.[6] This division compels us to ask a fresh set of questions. How can we explain the failure of the Korean War to gain wide support at home? Does this help explain why the war was "forgotten" in public memory and school textbooks? How does this contradiction challenge our view that a cold war identity permeated postwar America? To answer these questions, I will follow a road rarely traveled by historians. First I will focus on the politics and language rituals that surrounded the making of Hollywood films to promote the Korean War. As state leaders and moviemakers alike promoted this new departure, they saw the mass arts as a vehicle not to reflect group life, but to recreate American myths and symbols. Against the backdrop of New Dealers' Depression-era promotion of isolationism and class conflict, moviemakers in the postwar era dramatized a new American way rooted in consensus, internationalism, and liberal capitalism. Yet as the Korean War provided the opportunity to spread these values from cold warriors to the population, films made to advance a hegemony in which state goals received the voluntary support of the population failed to attract mass audiences. These events will thus provide a focal point for exploring how and why the Korean War was forgotten and for revising the view that a "cold war identity" permeated the American population.[7]

### Hollywood and the Making of Cold War Americanism

Our story does not begin with the Korean War itself, but rather with the exploration of why Hollywood moviemakers and state leaders saw the war as a prime opportunity to promote an unprecedented cold war Americanism. Nowhere was that notion more in evidence than in the rise of Erik Johnston to the presidency of the Film Producers Association in 1946. Johnston had served as a reformist president of the United States Chamber of Commerce and as President Roosevelt's business ambassador to the Soviet Union. Like his early mentor, Henry Luce of *Time* magazine, Johnston perceived that World War II had launched the

"American Century." Seeking to shed the "nightmare of class conflict" and isolationism that characterized the recent past, he saw that many viewed America as a new world removed from foreign affairs. In the past the people also identified democracy, equality, and fraternity with opposition to the capitalist order during the depression. But Johnston saw that unity against an external enemy in World War II created class unity and affluence, setting the stage for a new age of internationalism. Seeking to perpetuate that realignment in the postwar era, Johnston called for cooperation to create economic growth and defend the world against communism. Hollywood also had a great role to play in that recreation of public opinion:

> It is no exaggeration to say that the modern motion picture sets the styles for half the world. There is not one of us who isn't aware that the motion picture industry is the most powerful medium for influencing of people that man has ever built. . . . We can set new styles of living and the doctrine of production must be made completely popular.[8]

Johnston's promotion of the doctrine of "production" meant that he was also part of a generation of United States policymakers who, as recent scholars have shown, envisaged the economic growth stimulated by World War II as a utopian model for reconstructing the postwar domestic and international economy. Yet what has been overlooked is how these policies converged with a struggle over the values that scholars such as Benedict Anderson have called the "imaginary community" that defined nationality.[9] Filmmaking was critical to that project, for like many moralists Johnston feared that mass culture and consumerism could undermine order. Not only did movies draw on the population's quest for a revolution in morals and abundance, but in the depression films they were permeated with a republican ethos that modernized a producer's democracy in opposition to class inequality and internationalism. Yet Johnston saw as the nation's destiny the assumption of a global role as a model of liberal capitalism and defender of the world from communism.

It followed that all ideas that had once been "American" but were hostile to capitalism were seen as subversive. Johnston's response to these threats was sure and quick. With the aid of the House Un-American Activities Committee he helped purge radicalism from Hollywood unions, and sanctioned the influx of Central Intelligence Agency (CIA) officers to censor films and the Academy Awards. Similarly, he cooperated with the State Department to distribute acceptable films abroad and told civic groups that "the American film industry must be careful about what kind of pictures it sends overseas at this time to prevent a false impression of the U.S." Johnston also helped ban foreign export of Lewis Milestone's antiwar masterpiece *All Quiet on the Western Front* and Frank Capra's *Mr. Smith Goes to Washington* because each promoted pacifism and criticized big business. A systematic sampling of film plots released every year showed that these efforts yielded results. Films critical of monopoly capitalism or affirmative of alliances with the common people in opposition to corrupt leaders declined, whereas hostility to deviant women and men who defied official norms and values rose dramatically. Bathing in the glow of success, Johnston told screenwriters, "We'll have no more *Grapes of Wrath,* we'll have no more *Tobacco Roads,* we'll have no more films that deal with the seamy side of American life. We'll have no more films that treat the banker as a villain."[10]

Simply put, the advent of the Korean War provided a golden opportunity for Johnston and his allies to promote to a wider audience the call for containment at home and abroad. He and his allies saw that the public could screen themselves from revolutionary changes by dressing in the cultural clothing of a past to be restored. That past revolved around the model of World War II unity and victory. Where many might have resisted the appeal for a new wartime consensus, the North Korean communists' move into the South meant that American soldiers were once again dying in Asia. Suddenly the trade press observed that "Hollywood was going to war again," and ran advertisements that condemned critics of foreign policy as "traitors." They also backed the House Un-American Activities Committee's efforts to purge Hollywood of subversives. Symbolic of that alliance, the Screen Actors Guild, led by a future president of the United States, Ronald Reagan, no longer resisted implementation of loyalty oaths, and the conservative labor leader Roy Brewer called for a boycott of Charles Chaplin's *Limelight*. Why? As Brewer saw it, Chaplin's promotion of radical unions, his support for Vice President Henry Wallace's "Century of the Common Man," and criticism of the cold war meant that Chaplin was "un-American." Brewer worked to ban *Limelight* claiming that Chaplin's films promoted these "subversive" messages.

Yet that was not the end of it. As Brewer explained, "We are now engaged in a shooting war," and moviemakers must realize that "the artist, as well as his art, is a part of this fight."[11] The convergence of that fight with activist government support began when President Harry Truman called film producers to the White House at the start of the Korean War. There he explained that because Hollywood had done a "terrific job" mobilizing the population in World War II and "no organization in the world can make a better contribution to truth than yours," Hollywood must launch a "repeat act." To facilitate that contribution, producers met with the secretary of commerce, the army chief of staff, and the assistant secretary of state for public affairs to coordinate propaganda. Along the way a senator offered five thousand projectors to release films in South Korea, and Cecil B. De Mille offered his skills as the "voice of America." Not to be outdone, Johnston served as President Truman's economic adviser, explaining that "films are an important link between the government and the people and a great aid in time of war."

What this meant was that studios cooperated with the Defense Department to spur the nation's fighting spirit on several interdependent levels. Rare was the Korean War film that did not utilize official advisers from the Defense Department and the FBI to supply the proper facts and ideas for story lines. The producers of *Tokyo File 212,* for example, worked with the American occupation authorities in Japan to make films condemning communist labor strikes. Similarly, the director of *My Son John* noted that the FBI supplied secret files so that he could accurately portray the work of communists who subverted the Korean War effort. Repeatedly, the screen credits for Korean War films thanked the military for supplying advisers and facilities. Indicative of this union, *The Bridges of Toko-Ri* and *The McConnell Story* featured credits that thanked military advisers for their cooperation, and the FBI investigated and supplied security clearances for performers who entertained American troops in Korea.[12]

## Conversion Dramas: Cold War Containment at Home and Abroad

The creation of over thirty-five Korean War films from 1950 to 1960, therefore, converged with government and Hollywood anticommunist efforts to build a postwar consensus. This was no small undertaking, since what were labeled as enemy beliefs resembled many of the ideas that lay at the core of politics and a republican national identity for over a hundred years: hostility to corporate capitalism, class inequality, and international commitments. Operating as a mechanism to encourage the population to see these ideas as anathemas and even communistic, the Korean War films had many different locales and stories. Yet several patterns and formulas informed the whole. Conspicuously absent were references to the uniqueness of Korean history, or the distinctiveness of the nation's place within the story of colonialism in Asia. Typically stories focused on conflicts and traditions among the people who had to be forgotten and put aside in support of the war. In order to encourage historical amnesia, the younger generation was asked to shed memories of isolationism and class interests in favor of obedience to the fathers who fought in World War II. Because that reformation involved an inner struggle, plots often centered on the characters' guilt for not obeying the call to war, and their eventual conversions that presumably revitalized American life.

At the center of that purification drama, moviemakers masked the nature of this revolutionary departure in glorious memories of World War II victories. To reinforce the linkage, opening prologues featured a noted World War II hero, such as Audie Murphy, or a prominent officer. Looking at the camera from behind an imposing desk, a general in *The McConnell Story* explained that because viewers "lived in freedom" they could choose their religion, work, and home. But these liberties were guaranteed by heroes who stopped fascism and Korean communism. Soundtracks reinforced the message with patriotic tunes such as "Marine Hymn," "Anchors Away," and "Battle Hymn of the Republic." Performers like Humphrey Bogart, June Allyson, Robert Mitchum, William Holden, Grace Kelly, and Frederic March had gained fame in the World War II era playing characters fighting Germans and Japanese. By appearing in Korean War films, they carried that association into their new roles, while the actors who had previously performed as Japanese and Germans tyrants now played Russian or Chinese villains. Studios also emulated the pattern of World War II by turning premieres into civic rituals. Outside theaters military bands, gala parades, generals, and politicians complemented recruiters who encouraged men to enlist for the new war. Along these lines, at a premiere for *Torpedo Alley,* reporters noted that "the Navy made a twenty-two-foot atomic torpedo available for a local department store and placed a miniature submarine in the theater lobby."[13]

Moviemakers equated the doctrine of containment with continuing the task begun in World War II. For example, *Why Korea?* was made by Darryl Zanuck of Twentieth Century Fox in cooperation with John

Steelman of Truman's White House staff. Focusing on the need to arouse the population to stop North Korean invaders, Zanuck's 1950 documentary drew on the same newsreel techniques popularized in Frank Capra's World War II series *Why We Fight*. Capra's film aimed to convert the population from isolationism to internationalism. Seeking to link that same formula to the new doctrine of containment, Zanuck wrote to Steelman, "I produced in the past anti-Nazi films." Seeing no difference between the current battle and the last, he made this new documentary "without profit in an effort to help enlighten and to unify the American people." Steelman responded by using the White House stationery to send letters to theater owners across the nation, urging them to show the film as a patriotic service. When *Why Korea?* won the Academy Award for the best documentary, the press noted:

> American men are dying in Korea and there are many American People who want to know why we are involved in a war half way around the world. This film presents an answer.... In 1948 the world was concerned with the Cold War being conducted in the Soviet Union. This film presents an account of Communist aggression in Poland, in Czech Slovakia, etc. and how as country after country fell, the Communists continued to use international meetings to claim they were for peace. It shows how the Cold War has left no part of the Globe untouched and draws the history up to the Communist aggression against South Korea.[14]

At the same time that the doctrine of containment gained legitimacy through its association with the revival of a glorious past, the drama focused on a conversion narrative that asked the audience to forget and see as un-American interests and memories that clashed with the drive for victory and success in the new cold war. Nowhere was the equation of victory with forgetting more evident than in *The Bridges of Toko-Ri* (1954). A big-budget film featuring major stars, the film's narrative focused on Lieutenant Brubaker, played by William Holden, a jet pilot on an aircraft carrier off the North Korean coast. After fighting in World War II, Brubaker is at first unwilling to return to the site of horror. After being called back into service as a skilled officer and jet pilot in Korea, he tells his admiral—who was a hero in World War II—that he is "bitter" and believes "we should pull out" of this Asian endeavor. In harking back to dreams of isolationism and expressing class antagonism toward the "fathers," Brubaker both expresses subversive ideas evocative of communism and aligns with an Irish rebel enlisted man, played by Mickey Rooney, who evokes class resentment for the military hierarchy, particularly the officers.

Just as the lieutenant yearns for "home" and aligns with the Irish rebel, so Brubaker's wife is " bitter" because he has been called back to service. The conflict between their interests and the demands of the state comes to a head when Brubaker, his wife, and children arrive for a holiday in Tokyo. As they enjoy baths and hotels that highlight the lures of private life and the potentially disruptive effects of consumerism, the admiral calls him "son" and sympathizes with his wife's deep attachment to civilian life. But Admiral Terrant also reveals that he lost a son in the last war, with the result that his daughter-in-law became sexually promiscuous. Most important, he explains that this is "the wrong war, at the wrong place." Yet he draws on his authority as a World War II hero to explain that we must stop "Joe Stalin" or lose Southeast Asia and the Philippines, leading even to the invasion of the United States. To stop that domino effect, his pilots must send Stalin a message by destroying a highly fortified bridge at Toko-Ri, a mission that will most likely lead to the death of the American pilots.

Initially Brubaker and his wife resist the call to sacrifice. But Brubaker also feels deep guilt for expressing his isolationist beliefs and aligning across classes with a rebellious, Irish enlisted man. In order to purge himself of these oppositional desires and interests, he responds to the patriotic call to wash away his sins. Affirming class consensus and the doctrine of containment, he attacks the bridges, only to be shot down. The Chinese ground troops advance en masse and shoot the Americans. Just before death, Brubaker tells his Irish friend that Admiral Terrant was right: we have to stop the enemy. Turning his guns on the communists, who represent the demonic evil that the nation must destroy to bring peace, Brubaker dies as a martyred scapegoat, validating loyalty to the cold war and the new military and corporate hierarchies of the postwar era.

Brubaker's death scene links his sacrifice to the rebirth of the American civil religion. It begins as the camera tracks in to reveal Brubaker's body spread exactly like Christ on the cross. As the crucifixion gives way to a double exposure, the scene fades to images of rebirth and power, including that of the aircraft carrier, a great engine of technology gliding across the sea, framed by the expansive sky. Inside the cockpit, the admiral sits high above the fray like Jehovah himself. Told that the mission was a success, and "his boy" died a hero, the admiral looks at jet planes leaving the deck like angels shooting into the wide horizon. Then, as the patriotic music comes to a crescendo, the admiral asks, "Where do we get such men? Where do we get such men?" In other words, the wayward son has become a man. Shedding his past, he has created a new mission for the United States as the promoter of containment and consensus. The members of the younger generation are men in direct proportion to their capacity to sacrifice their memories for the new American way.[15]

Although other Korean War films took place in different settings, their plots continually focused on the need to convert the characters away from oppositional desires and interests to forge the new consensus. In so doing these films evoked audiences' fears and anxieties, only to resolve them by promoting a utopian crusade that served the interests of official leaders and the cold war. Take the isolationist and pacifist traditions that had been one of the key themes in American popular arts in the thirties.[16] A flyer in *Torpedo Alley,* for example, recalls that in the last battles of the Pacific War he was so afraid that his paralysis led to the death of his copilots. Entering into civilian life, he dislikes the new corporate order that demands that he conform to the optimistic vision of America. Another pilot in *Battle Hymn* experiences guilt because he bombed a German orphanage and killed children during World War II. To atone for his past, he becomes a Presbyterian minister and preaches the need to accept one's sins. He even emulates Christ and climbs a mountain to wrestle with his torment. The coming of the Korean War heightens the problem as protagonists in *One Minute to Zero* fire on enemy troops who use civilians to advance their cause.

Eventually the hero of a Korean War film finds redemption by perceiving that his pacifist impulses have to be shed in order to defeat the communist enemy. In so doing, the American soldiers also expurgate their class and racial interests.[17] *The McConnell Story,* for example, focuses on a white working-class rebel, played by Alan Ladd, a star known in the late forties for his portrayal of gangsters. Expressing the resentment of an ethnic outsider toward authority, McConnell initially refused to obey his superior officers. At the same time, his wife, played by June Allyson, is antagonistic toward the military that calls her husband to fight another war.

A similar conflict played in a racial key informs *Pork Chop Hill.* Symbolic of the new ethos of racial pluralism forged in World War II, the film features a Japanese-American officer who emulates the language and the behavior of his superior officers. But an African-American sol-

Colonel Steve Janowski, played by Robert Mitchum, in *One Minute to Zero* (1952) confronts the reality of civil war and atrocities: a column of refugees infiltrated with North Korean soldiers and arms. He responds with direct mortar fire on a civilian column composed of women and children, explaining that "War is the most malignant condition of the human race. . . . We sometimes have to cut out the good tissue with the bad." *(Courtesy Academy of Motion Picture Arts and Sciences Library)*

dier rebels from the pluralistic groups and threatens to shoot his commander. Why? As the black soldier tells the captain, he faces poverty and discrimination at home. For this reason, going to jail for defying the orders of those who resemble the oppressor is preferable to death in Korea.[18]

Even more threatening to social order in the Korean War era was the willingness of the population to equate the new corporate order and consumerism with cold war goals. And the reason was not hard to find. Hostility to big business had permeated politics from the Progressive era through the New Deal. In the depression many identified movies and swing music with an Americanism at odds with monopoly capitalism. A film such as *I Want You* (1950) showed how these memories had to be overcome. Evoking the personalities and imagery of *The Best Years of Our Lives* (1946), the film tells the story of a veteran who has returned home from the "war to end all wars." After helping to defeat the fascists, he attained the dream of a consumer with a house and an ideal wife, along with employment as a builder of vacation homes and hotels to supply the market for pleasure that drives the new consumer economy. Yet he finds that in the postwar era, in which the corporations predominate, his work threatens to become meaningless and devoid of public commitment. Seeking an alternative, his young brother drives hot-rod cars, listens to jazz, and loves a local girl. In an environment where inequality and discontent with big business reign, a radio announcer reports the start of the Korean War. The young brother rebels against the elites who operate the local draft boards. Similarly, the war hero's wife resists making yet another "sacrifice," and her mother-in-law destroys her husband's own trophy room filled with war medals. Eventually, however, the protagonists see military service and patriotism as a means to give life a larger purpose. Coming together across classes and generations, they link the cold war to a regeneration of American life at home and abroad. After seeing the film, a newspaper editor praised *I Want You* because it answered the key question of the day:

> What can one poor little citizen do about such gigantic waves on a vast ocean of people churned into an awesome storm by sinister forces he can't see or measure? His normal instincts compel him to seek a snug harbor for himself and his family. As the storm without increases in intensity, the inner desire for love, peace, home and security becomes almost an obsession. But his sense of duty tells him he must do his part along with others in fighting the storm. His intelligence tells him about the doubts that beset millions in the United States today and because it

In a climactic scene from *I Want You* (1951), Mrs. Thomas Greer, played by Mildred Dunnock, discovers that her sons have been drafted to serve in the Korean War. She reacts not with a spirit of heroic sacrifice, as in Word War II. Instead she destroys her husband's war trophies from World War I and II, seeing them as emblems of false values that threaten family life. *(Courtesy Academy of Motion Picture Arts and Sciences Library)*

shows that the citizens must accept their responsibility for the war that is why it is a great drama.[19]

Accepting responsibility for the war also meant that the protagonists identified the demonic communists with the disorders that had to be expurgated to create personal and social order. In so doing, the Korean War drama indirectly revealed that the anticommunist crusade projected onto the enemy those disorderly impulses that had to be forgotten as having been a part of American life. A rebellious son in *My Son John,* for example, enjoys consumer pleasures and pioneers, as in the thirties, a youth culture in opposition to mainstream values. Carrying that ethos into the fifties, he refuses to join his brothers in fighting the Korean War. Instead, he joins the Communist Party and resists the draft. In the end the hero converts, informs to the FBI, and tells his fellow students to shed the decadent ways that lead to moral laxity and communism.

Other films played the same song in a different key. In *Tokyo File 212,* a Japanese student trained to be a kamikaze pilot finds at the end of World War II that he cannot die to destroy the white imperialists. Seeking to continue his racial struggle, he joins the Communist Party and launches labor strikes to thwart industries of defense. Similarly weary soldiers in *Cease Fire* complain of being "cogs inside a machine" of the military hierarchy. And the hero and his lover in *One Minute to Zero* feel guilty for committing atrocities on Korean civilians. But the communists have to be destroyed because they perversely kill women and children, and because they like to promote bureaucratic organizations that are at odds with individualism. The result is that when American soldiers destroy the enemy, they have purged disorder from the self and society, giving birth to the promise of class consensus.[20]

Given that the promotion of the cold war demanded the repression of subversive isolationist traditions, class interests, and the oppositional values of consumerism and mass art, it followed that the Asian enemies were doubly dangerous because they appealed to these un-American desires to gain converts to their cause. This was not an idle concern, since at the end of the Korean War over twenty American prisoners of war refused to come back to the United States. To provide a dramatic answer to these troubling facts, the studios mobilized militant anticommunist liberals to create scripts to counter the charge that the communists had a better system. The writer of *Prisoner of War,* Alan Rivkin, was the president of the Writers Guild who eliminated radicals from the industry, and promoted President Truman's election campaign in southern California. As a militant supporter of the president's doctrine of containment, he was engaged in the new "war of ideas."[21] Similarly, an anticommunist writer showed in *Pork Chop Hill* that things are bad on the American side. Officers have to refuse the requests of soldiers who complain that they are now due to be rotated back home to enjoy Cadillacs and security. As the men fail to be supplied at the front, they listen to Chinese radio broadcasts that tell them there is no reason to die in advancing the cause of "Wall Street." And as the enemy plays romantic swing music, one American soldier even prepares to go over to the communists until his friends stop him.[22]

Once the communists captured a few wayward men, the reasons why soldiers had to resist the lures of communism became even more tangible. Rivkin, for example, observed that American collaborators were men who went over to the enemy for three reasons: they were weakened

The American officer Web Sloane, played by Ronald Reagan, masquerades as a turncoat in *Prisoner of War* (1954). As he broadcasts a confession of Korean War atrocities by the American army, the enemy officers observe with approval. The scene implicates both the Russians and Chinese in starting the Korean War, and portrays the collaboration of United States' prisoners not to a disenchantment with the war, but to a larger American plot to attain access to enemy secrets. *(Courtesy Academy of Motion Picture Arts and Sciences Library)*

by their mothers, weakened by a poor education, or weakened by a lack of education. As this explanation reinforced the view that the country was middle class, Rivkin interviewed ex-prisoners for his film *Prisoner of War*. Although he found that well over half of those captured by the Chinese and North Koreans were men of color, he ignored this fact in constructing his film. Expressive of the fact that the new middle-class consensus was implicitly rooted in the norms of white civilization, Rivkin's characters were all Caucasians. The central traitor, played by Ronald Reagan, was a secret agent who pretended to be a communist by mouthing communist ideas to get behind enemy lines to spy for the free world. The result was that, as in other Korean War films, the battle against communism made it possible for Americans to see that the people had not been corrupted by foreign wars, but remained part of an innocent people and nation.[23]

Beneath this conversion narrative lies more than meets the eye. Taken as a whole the Korean War films' central story was not the realities of the Korean War, or a story of the enemy. Rather, the films asked their protagonists, and by implication their audiences, to reveal their class interests and oppositional beliefs as subversive and potentially communistic. This struggle gives birth to a new type of ideal American man and woman. The magnitude of this change comes into high relief when one compares central characters in World War II and Korean War films. In the battle against fascism, heroes embodied a depression-era populism. Whether played by well-known stars like Humphrey Bogart in *Casablanca* or John Garfield in *Air Force,* they found their roots in a vernacular culture that created a communal reciprocity between leaders and their men. By way of contrast, the protagonists in Korean War films are officers who no longer share a close bond with the "grunts" or speak in the localized speech of the enlisted men. Symbolizing this shift in cultural authority, stars such as Humphrey Bogart and Alan Ladd, who had been the ideal heroes of World War II films, now perform as officers who operate as masters of science and management.

At the same time that they serve in large organizations, these heroes fight to protect an American way rooted in the white ideals of middle-class suburban life and normative sexual roles. Whether the narrative takes place in the United States or in Korea, many films feature a woman who sheds her career for the larger goal of creating a secure home for her man. The result is that if she has had a career, as in *Sabre Jet,* she too must undergo a conversion.

As in World War II films, the heroine of a Korean War film expurgated her desire for an independent life, and subordinated her interests to domesticity. If she went into battle, it was as a nurse subservient to male desires. As exemplified by a star like June Allyson in *Battle Circus,* the heroine performed as both a lover and mother who supported men engaged in attaining victory. Far more than in World War II films, the new heroine was weak and needed a strong male to protect her. In other words, as men shed the old definitions of manhood and community—their class, racial, and pacifist commitments—heroines supported the new heroes' "manhood" by becoming more needy of protection and support.[24]

All in all, the thirty-five Korean War films reveal that the revolutionary departure in foreign and domestic policy attendant upon the cold war demanded an alteration in nationality. Out of this conversion narrative there emerges a central theme: guilt and forgetting. On the one hand, the characters' patriotism inspires guilt for retaining loyalty to an older republican tradition. To free themselves of anxiety they affirm their patriotic duty to advance a new international mission for the United States. In resisting that mission, the characters initially feel guilty for retaining their localized class, racial, and antiauthoritarian values. Yet they expurgate guilt by affirming the memory of World War II and find success in building the new order of victory over communism. As the demonic adversary meets defeat, the protagonists create an Americanism rooted in the new corporate order, classlessness, and the normative sexual roles of the suburban home. At the same time, this ideal has its roots in white civilization as the model for the world. As a general in *Pork Chop Hill* explains, the Chinese are treacherous because they are both "Asians and communists."

## "I Lost My Shirt," or the Audience as Subversives

What was most important about these Korean War films, then, was that they were far more than just entertainment or fictional documentaries that reflected the facts of the war. On the contrary, they converged with the efforts of men like Erik Johnston, government agencies, and the anticommunist effort to forge a cold war consensus at home. Yet there was one problem with the new tune: producers found that the audience did not want to dance. This was indeed a tough pill to swallow. Looking back to World War II, when Hollywood made vast profits, reporters saw in 1950 that films geared to war "headlines" would surely yield "boom times ahead." To stimulate that boom, they advertised productions like *Glory Brigade* and *Cease Fire* as winners because they received "approval in advance by the Department of Defense." Gala premieres attended by "General Mark Clark, the Commander-in-Chief in Korea" were expected to spark demand for all Korean War films. Unfortunately fans "failed to show up with their dollars and cents" and theater owners complained that in showing the new films they were fast "losing their shirts."[25]

To add insult to injury, producers identified the Korean War with victory culture and the great success story of World War II. But audiences did not make the same association. In fact, because the country itself had not been attacked, as at Pearl Harbor, the population did not voluntarily rush to support the war at home. From 1940 to 1945 Hollywood war dramas comprised three or four of the top five commercial suc-

cesses. Critically, many won Academy Awards and made enormous profits as markets expanded to new audiences. The result was that producers
had the best of all possible worlds: they bathed in the glow of patriotism
and financial gains. Working with that same memory in mind, Hollywood producers foresaw that Korean War films would reap vast profits.
Yet no Korean War film reached the top five moneymaking productions
during the 1950s. Instead, thirty-two failed to reach the top fifty grossing films in any year. Further, no artist or director ever won an Academy
Award for a Korean War or anticommunist drama. In fact, the vast majority of films in all these categories experienced financial failure. Only
three reached the top fifty and none reached the top fifteen commercial
favorites through the entire decade. One thus had to report that the effort
to create a cold war consensus and voluntary support for the war failed
on all fronts.[26]

When trade reporters explored why this failure occurred, they con-
fronted a sharp contrast between what the literary scholar Kenneth Burke
called "cultural frames of reference" and facts that contradicted the frame.
The president and "cold warriors" alike evoked World War II victory
culture to demand obedience and support for the war. Yet as Burke observed, "the rise of new material, which it has not been designed to
handle, endangers the frame." It was not that people shed the glorious
memory of the last war. From the late forties through the fifties, films
focusing on World War II, such as *The Sands of Iwo Jima*, *Battle Cry,*
and *Twelve O'Clock High* became box office successes. But when filmmakers turned to "current headlines" on Korea they dealt with facts that
endangered the "serviceability" of the World War II "victory culture"
on all fronts.[27]

Even though moviemakers tried to turn tragedy into a success story,
it just did not seem to work. Take *Retreat Hell,* which told the story of
the Marine landing in 1950 at Inchon and the march north to the Yalu
River. Yet the Chinese entered the war and the Marines moved back
down the Korean peninsula in bitter snow, reminding viewers far more
of Napoleon's tragic withdrawal from Moscow in 1812 than of victory
over Japan in 1945. The soundtrack included the triumphal music of the
"Marine Hymn," and moviemakers tried their best to turn retreat into an
ode of victory. But a viewer noted that "it hurts to watch it thinking how
small the accomplishment of our effort in Korea has proved to be." It
reminded perceptive viewers of the "only war we have lost." Another
saw that *Cease Fire* showed that the "business at hand in the Orient" had

A Hollywood producer receives pointers from Captain Ben Russell, the technical advisor assigned by the United States Marine Corps to monitor the script of *Retreat Hell* (1952). This is typical of the script consultation provided by the Defense Department in the making of most Korean War combat films. *(Courtesy Academy of Motion Pictures Arts and Sciences Library)*

"no solution." And *Pork Chop Hill* revealed that war movies were not as simple as they used to be, because viewers no longer wanted to be "reminded of the Korean blunder" and this great "mistake in United States history." Summarizing the problem, one critic noted:

> I guess the main trouble is that our vastly troubled times cannot be dealt with by ringing platitudes. The result always seems to look, no matter how close it comes to actual problems and fears, simply like another of those staple mixtures of soapsuds and molasses.[28]

Observers and audiences also rejected what they saw as moviemakers' evocation of "platitudes" and "mixtures of soapsuds and molasses" designed to mask the reality of stalemate and tragedy. As producers called upon distributors to "intensify merchandising drives to overcome public apathy," viewers noted that characters spoke in dialogue "overloaded with primitive propaganda." Dialogue that evoked success and victory in the new setting appeared "dated and hackneyed" and plots were filled with "old cliches." To top it off, these narratives generated the unthinkable: active protest against the war.[29]

Symbolic of that larger issue, the owner of the largest movie theater chain in Ohio refused to show *Why Korea?*—a documentary made with the cooperation of the White House itself. Presidential advisers found that the recalcitrant theater owner was a supporter of Robert Taft, the Republican senator who wished to perpetuate the isolationist tradition into the postwar world. The owner accordingly saw the Korean War as a disaster. Writing to the White House, he noted:

> As you know, there are millions of people in disagreement with the administration's policy in Korea, many of whom will be forced to sit through the showing of this subject and in such instances the exhibitor will lose the good will of many of his patrons. Before this organization requests its members to show this subject, advise if it is the intention of the administration to show the other side of the controversy by authorizing the making of a film titled *Why We Should Get out of Korea.*[30]

The producer, Darryl Zanuck, called the protester a traitor, but the exhibitor refused to back down. In a similar vein, a censorship board in Tennessee had the temerity to ban a prisoner-of-war film engaged in the "battle of ideas." The Memphis censors had apparently failed to realize that the good American in *The Bamboo Prison,* who condemned Wall Street and the imperialist war in Asia, was in reality a secret agent. Only when the film producer explained the plot's finer points did the Memphis regulators relent, even though one censor had the last word, for as she saw it *The Bamboo Prison* was still a "rotten picture."[31]

By the third year of the Korean War it was also clear that discontent with the conflict was not confined to moviegoers. In fact, the reality of the "lost audience" for Korean War films was part of a much larger trend. Symbolic of the process, pollsters found that the majority of the people saw the war as a clear "mistake," and the Truman administration's popularity slowly waned. Dwight D. Eisenhower won the presidential election of 1952 promising to end the stalemate in Korea. Yet, because the public found that the president's most admirable quality was his leadership in World War II, the president drew on the ethos of the victory culture to transform the tragedy of the Korean War into a success story. Far from being united under capitalist-friendly and militarily strong regimes promoted by the United States, two Koreas emerged from the conflict. Yet the new president drew on his prestige as the most important general of World War II to encourage increased support of the South and containment around the globe. The president and his secretary of state, John Foster Dulles, increased United States military commitments, supported Chiang Kai-shek in Taiwan, and aided the French against the Viet Cong in Vietnam.[32]

Ironically, these leaders' actions, as in the Korean War films, promoted a cold war ideology of forgetting as the heart of anticommunist doctrine. Officials implicitly asked the public to forget about the failures of the war in Korea and to see it as a great victory. On some levels it seemed to work. At the local level the anticommunist crusade stifled dissent, while government-sponsored reports ignored detailed descriptions of the war, leading to the "forgetting" of the Korean conflict in the public discourse of the United States. If silence in official circles suggests the people's acquiescence, it could be argued that the people did forget the tragedies of the Korean War. In fact, however, a sober second look leads to a more complicated assessment of the war's impact. The fact that the public failed to attend Korean War films, and that the majority of the population turned away from Truman's policies in Korea, did not seem to suggest that forgetting predominated.

On the contrary, the market for mass art revealed that in realms of popular memory a different story gained a hearing. Where this was most evident was in the few pacifist and Korean War films that did make a commercial profit. A theater owner in New York City, for example, defied industry guidelines and rereleased the antiwar classic *All Quiet on the Western Front* to "standing-room-only audiences." Watching the patrons' response, a critic saw that the audience applauded the characters' antiwar sentiments and criticism of big business, suggesting that support for the Korean War was going to find among the young a "tough customer." Similarly, *The Bridges of Toko-Ri* emerged in 1954 as one of the few successful Korean War productions. The reason for its moderate success was not that it dramatized a conversion narrative; it was that it brought to the center an Irish-Catholic comic, played by Mickey Rooney, who mocks the whole enterprise. He disdains officers, rebels from military authority, and turns to the joys of nightclubs, play, and consumer culture for an alternative. *Battle Hymn* also gained moderate success by portraying an Air Force officer who atones for bombing civilians by constructing orphanages for Korean children. In other words, he atones

for his war guilt not by killing communists, but by the act of constructing homes for children whose parents have been killed in the fighting.

To top it off, one of the most popular films gained success in proportion to its ability to undermine the official view of the war itself. Critics
saw that Samuel Fuller's *The Steel Helmet* was a "great war picture"
because no one "mouthed heroic or vainglorious declarations." Working in an independent studio, Fuller noted that "all my films are antiwar" and his admirers called him the Ernie Pyle of Hollywood
moviemaking, after the World War II columnist who admired the common soldiers. But the Defense Department told theater owners that "any
attempt to say, or even to imply, that this picture was in any way cleared
or approved is a deliberate lie." A conservative columnist chimed in to
note that *The Steel Helmet* was a "vicious attempt to show the military
in a bad light." Fuller showed that racism permeated the army, that common soldiers viewed patriotism cynically, and that veterans disdained
the new corporate officers. Military spokesmen condemned the film
because the "impression is clearly left that the American either has no
idea why he's fighting, or doesn't really believe he should be fighting."

One of the central characters in *The Steel Helmet* is a young Korean
boy who has not been clearly socialized into the ideological views of
adults who fight the war. Unlike the Korean or the American soldiers,
the youth believes in the loving philosophy of Buddha and rejects the
closed systems of the communists as well as that of the promoters of the
free world.

As Fuller noted, "at the end of the film . . . the three survivors are all
outcasts in some way—the Negro, the Oriental and the bald-headed. This
adds a very downbeat note to the 'victory' over the North Koreans."[33]

Five years after the end of the war, the erosion of victory culture in
the popular if not the official arena continued with the production and
release of *The Quiet American*. Filmed with the full support of the South
Vietnamese government in the streets of Saigon in 1958, and geared to
gathering mass support for the United States' commitment in Asia, the
narrative drew on a Graham Green novel. The film featured the single
most decorated soldier of World War II, Audie Murphy, playing an
American reformer who offers Asia a "third way." A critic noted that
Murphy played an "innocent abroad, a do-gooder for the U.S.A." The
hero worked for an organization called the "Friends for Free Asia" and
advocated a "third force—something between democracy and communism." Yet trade critics saw that the film failed because it contained "too

Sergeant Zack, played by Gene Evans, peers behind a statue of Buddha in *The Steel Helmet* (1951). Written and directed by Samuel Fuller, the film portrays a platoon where tension along race lines and between officers and men is an everyday factor of life. And in contrast to the killing and atrocities, an innocent Korean boy and the spirit of a Buddhist temple present an alternative to brutal war and demonic conflicts. *(Courtesy Academy of Motion Picture Arts Sciences Library)*

much ideology" and dialogue "more concerned with intellectual and political problems than with dramatic entertainment," with the result that the characters were "symbols with each mouthing a given ideology." Prophetically, another critic observed that while some would support these anticommunist views, "there are likely to be an awful lot of people who'll come out of this film saying, 'Who gives a damn about the "clash of ideologies" in Asia?'"[34]

At this point of "giving a damn" we can also begin to answer the questions with which we began: Why was the Korean War forgotten, and how pervasive was the "cold war American identity" that scholars uncritically assume pervaded the late forties and fifties? Within Hollywood, anticommunists like Erik Johnston and Ronald Reagan sought to purge left-wing influences and forge an American way rooted in classless ideals and the normative family. The Korean War films evoked the historical memory of World War II to demand unity and expurgation of dissenting ideas. The Korean War films popularized this ideology by focusing on themes of guilt, forgetting, and redemption. Although the Eisenhower administration perpetuated this ideological change when it expanded the cold war in areas like Vietnam, audiences failed to support films promoting cold war goals. In many ways this suggests the truth of Milan Kundera's insight in *The Book of Laughter and Forgetting*: "The struggle of man against power is the struggle of man against forgetting."[35] Unlike in World War II, audience behavior exhibited a resistance to the official "truth" that Korea was not a tragedy, but a victory. And as audiences supported alternative films, they validated the power of mass art to evoke counternarratives of American culture. All in all, these events reveal that officials used established institutions to advance a triumphal cold war ethos. But to assume that their doctrines struck deep roots is to ignore that the public failed to join in that celebration—a reality that foreshadowed the Vietnam War and the conflicts of the sixties.

## Notes

1. Kenneth Burke, *Attitudes Towards History*, 3rd ed. (Berkeley: University of California Press, 1984), 132; *"My Son John," Motion Picture Herald*, 25 April 1953, 35.

2. Barton J. Bernstein, "The Truman Administration and the Korean War," in *The Truman Presidency*, ed. Michael J. Lacey (Cambridge: Cambridge University Press, 1989), 410; Charles E. Bohlen, *Witness to History, 1929–1969* (New York: Norton, 1973), 295.

3. Tom Engelhardt, *The End of Victory Culture: Cold War America and the Disillusioning of a Generation* (New York: Basic Books, 1995), 5–7. For a review of the current literature of the war, see Philip West, "Interpreting the Korean War," *The American Historical Review* 94, no. 1 (February 1989): 80–96; *The Gallup Poll: Public Opinion, 1935–1971*, vol. 2 (New York: Random House), 968.

4. Bruce Cumings, *War and Television* (New York: Norton, 1994) 148, 269; Dan B. Fleming and Burton I. Kaufman, "The Forgotten War: Korea," *Education Digest* (December 1990): 70–72.

5. See, for example, Alan Wolfe and Jerry Sanders, "Resurgent Cold War Ideology: The Case of the Communist Committee on the Present Danger," in *Capitalism and the State in United States–Latin American Relations*, ed. Richard R. Fagan (Stanford: Stanford University Press, 1978), 41–75.

6. Ellen Schrecker, *The Age of McCarthyism: A Brief History with Documents* (New York: Bedford Books of St. Martin's Press, 1994), 144–46; "Most Important Problem," interview, 19 November 1953, *The Gallup Poll,* 1199.

7. On hegemony, see Jackson Lears, "The Concept of Cultural Hegemony: Problems and Possibilities," *American Historical* Review 90, no. 3 (June 1985): 567–93.

8. On Erik Johnston and postwar Hollywood, see Lary May, *The Big Tomorrow: Hollywood and the Politics of the American Way* (Chicago: University of Chicago Press, 2000).

9. See Charles Maier, "The Politics of Productivity," *International Organization* 31, no. 4 (1977): 607–31; Benedict Anderson, *Imagined Communities: Reflections of the Origins and Spread of Nationalism* (New York: Verso, 1991). On memories of radical films and their effects on politics, see James Jones, *From Here to Eternity* (New York: Dell Publishing, 1951), 272–73.

10. See May, *Big Tomorrow*, 175–225; and "Urge Care on Pic Kickbacks O'Seas," *Variety*, 16 August 1950, 1.

11. "Roy Brewer Gives Answer on Chaplin and 'Limelight,' " *Motion Picture Herald*, 28 February 1953, 8–9; "Say Screen Saved from Communists," *Motion Picture Herald*, 3 January 1953, 25; "COMPO Pledges Full Cooperation to Truman in War Emergency," *Variety*, 13 September 1950, 4–12; "An Anti-Red Oath Wins SAG Vote," *Motion Picture Herald*, 1 August 1953, 29.

12. "Hollywood Scurries to Capitalize on Korean Shooting," *Variety,* 4 July 1950, 1; "Government Eyes Reception of Its War Pix with Korean War Flare-Up," *Variety*, 28 June 1950, 3; "Industry Mobilizes in National Emergency," *Motion Picture Herald,* 13 January 1951, 13; *My Son John* file and *Tokyo File 212* file, Academy of Motion Picture Arts and Sciences Library, Los Angeles (hereafter cited as AMPAS). For FBI clearances, see *Variety,* 7 March 1951, as in Korea file, AMPAS.

13. *The McConnell Story* is on video. See Leonard Maltin, *1999 Movie and Video Guide* (New York: Signet Books, 1999); "Torpedo Alley Uses Intensive Exploitation," *Motion Picture Herald,* 28 February 1953, 44.

14. "23rd Awards, Documentary, Short Subjects," *Why Korea?* file, AMPAS; "Darryl Zanuck to John R. Steelman," 2 February 1951, in John R. Steelman file, *Papers of Harry Truman,* Harry S. Truman Library, Independence, Missouri (hereafter cited as Truman Library).

15. *The Bridges of Toko-Ri* (1954) is available on video. See Maltin, *1999 Movie and Video Guide.*

16. See Frederic Jameson, "Reification and Utopia in Mass Culture," *Social Text* 1 (1979) for a general theory of how films accomplish the task of resolving anxieties within acceptable themes.

17. *Torpedo Alley* (1953), *Battle Hymn* (1957), and *One Minute to Zero* (1952) are all available on video. See Maltin, *1999 Movie and Video Guide*. Also see Steve

Fore, "Howard Hughes' 'Authoritarian Fictions': RKO, *One Minute to Zero*, and the Cold War," *The Velvet Light Trap*, no. 31 (spring 1993): 15–26.

18. All the cited films are available on video. See Maltin, *1999 Movie and Video Guide.*

19. *I Want You* (1951) is available on video. See Maltin, *1999 Movie and Video Guide.* The editorial is from *The Los Angeles Daily News*, 19 December 1951, as in *I Want You* file, AMPAS.

20. *One Minute to Zero, My Son John, Tokyo File 212*, and *Cease Fire* files in AMPAS.

21. The writer was an important anticommunist in Hollywood who helped purge the left from the Screenwriters' Guild. See "WGA Pioneer Rivkin Dies," *Variety*, 20 February 1990, 26; and *Prisoner of War* file, AMPAS.

22. *Pork Chop Hill* is available on video. See Maltin, *1999 Movie and Video Guide.*

23. See *Prisoner of War* scripts and Rivkin's notes in *Prisoner of War* file, University of Southern California Film Library, Los Angeles.

24. The equation of Korean battles with other sacred events in American history can best be seen in the climax of *Pork Chop Hill* (1959). All the cited films are available on video. See Maltin, *1999 Movie and Video Guide.*

25. *Motion Picture Herald*, 25 July 1953, 25 and 21 November 1953, 28.

26. "Top Grossing Films," in *Motion Picture and Television Almanac*, ed. Charles S. Aronson (New York: Quigly Publications, 1954) has data on the top one hundred grossing films of all time: ten derived from World War II, none from the Korean War. Staff of Academy Library, "*Variety* Top Grossing Films, 1946 to the Present" lists the top fifty grossing films in AMPAS. On World War II, see *Reel Facts: The Movie Book of Records*, Updated ed. (New York: Vintage Books, 1982), 3–9, 193–250.

27. Burke, *Attitudes Towards History*, 35; *Reel Facts*, 20.

28. Hollis Alpert, "*I Want You*," *Saturday Review of Literature*, 22 December 1951, unpaginated clipping in *I Want You* file, AMPAS; "*Retreat Hell*," *Los Angeles Examiner*, 16 February 1952, unpaginated clipping in *Retreat Hell* file, AMPAS; unidentified clippings in *Pork Chop Hill* and *Cease Fire* files, AMPAS.

29. "Hollywood Scurries to Capitalize on Korean Shooting," *Variety*, 4 July 1950, 1; *The Hollywood Reporter*, 7 July 1953, unpaginated clipping in *Mission Over Korea* file, AMPAS; "*Retreat Hell*," *Box Office*, 16 February 1952, unpaginated clipping in *Retreat Hell* file, AMPAS.

30. P.J. Wood, "Public Service Propaganda or Politics?" *The Independent Theatre Owners Bulletin*, 23 January 1952, 1. Steelman Papers, Truman Library, Independence, Missouri.

31. "The Independent Theater Owners of Ohio, Service Bulletin," Steelman file, Truman Library; *Bamboo Curtain* file, AMPAS.

32. "President Eisenhower," 14–19 July 1955, *The Gallup Poll*, vol. 2, 1351. Unidentified clipping, *Pork Chop Hill* file, AMPAS. On the aftermath of the Korean War, and its effects on Eisenhower, see Bernstein, "The Truman Administration and the Korean War."

33. For the box office success of these films see "Top Grossing Films from *Variety*," AMPAS. Victor Riesel, " 'Steel Helmet' Stirs Protests," *Hollywood Citizen-News*, 17 January 1951; "War Department Withholds Full Approval of 'Steel Helmet,' "

*Variety,* 10 January 1951; *"The Steel Helmet," Motion Picture Herald,* 6 January 1951, unpaginated clippings in *Steel Helmet* file, AMPAS.

34. "Saigon Film Tragic Study," *Los Angeles Times,* 24 January 1958; *"The Quiet American," Hollywood Reporter,* 22 January 1958; *"The Quiet American," Variety,* 10 January 1958, unpaginated newspaper clippings in *The Quiet American* file, AMPAS.

35. Milan Kundera, *The Book of Laughter and Forgetting* (New York: Viking 1981), 4. Kundera refers to the conflicts in Soviet-occupied Czechoslovakia in the 1970s.

# 8
## The Korean War in Korean Films

*Suh Ji-moon*

Given its profound impact on all aspects of life on the Korean peninsula today and its continuing irresolution, one could argue that the Korean War, directly or indirectly, touches upon almost all of the stories and characters in Korean films made over the past half-century. Among some of the most popular and highly respected films made by Korean directors are many that explore themes related to the Korean War: its setting, the war itself, and its legacies and impact on Korean life. It would be impossible in this brief chapter to address all of these films. So I have chosen to review three films in particular: *The Taebaek Mountains*, *To the Starry Island*, and *Spring in My Hometown*.*

In the 1950s and 1960s, Korean movies dealing with or featuring aspects of the Korean War naturally strove to show how evil and inhuman communists were. I say "naturally" because not only was anticommunism the primary national policy line under the Syngman Rhee and Park Chung Hee governments, but there was a very strong anticommunist sentiment among the general population as well. Most South Koreans had suffered excruciating hardships because of the communist invasion that started the war. Many of them lost family members in the war as casualties in combat or through the communists' torture, execution, and abduction of civilians. Today's younger generation tend to think

---

*All three films are subtitled in English and have been screened for review and study as part of the Mansfield Center's project "America's Wars in Asia: A Cultural Approach." *To the Starry Island* was screened in July 1995 as part of the Center's National Endowment for the Humanities–sponsored Summer Institute, which launched the project; *The Taebaek Mountains* and *Spring in My Hometown* were screened in the course of the Korea/America Dialogue on the Korean War, June 19–25, 1999.

that the anticommunist sentiments of the fifties and sixties were little more than government indoctrination, but this is certainly not the case. Because I never liked war films, I saw few of the 1950s and 1960s movies on the Korean War. These early films are rarely revived today (because of the lack of commercial viability and the poor state of film preservation), so I cannot compare them with the three selected here. But I vaguely recall the portrayal of communists as cruel monsters in the Korean movies of bygone years. One movie I remember, which was entitled *The Barber of Changmaruch'on Village,* is about overcoming the fatal wound left by the Korean War through love that transcends the physical.

The hero of this movie returns from the Korean War impotent. Because he is a noble youth, he pretends that he is not interested in his fiancée any more, and she leaves the village in wretched despair. He becomes the barber of his hometown and tries to console himself with the thought that he did not make his fiancée a victim of the war. His fiancée has a very eligible new suitor, but returns to the village to make a last effort to win back the protagonist. Discovering the truth behind his ostensible change of heart, she vows she will never leave him. So the wound of war is overcome by love greater than the sensual. There is a communist featured in the film, and of course he is portrayed as an ignorant brute, who hates the noble protagonist just because he is the son of a landowner and because he wins the love of the woman he covets. When the war breaks out, the villain becomes a communist and soon after attempts to rape the heroine. Failing that, he tries to blow up the protagonist's house and kill his entire family, but meets his own death at the hands of the protagonist. The communist often plays the role of the villain in movies set in this period.

With the coming of age of the generation that experienced neither the Korean War nor its painful aftermath, and that came to hate and distrust any action of the government they lived under, these tables were turned. In resisting successive military regimes this generation, often led by students, not only held antigovernment demonstrations but also became interested in and began the study of Marxism as an ideology that they could use to oppose capitalistic democracy. They came to regard communists generally, and even the leadership of North Korea, as friends of the downtrodden masses, whereas they saw the upholders of liberal democracy, as represented by the government of the South, as corrupt opportunists.

Literature and the arts followed this trend, and also defied the taboo against representing communists as anything other than inhuman perverts by portraying them with compassion, even admiration. This emerging sympathy toward communism made inroads into filmmaking too, even though cinema tends to be the most ideologically conservative medium. The revisionist trend was of course most pronounced in literature, which incited it and was fed by it. Many multivolume sagas were written, which explored the whole course of events leading up to the Korean War and its consequences, and most of these novels featured several communists among the gallery of main characters. In the fine arts, the Minjung—mass or grass-roots—art school was formed and was a strong force in painting, sculpture, video, and installation art.

Partly because the government exercised stronger censorship on films, and partly because the audience tended to eschew movies that dealt with disturbing questions, revisionism had an impact on cinema only much later. But with the appearance of a new generation of directors who were willing, even eager, to take risks and knew how to excite public interest by treating risky subjects, certain taboos were lifted from cinematic subjects as well. Most of the risks were taken in the area of portraying the student movement and the sensibilities of students in the 1980s, but the Korean War and the ideological conflict at the base of it also began to be treated with unprecedented freedom.

*The Taebaek Mountains* is a cinematization of the ten-volume river novel of the same title by Cho Chŏng-rae, published in 1986. The original novel is perhaps the most ambitious exploration to date of the left-right conflict that tore the country apart in the wake of liberation from Japanese colonial rule, though it is not the first fiction in which socialists are treated sympathetically. The author spent more than ten years gathering materials and visiting all the villages, hills, and valleys that were the loci of the communists' subversive efforts against the government of South Korea. It was not only a most ambitious undertaking, but also an extremely courageous one. Cho Chŏng-rae's writing reflects the experiences and memories of his childhood, when his father was imprisoned for being a communist sympathizer. Cho grew up in the South Chŏlla Province region, where the left-right struggle was fiercest. Like many other writers, he says, he did not so much choose to write the novel, but was compelled to write it by an "irresistible inner momentum." He said he was prepared for persecution on account of the subject matter and his treatment of it, and he did receive threats and abuses, but fortunately not to the degree he might have suffered had he written the novel ten years earlier. Indeed, his novel brought him great acclaim and wealth, far exceeding his most sanguine expectations. The success of his novel can serve as a gauge of the growing freedom of expression in South Korea and the South Koreans' emancipation from their communist phobia.

Director Im Kwon-taek, who undertook the cinematization of the novel, also had a father who was a follower of communism and had a miserable adolescence and youth as a result. Like Cho Chŏng-rae, he is from Chŏlla province. So the original author and movie director were well matched. The movie version (released in 1994) is, of course, a mere outline of the magnum opus. But it shows effectively in concentrated form the major events and causes of the left-right struggle in Korea. The movie revolves around three central characters. The first is Yŏm Sang-jin, who is a communist of firm convictions and sterling virtue. The second is Kim Pŏm-u, a humanist who distrusts ideologies and is skeptical of revolutions and utopias. And the third is Yŏm Sang-jin's brother Sang-gu, who, as the younger son of a poor family, saw his elder brother favored in everything and became an extreme anticommunist simply from hatred of his older brother. Most of the other important characters tend to be communists, since the novel is among other things a study of what made so many Koreans turn to, or be susceptible to the promise of, communism. Some of the communists are highly educated intellectuals from the bourgeois class; some of them are exceptionally bright youths from the lower class who rise above their origins; and some are ignorant farmers and country folk motivated by their hatred of the rich and powerful and seduced by the promise of free land and classless society. Like the novel, the characters in the movie are allowed some nonideological activities, and the film includes a wide range of romantic and erotic episodes that cover the spectrum from devotion to idealism and comradeship to crude eroticism and reluctant yielding to the call of the flesh.

The movie begins with the Yŏsu Uprising, which was a rebellion staged by the leftist elements in the South Korean regular army in October 1948. There was a large contingent of leftists in the South Korean army, because the United States allowed anyone who swore an oath of allegiance to democratic ideals to join the army when it was founded as a "constabulary force in national defense" shortly after national liberation. In the film, the rebels seize Yŏsu and Sunch'ŏn by surprise attacks on the police stations. The first typical action of the communists when they take a town is to hold a "people's court" and execute landowners, government officials, and police officers. But government forces recapture the cities in less than five days, and the communists flee into the Chiri Mountains to become guerrillas. Retaliation inevitably follows. The punitive forces ferret out collaborators and communist sympathizers and execute them.

This cycle of retaliation—in which ideological adversaries try to eliminate each other, and plain folk settle private scores by accusing hated neighbors of communism or democratic republicanism—goes on throughout the movie. The movie shows that in that period no one was safe; a neighbor's false testimony or the mere fact of having a county office clerk for a nephew or a former school friend who became a communist was enough to get a person stood up against the wall before a firing squad or pierced by a bamboo spear. Anyone defending others who faced such charges could also be accused of sympathizing and secret alliance. In one place in the movie, the chief of the punitive force, who has lost his landowner father to the communists' purge, declares: "You must be [a communist], if you want due process of law observed for [executing] the communists." In such times, the vast majority of people were like "tiny shrimps in a sea in which giant whales are fighting." One hapless communist's wife cannot but submit to the sexual aggression of Yŏm Sang-gu, who has done her the fatal favor of getting her out through the back door on the day communists and their families were culled out for execution.

The support and sympathy communists inspired in the underprivileged masses is encapsulated in an exchange between a young shaman and a young leftist intellectual. The young man, seeking refuge from the police in the shaman's isolated abode, asks her: "What do you think of communists?" and she answers, "I guess they can't be very bad if they are friends of the poor."

Kim Pŏm-u, the skeptical intellectual who stays above the bloody fray of the ideologists, sees land as the source of all the conflict. The farmers, who gave up 70 percent of the yield for rent and lived in constant penury and hunger, once regarded their lot as ordained by heaven. However, once the communists persuaded them that they had been exploited and wronged for centuries and that they had rights equal to those of their landlords—their virtual masters—they became explosive materials ready for detonation. Land reform thus becomes an issue throughout the movie. After Korea's liberation from the Japanese colonial occupation, land reform was expected as a matter of course. The delay in land reform in the South helps explain why many farmers became communist sympathizers and followers. The movie casts a cold eye on the landowners' attempts to sell their land cheaply, before land reform is enforced, or to convert their planted rice paddies into salt farms without even notifying, to say nothing of gaining the consent of, the tenant farmers. And the times did not allow people to remain neutral. A doctor who treats a wounded communist gets into trouble with the law, and the communists criticize him for saving the life of a police officer shot by communist guerrillas.

There is little doubt that the writer, Cho Chŏng-rae, and the film director, Im Kwon-taek, had great sympathy for the communists, but the latter are not idealized unrealistically. The communists are as brutal as the supporters of "capitalistic democracy" in executing their ideological enemies. They too punish "traitors," and even kill off innocent people who happen to witness their activities, to ensure their own safety. There is also a deadly power struggle between communists belonging to the Southern Labor Party and party members from North Korea after the outbreak of the Korean War, during the brief period when the communists occupied most of South Korea. Of course, the South Korean authorities are just as brutal, and in one scene South Korean soldiers tell all the villagers to evacuate their village and then set fire to the entire village, "to drive out the red bastards."

Two short dialogues toward the end of the movie fairly well sum up what the ideological struggle achieved. While the communists are still holding the town, Sang-jin finds his evil reactionary of a brother hiding in an underground dugout in his house. He aims a gun at his brother, and the latter tells him to go ahead and pull the trigger. Then Sang-jin makes an appeal to their brotherhood and asks him why he became an evil reactionary. Sang-gu replies that both of them simply chose the path that seemed the best for them, but that, come to think of it, "we did nothing but slaughter people." He observes, wryly, "Seems to me you're mighty careless about people's lives, for guys claiming to work for the people," and quips that his brother's talk of equality "looks like a fine fiction."

In the penultimate scene, the communists, before being driven out by the combined Korean and UN forces, frantically slaughter anybody in sight and indiscriminately set houses and buildings on fire. Pŏm-u desperately seeks out Sang-jin and demands that he put a stop to the carnage, whereupon Sang-jin gives the command but is told that the situation is totally out of control. Pŏm-u observes that Sang-jin's utopia is a completely failed idea. In response, Sang-jin muses dreamily, with flames soaring on all sides and his subordinates urging him to flee, how moved he was when he first read Marx and how he vowed to give his life to make his dream of "a world where everybody was equal and free" come true. Then Pŏm-u remarks that no ideology based on hatred can save people.

The movie ends with a ritual the town's shaman performs to lay to rest the embittered ghost of the woman who took her life after giving in to Sang-gu's sexual importunity. Pŏm-u tells the young shaman that he is moved by her taking such great care to comfort a ghost when everywhere people are committing mass slaughter. The shaman replies that her rituals are performed to console the living people in their sorrow. To provide that comfort, Pŏm-u observes, there will have to be many such rituals. The ending, thus, is a typically Buddhist-shamanistic resolution to human conflicts and the urge to seek revenge. It is a transcendence of all hatred and resentments through the recognition of the common basic flaw in human nature.

Director Pak Kwang-su's *To the Starry Island* (Kŭ Sŏm'e Kago Sipda, literally "I Want to Go [Return] to That Island"), released in 1993, does not concern itself directly with the ideological issue. But it does illuminate the horrendous consequences of one man's taking advantage of the ideological confrontation during the Korean War period to satisfy his grudges and resentments. The movie opens with a boat carrying a coffin and mourners approaching an island. The body in the coffin is that of a man who had been an inhabitant of the island forty years before, but was exiled after causing the death of scores of the islanders. He had requested, as his last wish, that his body be buried on the island where he was born. But before the boat and the mourners reach the island, they are intercepted by a boat carrying the islanders, who threaten to sink the funeral boat and kill everyone in it if the boat dares approach any further. Among the mourners on the coffin boat is a poet who is a friend of the deceased man's son. The poet spent his childhood on the island because his father, a schoolteacher from the mainland, devoted his life to enlightening the islanders. Counting on the islanders' goodwill toward himself as the respected teacher's son, the poet shouts his appeals to the islanders, but is rebuffed by them. He thereupon tries to jump over to the other boat to reason, or plead, with the islanders, but misses his footing and falls into the sea.

Fished up from the sea and brought onto the island to be revived, the poet recalls what happened forty years before, when he was a small child. Life on the island then had all the features such remote islands of those times had—a half-wit nubile girl, a habitual wife beater, a sex-hungry widow abused as an easy lay, a (relatively) rich playboy who flagrantly neglects his rustic wife and spends most of his time on the mainland with his mistress, and so forth. What the island didn't have was anyone with any ideological orientation, even though there was a landlord who was also a ship owner and some discontented tenant farmers and hired fishermen.

The mass slaughter that assumes the character of an ideological "purge" is ushered onto the island by the playboy, whose wife goes mad on account of his heartless neglect of her and the death of their cretin daughter. The playboy does not even return to the island for his daughter's funeral, but takes his demented wife away to the mainland on a stretcher, saying that he will put her in a mental hospital. Given the islanders' distrust of, and hostility toward, institutions on the mainland, it is an act that earns the islanders' grave disapproval and anger. Very shortly afterward he brings his very pregnant mistress to the island, and tells people that his wife died after breaking out of the mental asylum. The islanders suspect him of doing away with his demented wife. Even if he has not actually killed his wife, bringing home a pregnant mistress as soon as his wife has died is a breach of morality and decorum that the simple villagers cannot brook. So the village council convenes a summary court and gives him a mass thrashing.

Soon after that, a ship carrying soldiers lands on the island. Declaring themselves communists who have come to liberate the oppressed, the soldiers round up all the villagers in a square and divide them into groups of revolutionaries and reactionaries. Of course, many people desperately try to be put into the revolutionary group, declaring their allegiance to communism and accusing their neighbors of being reactionaries. Those who succeed in being identified as revolutionaries shout "Long live communism!" Then the playboy appears with several more soldiers, who are in South Korean military uniform and who proceed to execute all the self-declared communists. A massive burial plot is thus created. Even though it is never proved in the movie, the villagers believe that the scam of pretending to test the villagers' loyalty to communism was the playboy's idea. It goes without saying that the playboy cannot stay on the island another hour.

How much he must have re-
pented is to be surmised from the
fact that his last wish was to be
buried on the island. But such a
sign of repentance cannot assuage
the islanders' hatred and fury,
which was handed down to the
next generation unmitigated. The
son protests, "My father was a victim, too!" but the protest is met
only with scorn. So when the son
attempts a clandestine landing under cover of night, the villagers set
fire to the boat. The poet sighs
helplessly, but turns his eyes from
the burning boat to see a vision of
the ghosts of the victims and vic-
timizer dancing in joyous communal harmony in the next world,
released from the vicious cycle of

Director Lee Kwang-mo had worked on
the script of *Spring in My Hometown*
for almost two decades before finding
the means to produce the film, which
he directed. The film received numerous international awards and superla-
tive accolades.

bad karma giving birth to more bad karma. The extreme respect and
awe Koreans have for the dead and the tradition of not passing judgment on anyone who has just died, added to the intercession of the shaman who owes a debt of gratitude to the poet's father, bring about a
change of heart in the villagers. The last scene is a long shot of the coffin
boat beached on the island. The reconciliation is not a logical resolution of
the conflict, but again a Buddhist-shamanistic transcendence based on recognition of the imperfection of all human beings and the concept of life as
full of moral pitfalls and an endless series of tribulations.

Director Lee Kwang-mo poured his heart and soul and unstinting labor
into *Spring in My Hometown* (Arŭmdaun Sijŏl, literally "Beautiful
Times"), released in 1998. The result is a heartbreakingly beautiful film
that bears repeated watching. The director worked on the script for more
than ten years, and dedicated the film to his father and grandfather, "who
did not lose hope and courage even during those difficult years." The
movie is full of contradictions and paradoxes. The lyrical English title,
*Spring in My Hometown*, like its equally lyrical and peaceful Korean
title, is a paradox. What happens against the backdrop of the consum-

The boys of the village enjoy peeping in on American GIs having sex with Korean women in a ruined flour mill. But the two boys are devastated one day when they steal up to the mill and find Chang-hee's mother offering herself to a GI, and Sung-min's father acting as procurer.

mately beautiful and poetic scenery and the deceptively peaceful rural setting is debasement, treachery, corruption, arson, and murder.

The film begins with a group of villagers dragging a "red squealer" out of a well where he has hidden himself to escape their fury. The thread of the ideological divide runs throughout the film and surfaces from time to time, but it is really secondary to the issue of the Koreans' loss of innocence in the course of the war. Of course, ideological strife is itself a symptom of the Koreans' loss of innocence, but the movie deals more with the impact of the war, which was a result of the ideological conflict. The main cause of this loss of innocence, as portrayed in this film, is the presence of the U.S. army base near the village. In the second scene, boys are seen at play, running and tumbling as children used to do everywhere, especially in rural Asia, before the advent of computer games. The boys, ten to twelve years old, become excited by the appearance of an army jeep driven by an American GI. After raising dust on the dirt road, the jeep stops before an abandoned flour mill, and the soldier goes into the mill to have sex with a Korean girl.

As boys will do, the children greedily peep in through cracks and rents in the wall. After a while, the GI emerges from the mill, remarks "That was pretty good," to the procurer standing guard in front of the door, and drives away. A rustic girl emerges from the mill guiltily, and the procurer hands over a few notes to her, telling her to buy medicine for her father with that and praising her filial piety. After the procurer and the girl leave, the boys who had been hiding behind the wall and shrubs rush into the mill. Some of the boys are excited by finding a nude magazine. Sung-min (Sŏng-min), the protagonist in the film, finds a gasoline lighter, which becomes his most cherished possession. The

An American GI walks out of the flour mill, which has become his sexual haven, leaving the Korean woman to gather herself together again.

gadgets that the GIs carry, such as gasoline lighters and binoculars, are miraculous treasures and irresistible temptations to the boys. The year is 1952. Throughout the movie, related incidents are noted or explained in subtitles on the screen. Below the subtitles appear references to incidents in contemporary history that happened at the same time, such as riots in the POW camp or U.S. Vice President Nixon's visit to Korea.

The movie revolves around the friendship between two boys, Sung-min and Chang-hee (Ch'ang-hi), and the fluctuations in the fortunes of their families. Chang-hee's family of mother and two young children are nonpaying tenants in Sung-min's house. Chang-hee's mother had moved into a room in the house when Sung-min's family left the house vacant to take refuge and, though irked by their neighbor-turned-squatter's constant pleas for loans of rice and other necessities, Sung-min's family does not have the heart to actually throw her out, so the two boys live in the same house. The fortunes of Sung-min's family keep rising, while those of Chang-hee's only go downhill.

We learn later that the absence of Chang-hee's father is due to his being in a POW camp for South Korean soldiers. Sung-min's sister gets a job at the U.S. military base and is befriended by one "Lieutenant Smith," who never actually makes an appearance in the movie. Before long Sung-min's father gets a job at the base, thanks to Lieutenant Smith's "pull." Like most employees at U.S. army bases, Sung-min's father be-

Since U.S. troops came to be stationed in the village, the camp becomes a source of livelihood for many villagers. Here, GI uniforms laundered by Korean women, including Chang-hee's mother, are hung out to dry.

gins to smuggle out things from the base, such as a radio. And Sung-min's mother gets a job as a washerwoman at the army base, laundering the uniforms of the GIs. The family becomes richer and richer, and moves to a house that is like a mansion compared to the homes of the villagers. Meanwhile, the undergarments of some GIs that Chang-hee's mother had laundered to earn some money get stolen and she is reduced to selling herself to GIs, with Sung-min's father acting as the procurer. One day Chang-hee and Sung-min see a GI jeep stopping in front of the mill and excitedly rush to take a peek, and they witness Chang-hee's mother having sex with the GI and Sung-min's father acting as procurer. Both boys are completely shattered. Chang-hee runs away from home and later sets fire to the mill, apparently while a GI (presumably the same GI) is using the mill again for a sexual haven. The reaction of the U.S. Army indicates that the American GI is killed in the fire.

In a bitter parody of the Cinderella story, American military police come to the makeshift tent classroom of the village school with a homely black rubber shoe that was found near the mill and try the shoe on every child, girls as well as boys. Sung-min is so disgusted with his father that he refuses to ride on the backseat of his father's bicycle any more, and when a neighbor remarks, "You must be happy, moving to a big house," he rejoins, "Why should *I* be happy? It's my father's house, not mine."

The boys are holding a funeral procession for their friend, Chang-hee, who was found a drowned corpse after being missing for a few months subsequent to setting fire to the mill, killing the GI who had sex with his mother.

Chang-hee's father is released from the POW camp in 1953 and returns home, broken in body and spirit. Shortly after his return, a boy's body is found in a marsh, too decomposed to identify, but tied all over with ropes that are clearly from the U.S. army base. Villagers whisper that the body must be Chang-hee's, and his friends give the body a burial, building a coffin and a hearse and performing the traditional funeral ceremony complete with a hearse-carrying procession. Their ritual of mourning is significant because traditionally the funeral ceremony was not performed for dead children. In Confucian thought dying young and causing one's parents sorrow was seen as an unfilial "crime." Chang-hee's father, still not well enough to work, roams the village trying to find out why his son left home and why the village people think the corpse is Chang-hee's. But he fails to find any answers.

Sung-min's family's luck runs out, from being taken too great advantage of by the father, it seems. Sung-min's sister is pregnant, but Lieutenant Smith is too busy to come to see her, although he shows some generosity by presenting things like a gramophone as a gift to the family of his pregnant sweetheart. Because he is employed at the U.S. army base, Sung-min's father does not seem to mind his daughter becoming an unwed mother. Although the mixed-blood child is sure to make her an outcast from Korean society, her father uses her condition to secure his job and access to the base. Even her mother seems to stop worrying and complaining, as the family becomes more and more prosperous and an object of envy for the whole village.

When the father finds that his son Sung-min has in his possession a gasoline lighter and other small items that he cannot but suspect the boy had stolen from the GIs, he reads him a solemn moral lecture and gives him a flogging—for doing on a small scale what he himself is doing on a large scale. He even admonishes the boy, as he cringes under the blows, to take his punishment "like a man."

Right afterward, the father is thrown out of his job and severely "tarred" with red paint by the Americans, for getting caught smuggling things out of the army base. In those days, the film tells us, the U.S. Army, which could have its way in everything, simply meted out that kind of summary justice to Korean employees caught stealing, rather than turning them over to the law (whether their own or Korean). With the father's disgrace and loss of his job, Sung-min's family is forced to move out of their "mansion." They can no longer hold up their heads (or "face" in the Korean idiom) in the village, and they leave, piling their household effects and their pregnant daughter onto an oxcart, trailing off into the countryside.

Throughout the movie, the peaceful and innocent landscape of the boys' hometown—the typical hometown of most Koreans in the early 1950s—is contrasted with the drama of corruption, disgrace, and violence enacted by the men and women in it. The strongest factor in the drama, which triggers many of the incidents, is the presence of the U.S. troops. The movie does not place all the blame on the Americans, and points an accusing finger at Sung-min's father's greed, hypocrisy, and insensitivity, but the American presence is shown to be a terrible temptation.

The three movies reviewed here were successful movies, which indicates that Korean moviegoers are now ready to see such serious issues as the national tragedy caused by the ideological confrontation and the meaning of the presence of the U.S. armed forces in Korea played out on screen. The movies give visual and artistic pleasure while forcing the audience to do some soul-searching. They give no ready answers. *The Taebaek Mountains* and *To the Starry Island* suggest transcendence of animosity and resentments through the recognition of universal human fallibility. *Spring in My Hometown*, while obviously enjoining self-scrutiny, also suggests that we have survived the years of humiliation and broods on the Koreans' collective past with compassion as well as judgment. Although such "soft" tenors may result from the inevitable limitation of the cinematic medium, they may also be the true reflections of popular feeling toward those issues and are helpful guides for the younger generation of viewers. One only hopes that such artfully produced films will reinvigorate the Korean film industry by helping intelligent audiences probe the deeper meanings of the Korean War and better understand Korea's predicament in modern world history.

# 9
# Interior Stories of the Chinese POWs in the Korean War

## *Philip West* with *Li Zhihua*

Although I had been studying the Korean War for more than thirty years, I was not prepared for the shock of seeing the big scar on the arm of Zhang Da, whom I met in April 1999 at his restaurant in Beijing. The scar was created by his taking a razor nearly fifty years ago to remove the slogan *fan gong kang E*— "Oppose the communists and resist Russia"—that had been tattooed on his upper arm in the first year of his captivity as a POW. To complicate the story, other Chinese POWs who later chose to go to Taiwan volunteered to be tattooed with the same slogan. But Zhang's was done against his will, violently by the pro-Taiwan POWs, to persuade him against returning to China. At the time, this struggle between the pro-Taiwan and pro-China POWs mimicked the unfinished Chinese civil war, which continued in the POW camps under the American command. This account of Chinese POWs in the Korean War suggests one among many Chinese perspectives that enlarge—especially for American readers—an appreciation of the human dimensions of war. But it is only one, and the suffering and cruelty of tattooing is small compared to the casualties and deaths suffered by soldiers in the heat of battle on all sides of the conflict. And it is smaller still than the human suffering caused by the collateral damage inflicted on Korean civilians throughout the war.

The greater surprise and larger shock in Zhang's story is the anguish that he and six thousand other Chinese POWs suffered upon returning home in 1953. They were not treated as the heroes of Chinese propaganda at the time—and since, in popular culture. Rather, they were labeled as traitors and counterrevolutionaries, ostracized by their families and communities, and subjected to discrimination for thirty years. The reason? They had surrendered to the enemy instead of dying on the battlefield. Softening the shock, somewhat, was the surprise of discovering how Zhang Da, and many of his fellow POWs, had been politically rehabilitated after Mao Zedong's death, permitted to return to normal life, and in Zhang's case, to flourish.

Writing evenhanded histories about the Korean War is not an easy thing to do. Whose history and stories represent the war "as it really was"? Are they the books written and the films produced in Korea, in English, or in Chinese? Are they the familiar works of military historians? Can they be the works of poets and artists? Must they be the stories told by those who were there and knew the war firsthand? Or can they also include those told generations after the war is over? What weight do we give to stories from the high command, the generals, the heads of state, and the diplomats? How important are the voices of the soldiers who knew combat firsthand? And what about the voices of civilians, the millions of Koreans who were displaced, suffered, and died in the war? In attempting to be objective, we try to balance these differing and often conflicting voices. But what is the proper balance? Historians aspire to be fair, representing all important points of view, but pulling the many voices of war together is impossible. Unlike singing and musical instruments, the voices of war by nature cannot be made into a chorus or a symphony.

My study of the Korean War began some thirty years ago, while I was writing the concluding chapter to my study of Yanjing University in Beijing. Its students were enthused with China's entry into the war and early victories over American soldiers in the fall of 1950. Many volun-

A young Chinese soldier has his anticommunist slogan tattooed on his arm in Chinese. *(USIS, n.d., National Archives)*

teered to go to the fighting front, but few were chosen. The Chinese faculty at Yanjing, if more cautious in the wake of the Chinese Communist Party's rise to power, were also patriotic. Along with the students, they seemed to welcome the austerity and sacrifice forced upon them by the war and were willing, if necessary, to put up with the loss of financial support from the United States. The letters and diaries of the Chinese and Western faculty had told a story of the Korean War quite different from the abstract language of military history, ideology, politics, and diplomacy—the language of graduate training.[1] Before meeting Zhang Da, I had read a book on the Chinese POWs—*Zhiyuanjun zhanfu de jishi,* by Jin Daying, published in 1987 in Beijing.[2] Jin's book has sold over a million copies and has been translated into English by Li Zhihua as a master's thesis (1993) as "Accounts of the [Chinese] Volunteer Army's Prisoners of War." Zhang Da emerges as one of the key figures in Jin's account, and it was Jin who introduced me to Zhang in the spring of 1999. Jin's book tells the stories of the POW camps and how the term POW in Chinese, *zhanfu,* became a byword of infamy.

## The POW Issue as Stalemate

One can hardly overstate the effects of the impasse over repatriation of the POWs in the armistice negotiations. The moral and legal issues surrounding the impasse at Panmunjom are anchored in the ideological and political impasse of the Asian cold war, with powerful echoes heard still today. The delay in resolving the impasse in negotiations, even after the war had reached a military stalemate in the spring of 1951, goes far toward explaining the extension of the war by at least another year and a half and an added number of deaths and casualties, mostly Korean, reaching into the hundreds of thousands. In addition, the extension of the war and the escalation of American bombing accounts for much of the physical destruction of the Korean peninsula, both North and South. The heaviest bombing of the North occurred in the last year of the war, extending to "small cities and towns" as the "last currently vulnerable link in the supply and distribution system for the communist armies."[3] Apart from the postarmistice exchange of prisoners, Max Hastings observes, there was no aspect of the Korean War that was "more grotesque than the manner in which the struggle [over the POW impasse] was allowed to continue for a further sixteen months."[4]

The outlines of the exterior history—the negotiations themselves and the language used to justify the impasse at Panmunjom—are relatively clear.[5] We know that the Geneva Convention of 1949 was used not only by American negotiators to justify the voluntary repatriation of individual POWs—as opposed to the all-for-all pattern of repatriation of previous wars—but also by Chinese and North Korean negotiators to protest the treatment of their POWs in the American-controlled camps. We can understand why President Truman and Secretary of State Dean Acheson were genuinely committed to avoiding the mistakes of the repatriation policy agreed to at Yalta, for widely shared ethical as well as personal reasons. At Stalin's request, and with Roosevelt's and Churchill's consent at Yalta, hundreds of thousands of European citizens and soldiers residing in territories controlled by the Soviet armies at the end of World War II were forced against their will to return to the Soviet Union in 1945. We can also understand how the refusal of Chinese POWs to return to the mainland in 1953, and their desire instead go to Taiwan, was deeply embarrassing to the government in Beijing, which at the beginning of the Korean War was still mired in the civil war with the nationalist government in Taiwan. The communists would likely have won the civil war had it not been for the American military intervention in the Taiwan Straits two days after the Korean War broke out.

Faced with the fiercely anticommunist tone of Congress in Washington at the time, we can also understand Truman's frustration in negotiating with the communists. With characteristic frankness, he wrote in his diary that "dealing with the communists" was "like an honest man trying to deal with a numbers racket king or the head of a dope ring."[6] We can imagine that the frustration was mutual for the communists, who may have felt similarly about the United Nations and American negotiators. We know that members of Truman's policy planning staff disagreed with him, as did most members of the joint chiefs of staff, who accepted the Chinese position and in fact recommended an all-for-all repatriation, in anticipation that an armistice would be signed as early as the summer of 1951. We know that Stalin's death in March 1953 and the terrible drain on the Chinese economy of the process of rebuilding the country were factors that persuaded the Chinese negotiators to accept Truman's position on voluntary repatriation. And we know why Syngman Rhee, insisting that reunification of the peninsula be under his control, refused to participate in the armistice negotiations and defied his American allies by dramatically releasing tens of thousands of North Korean POWs the month before the armistice was signed.

A communist POW is questioned by his two UN captors. *(Defense Department, November 11, 1950, National Archives)*

We also know how the press was used on all sides. Exploitation of the domestic press in the United States and of the world press by China and North Korea did win respective political—and moral—victories, while continuing to demonize the other in the language of ideology and warfare. Even then, however, more dispassionate thinkers knew that demonization of the enemy makes poor military history. Qualifying the common perception and assertion that Chinese soldiers had little regard for human life and fought in "human wave attacks," U.S. Marine historian Lynn Montross wrote that "nothing could be further from the truth." It was not mass attacks, Montross wrote, but rather "deception and surprise which made the Chinese Red formidable." And it was the American political scientist Alexander L. George who gave a more humane picture of the Chinese soldiers, based on his interviews with ninety-one Chinese POWs on Kŏje-do, conducted in the spring of 1951 when the Chinese offensive was stopped. George depicted the Chinese "volunteers" as credible patriots, who sincerely believed in the justice of their actions and whose "spiritual values" commanded respect.[7]

What makes the POW stories particularly interesting is the great disparities, on both sides of the conflict, on the taking of prisoners of war, the numbers captured or surrendered, and the reasons for repatriating or not at the time of the armistice. The total number of Chinese POWs held by the largely American command at the time the armistice was signed on July 27, 1953, was over twenty-one thousand. Of these, less than one-third chose to repatriate to China; the other two-thirds chose instead go to Taiwan as civilians. The number of North Korean POWs released was much higher, over eighty-three thousand. Their repatriation rate, however, was quite the reverse of that of the Chinese, with over 90 percent choosing to return home. The total number of UN POWs released by the communists was over thirteen thousand, considerably less than that of the Chinese alone and but a fraction of that of the North Koreans. Of these, the South Korean POW number was by far the largest, over eight thousand, most of whom chose to return to the South, but including also a small number who chose to stay in the North. The number of American POWs released by the communists was over three and a half thousand. Among them were twenty-one prisoners who chose not to return to the United States, but rather to live in China. Their decision provoked a heated discussion in American journalism and scholarship for decades in interpreting not only the Korean War, but also more generally the political and intellectual life in China since the communist takeover in 1949.[8]

What does this numerical sketch of the POWs at the end of the Korean War suggest? Does the great disparity in the numbers of POWs released by the UN command and those released by the communists suggest that the communists were less humane and simply did not take prisoners of war? Were UN soldiers, and Americans in particular, more humane? Or does it suggest the results of two very different kinds of fighting, one of large numbers of soldiers on the ground and therefore more exposed to capture, and the other of heavy combat conducted from the air? How do the POW numbers compare with the figures on all sides for battle deaths, casualties, and by war's end the tens, perhaps hundreds, of thousands missing in action? Was one side or one group on the same side more brutal and less humane than the other? (American stories frequently suggest that Chinese treatment of American POWs was more humane than that of the North Korean soldiers and that American soldiers were more humane than South Korean soldiers in their treatment of communist POWs.) As for the word humane, how useful is it to compare the damage, both battlefield and collateral, caused by a soldier carrying a bayonet and a hand grenade with that of a soldier firing heavy artillery or piloting a bomber? What about medical care and diet for POWs? And how does one talk about the number of prisoners, on all sides, who died in the POW camps? Because the North Korean armies earned so few victories after the first three months of the war, how does one explain the apparently high morale of their POWs as reflected by the large proportion who, in their moments of repatriation, defiantly tore off clothing given to them by their captors as they crossed the line at Munsan in August of 1953? What does the large proportion of Chinese POWs who chose not to repatriate tell us about the Chinese soldiers at midcentury generally and their political orientation during the war, and the impact of the war on those who did choose to repatriate? And what about the organization and operation of the POW camps themselves?

However one tries to address or rephrase these questions, the story of the American POWs—and those of other UN POWs—is understandably the one best known to American audiences. But the largest POW story, that of the North Korean repatriates, including the nearly nine thousand civilian internees from both the North and the South, remains largely untold if not unknown, even for the people of North Korea, because of their political repression over the past half century.

From the mid-1950s to the mid-1960s, the story of the American POWs was highly acrimonious and became caught up in accusations and counteraccusations against both the captors and the POWs themselves, who, in contrast to British and Turkish POWs, were accused of "give-up-itis" and seen as emblematic of social decay generally in American culture. Others defended their behavior, if not the high death rates among them, as a function of the terribly harsh conditions they suffered in the winter of 1950 after China had entered the war.[9]

The passing of time can soften the controversies of war and allow us to tell stories of war more fully and faithfully. The exterior histories of the Korean War have become more complex and more nuanced with the opening of archives, the reexamination of national myths, and the relaxation of the ideological confines of military writing, first in Britain and the United States and then, to a certain extent, in South Korea and China, though not yet in North Korea. As for the interior histories, they may always have a hidden quality. While the battle rages they must be hidden and the enemy demonized. Otherwise it would be impossible to mobilize the home front and motivate soldiers to fight and kill. But in order to maintain the fighting spirit among allies, the stories of war are also hidden, at least for a while, by the differences in language and reasons for going to war. United behind ideology and politics, North Korean, Chinese, and Soviet soldiers fought together, but ideology was a thin veil for profound differences in national and foreign policies, historical legacies, culture, and language. The differences among American and South Korean soldiers fighting on the same side of battle also ran deep, as various chapters in this book attest.

Time also has a way of making the stories of war interesting and plausible to the other side and, in the process, moving them in a more "exterior" direction. The interior histories will never be fully told. There are too many to tell, and too many people with too many ways to tell them. The stories of soldiers and civilians who knew war firsthand will continue to be told by their children and grandchildren, and by historians, writers, poets, artists, filmmakers, and musicians who will continue to give them voice, decades and perhaps centuries later. Understandably, stories based on memory and told by writers of fiction are viewed with skepticism by historians. Memories are always personal; they adjust to the winds of time; they fade in and out, and they can misrepresent and distort the way things really were. Writers and poets are not interested in gathering facts in the way historians are. Despite these imperfections, when it comes to probing the human dimensions of war, fiction and poetry have an unmistakable ring of truth. Writing nearly a century and a half after the American Civil War, Charles Frazier's *Cold Mountain, a Novel* (1998) is a masterful illumination of the splendor, the savagery, and the sorrow of war, as seen in the lives of soldiers and civilians alike in North Carolina throughout the four years of that war. Frazier cites a number of historical books that were "helpful in the cultural and historical background for the novel." The truth of his story may be fair, and as accurate as any research based on archives alone, but his claim is that of the novelist. Given its popularity, one can only guess the impact his novel will continue to have in shaping American understanding, including that of historians, of the human dimensions of war for years to come. If the number of books on military history, novels, and films one can buy and rent today is any indication, the passion for writing about and hearing the stories of war has a long shelf life. It will inspire more poems, more short stories, more novels, more histories, more games, and more films for generations to come, even if all the archives are someday opened. The truths of war and the human dimensions of war are as elusive as they are universally and perpetually fascinating.

## Chinese Contexts

The appearance in 1986 of Jin Daying's book on the Chinese POW repatriates coincides with China's gradual political relaxation and opening up, both inside and to the outside world. For more than three decades the Chinese histories of the war were largely one-dimensional, closely following the main line as determined by the Communist Party. Although not forgotten in the same way, the Korean War in the Chinese context finds a striking parallel in the evolution of American histories of the war. Despite its vast significance to politics, foreign relations and life in general in China at midcentury, the Korean War for decades has received minimal attention both in Chinese publications and in public education. Some of China's most famous writers, including, for example, Ba Jin and Lao She, went to the front lines of the Korean War, lived for weeks at a time close to the fighting front, and wrote extensively in the service of propaganda. Their language for the most part was the language of battle—friends and enemies, heroes and villains—in which the Americans were uniformly portrayed as aggressors and villains. Their writings embraced the exterior Chinese version of the war as unquestionably righteous. They did not allow the reader to see the interiors, the suffering and the surrender of the Chinese soldiers, or the internal conflicts at the top over strategy and tactics.[10]

The paucity of Chinese writing about the Korean War from the mid-1950s through the late 1980s corresponds with the growing and eventually decisive split between China and the Soviet Union, which had provided substantial military aid in the course of the war. The Chinese silence on the war also correlates with the personal and political struggles among the Chinese leadership and the consequent demise of Marshall Peng Dehuai. Peng had commanded the Chinese troops throughout the war and returned home as a popular hero, but he fell out of political favor in 1958 as the result of his sharp criticism of Mao Zedong's Great Leap Forward. Similarly, it was Peng's rehabilitation in 1980 and the publication of his memoirs that signaled the beginning of renewed publications on the Korean War, over thirty volumes by the early 1990s.[11] Chinese films on the Korean War, extolling the victories and patriotic fervor of the Chinese soldiers, had become popular in the 1960s and 1970s, during the Cultural Revolution. These included prominently *Yingxiong ernu* (Heroic Sons and Daughters), based on Ba Jin's short story "Tuanyuan" (Reunion, 1960), and *Shangganling*, based on the most famous battle in Chinese popular memory, October 14 to November 25, 1952, and conspicuously overlooked in American battle histories. It is the songs from these popular films that Chinese over forty today recall and sing from memory. Chinese comic books about the Korean War, featuring heroic and self-sacrificing Chinese soldiers, became popular during the Cultural Revolution.

With Peng Dehuai's rehabilitation, we see beginning in the 1980s a burst of military histories on the Korean War, but their focus is on the first ten months of the familiar five military campaigns, from October 24, 1950, to June 10, 1951. They include detailed orders of battle, brief biographies of key Chinese figures, statistics on military strength, and informative maps, but the statistics on war casualties and war losses are those suffered only by the enemy. By the late 1990s we see for the first time mention in military histories of the Chinese POW repatriates. By then the Korean War had become once again incorporated into Chinese popular culture, more openly than ever before. Today, one can go into Chinese department stores and find in the entertainment section, alongside popular music both Chinese and Western, whole collections of CDs, VCDs, and DVDs containing documentary histories of the Korean War and digitized versions of famous films on the Korean War. It may be that the Korean War will hold both historical and entertainment value for Chinese young people today and that exposure to Chinese victories in the war will strengthen their patriotic pride, even as they absorb as never before the music, the films, and the fashions of Western, especially American, popular culture.

### The Value of Jin Daying's Book

Despite the growing openness of Chinese society and renewed interest in the Korean War, the question of the Chinese POWs remains highly sensitive. It is here that Jin Daying's book on the Chinese POWs becomes historically and intellectually significant. Born in 1954, Jin Daying eventually joined the navy, where he began his career as a writer. He has written broadly on key figures in the Chinese leadership, including Lin Biao and Luo Ruiqing, and has produced films for Chinese television. The publication of his book on the Chinese POWs provoked a broad public interest, and he has been invited to lecture in prominent Chinese universities, telling the stories both of the POWs' valor in the camps in

Korea and of their humiliation upon their return home. His book was published in 1987 during the period known as "bourgeois liberalization" and appeared first in serial form. This period of relative openness came to an abrupt end in 1989 following the incidents in Tiananmen Square. But if the growth of publishers, magazines, and bookstores— and the digital versions of films and popular culture that they sell—is any indication, the interior histories of revolutionary China are flourishing more than ever before in films, fiction, memoirs, and new histories.

Jin writes in the style known as "literary reportage" (*bagaowenxue*), which finds no clear equivalent in Western writing. It is a literary style developed after 1949 and is quite different from traditional Chinese poetry, the novel, and drama. One standard Chinese dictionary definition for literary reportage reads: "The writing of real people and real events directly drawn from actual life with a typical meaning, reported quickly and in time with proper artistic processing to serve the current political purposes."[12] Literary reportage is a hybrid of journalism and fiction. It is sometimes more one than the other, but its credibility in the minds of the hundreds of millions of Chinese who have read it over the years rests on the fact that it does contain sufficient truth to be credible in the contexts of their life experiences. For many Western critics the idea of serving "political purposes" reduces literary reportage to propaganda and renders it invalid as an account of what really happened in the war. Its failure to use footnotes and to include full citations, its obscuring of names and places, and its underlying patriotic tone call its veracity into question. By straddling both journalism and fiction, in the Western critique, it falls between both stools and winds up having neither the literary quality of fiction nor the veracity of journalism, not to mention scholarship. Whatever its weaknesses may be, it is a large component of popular culture and has the ring of authenticity in Chinese memories, including the hundreds of thousands who know the Korean War firsthand. Jin's book offers an approach to the Korean War that bears serious consideration.[13]

Jin's book contains much firsthand data. Most of the names of the 159 characters are verifiable. Many of the characters the author mentions in the book are still living.[14] The places and description of events in the camps where the Chinese POWs were held can be cross-referenced and follow closely the detailed account, though certainly not the tone, of one standard American account, *The Handling of Prisoners of War During the Korean War*, prepared by the Military History Office of

A group of Chinese communist prisoners is rounded up by U.S. Marines during the fighting in North Korean mountains. *(Defense Department, Fall 1950, National Archives)*

the United States Army in 1960. Jin's patriotic tone and use of a particular political and ideological vocabulary can be off-putting to Western readers, but he gains credibility with candid accounts of American soldiers and camp guards who are not merely villainous but can in fact be kind to the Chinese prisoners. Much of the material in Jin's account, although not footnoted, is taken from Chinese military archives, to which he was given access. Among them are the detailed confessions of the repatriated POWs both immediately after their return to China and during the Anti-Rightist Campaign of 1957, when many of them underwent severe criticism. Major arguments in Jin's account, furthermore, are supported by Barton J. Bernstein, based on his work in the American archives two decades ago.[15] With few exceptions, surprisingly, Bernstein's study has been largely ignored by subsequent American popular histories of the Korean War, despite the broad agreement that the POW stalemate is a major explanation for extending the war from the summer of 1951 into the summer of 1953.[16]

Although the POW issue—referred to as "question number four" at Panmunjom—lies at the core of the stalemate in negotiating the armistice, the history of the Chinese POWs begins already in the spring of 1951, during the fifth campaign in the Chinese order of battle. It was a time when General Matthew Ridgway, then commander of the Eighth United States Army and of the joint armies, halted the Chinese advance south of Seoul. In March and April of that campaign many Chinese soldiers had been taken as POWs. Prior to the winter of 1950–1951, most of the POWs captured by the UN command were North Korean, numbering over a hundred thousand by the end of October 1950. These North Korean prisoners were comprised of both Korean soldiers and civilians captured when the North controlled the South, and were held in three different locations, one in Pyongyang and two in the South, Inchon and Pusan. By the first of the new year all POWs were concentrated in Pusan, and by June of 1951, after some twenty thousand Chinese POWs were captured, most were transferred under the American command to the island of Kŏje, or Kŏje-do, forty miles south and west of Pusan. When the armistice was signed in July 1953, a sharp division arose between the six thousand Chinese POWs who chose to be repatriated to China and the fourteen thousand who chose to go to Taiwan. The lines dividing these two groups were already sharply drawn in the POW compounds two years before, and they defined the political and physical struggles that comprise the heart of Jin's book.

### The Tattooing of Chinese POWs

Already within a few years after the war, when the American controversy over the treatment and behavior of American POWs in the Korean War was high, William White, in his 1957 book *The Captives of Korea*, included some pictures of Chinese POWs. The captions and the accompanying text celebrated those POWs who chose Taiwan and the treatment given to them by the American command, while disparaging those who chose to return to China and the treatment given to American POWs in camps commanded by the communist side. Included are pictures of Chinese POWs playing mahjong, strumming banjo-like instruments made from rat skins, blowing trumpets made from tomato cans, and staging plays for fellow prisoners. But the one picture that stands out is that of a Chinese POW whose arm had been tattooed with the slogan in Chinese, *fan gong kang E*, or "Oppose the communists and resist Russia." The caption below the picture reads: "To show anti-communist fervor, this prisoner has tattoo marks first in Chinese and below them in English: 'To oppose the Reds and destroy Russia.'"[17]

Remarkably, Jin's study also includes similar pictures, including one of a Chinese POW with the same tattoo on his arm. But the captions and the point of his study convey an opposite impression and conclusion. Jin acknowledges the difficulty facing the Chinese leadership over the fact that two-thirds of the Chinese POWs refused repatriation. But in his account the Chinese repatriates are heroic, and the China to which they return is eminently worthy of their loyalty. In his colorful discussion of the Chinese POWs, White occasionally grants legitimacy to the repatriates, but it is grudging. Similarly Jin allows the reader to understand why so many Chinese POWs chose Taiwan over China, but he too is grudging.

Rather than pitting the two accounts against each other as merely political and ideological confrontation, it is well to remember that both sides, both repatriates and nonrepatriates, have sympathetic, if not heroic, stories to tell. Albert Biderman, whose study is focused on the American POWs in the war, reminds us that "prisoners everywhere must evolve some accommodation to their captors."[18] The question then becomes one not of the POW decisions alone, but of the larger contexts of those decisions, the conditions of the camps, the treatment of POWs, and the political orientations of the Chinese POWS and their soldiering on the Korean peninsula as continuing engagement in the Chinese civil war. The differences in treatment by the American command and that of the Chinese, after November 1950, are well known. The Chinese camps located near the Yalu River certainly were primitive by Western standards, in terms of food, medical treatment, clothing, and shelter—in that terribly severe winter. By contrast, the camps for the North Korean and Chinese POWs that came under the command of General Ridgway after January 1951, located first in Pusan, and then on Kŏje-do and still later on Cheju-do, were clearly more comfortable—better food, better medical treatment, and more spacious facilities in general, despite the severe crowding in the early months. These disparities were not merely the differences between humane and inhumane policies. With some exceptions, Chinese soldiers and commanders of the POW camps lived under similarly austere conditions. There is clear evidence of torture by the Chinese captors and subjection of the American POWs, in particular, to political indoctrination. (One result of widescale reporting of the

New prisoners of war arriving at UN POW camps at Pusan are given a thorough dusting with DDD by other prisoners. (*State Gahn, April 1951, National Archives*)

American POW experience in the press was the introduction of the word "brainwashing" into the American vocabulary.)

But what of the camps commanded by the American army? How were the North Korean and Chinese POWs treated? Here Jin's story of the tattooing comes into play. The tattooing had begun in August 1951, when most of the POWs, 140,000 in all, 23,000 of them Chinese and the rest North Korean, had been relocated to the island of Kŏje. In addition to *fan gong kang E*, a common slogan tattooed on their bodies was *sha zhu ba mao,* literally "Kill the pig for its hair." Pig, or *zhu,* in Chinese is homonymic with the surname of Zhu De, commander-in-chief of the People's Liberation Army, while *mao,* or hair, in Chinese is homonymic with that of Mao Zedong. Other symbols tattooed were the characters for Guomindang (Nationalist Party), and POW officers above the rank of squad leaders were also tattooed with the map of China on their backs.

Tattoos were willingly accepted by those POWs who preferred then, and later chose, not to be repatriated. But the point of Jin's account is that thousands of those who wished to repatriate had been tattooed by March 1952, against their will.

Several factors in the camp setting help explain how and why the tattooing was carried out and why it becomes both physically and symbolically important in telling the interior history of the Chinese POWs who wished to repatriate. First of all, from the taking of the first significant number of North Korean prisoners right after the Inchon landing in September 1950, the camps were seen as being temporary and short-lived. As early as July 1951 all sides anticipated an armistice would be signed, and with each delay and new twist in the negotiations, the optimism would return as each side, firm in its own position, believed the other would yield. Second, the camps were commanded by a small number of U.S. military personnel, who in one authoritative description were of "inferior quality" and faced a "high turnover of camp commanders." In the American-controlled camps, "discipline was lax and morale among the officers was low."[19] Third, because of the glaring lack of language skills at all levels in the American command, the camp commanders were forced to rely on prisoner cooperation in managing the camps. Accordingly a staff of native speakers of Korean and Chinese were hired to work with leaders from among the prisoners to manage day-to-day operations. Able to function also in English, this staff included South Korean soldiers to manage the large North Korean prisoner compounds; and by summer 1951, American Chinese and former Nationalist soldiers from Taiwan to manage the Chinese prisoners. Despite their reputation after June 1951 for being well administered, the UN compounds in their first year of operation were characterized by poor food, over-crowding, lack of medical care, and disease. Suicide had become such a severe problem that by December 1951 six thousand of the combined North Korean and Chinese POWs had died at their own hands. Similarly, the POW camps commanded by the North Koreans and eventually the Chinese were also in their poorest conditions in the early phase of the war. All sources agree that the camps on both sides were greatly improved by the spring and summer of 1953. Indeed, when the prisoners were re-leased, each side for the most part was respectful of the other's efforts to bring this phase of the war to an end in an orderly and fair manner.

It is also important to recognize that the struggles in the POW camps mimicked the continuing civil wars in both Korea and China. The military struggle on the battlefield carried over to physical violence among prisoners who, by the summer of 1951, were divided into compounds according to their political preferences. Jin Daying goes to great lengths in describing how the pro-Nationalist groups early on, with American support, gained control of the camps. His account helps the reader understand the resistance and organization by those Chinese POWs who eventually chose repatriation. The titles of eleven chapters in Jin's book (out of a total of fifteen) outline this sequence of events, beginning with "initial silence" by those POWs loyal to China, followed by a long description of the "renegade" leaders among the POWs refusing repatriation, and ending some chapters later with "the end of the renegades" and their control over the camps by August 1952, when they were moved to Cheju-do. By then most POWs had already made up their minds on repatriation, and the political struggles were largely over.

The initial silence, according to Jin's account, came from the shock of having been captured at all and wondering if it were possible to survive. The POWs were also embarrassed to have been taken prisoner, as sayings from traditional Chinese culture echoed in their heads: "Better to die than to be disgraced"; "A good horse serves only a single master"; and so on (60). Right through the spring of 1951, when most of the Chinese POWs were captured, the pro-Nationalist soldiers, led by Jin's "renegades," were clearly in control of the compounds. They had the support of the American commanders, and already by June they had organized anticommunist indoctrination programs, known as CIEs, for Civil Information and Education. For the Chinese national holiday on October 10, they had forced all Chinese prisoners to celebrate under American, Chinese Nationalist, and South Korean flags. Chinese prisoners were also forced to attend religious services by one Wu Boli, a colonel-chaplain of the Eighth U.S. Army, who handed out Bibles and taught the prisoners Christian hymns.

The early Chinese repatriate response began with hunger strikes, but by October 1951 a group of them, all under twenty, all sons of former Guomindang military officers, and all from Sichuan Province, were led by Zhang Da to protest more forcefully. For his daring Zhang was himself imprisoned in a barbed-wire cage—within the prison of the camp—and tortured. The renegades, in Zhang's words, taunted him with, "Why did you not die on the battlefield?" and "The Communist Party won't know you died for them here." The anticommunist leaders, representing the larger number of prisoners, gained the upper hand and were able to

Group of Chinese communist soldiers recently captured by UN forces on a Korean fighting front. *(February 1951, National Archives)*

take control over most of the compounds, which at the outset had not been divided along political lines. Anticommunist control, however, was challenged first by the procommunist Korean prisoners, who, with much larger numbers, demanded their own organization and control over compounds, and who supported the procommunist Chinese prisoners, demanding that one of the compounds be under their control. By November the procommunist Chinese persuaded the American command to recognize their demands and designate compound number seventy-one as the first "CPV POW Repatriation Camp." In describing this process, Jin makes it clear that however favorable the American command was administratively to the pro-Taiwan prisoners and their leaders, individual American officers were sympathetic and granted the request.

The practice of using tattoos to influence the political views of the Chinese prisoners had begun already in 1948 during the Chinese civil war, when former Nationalist troops fighting under warlord Yan Xishan's command were tattooed with *shazhu bamao,* again with slights to Zhu De, then commander-in-chief of the PLA, and Mao Zedong. We know that political commissars held great authority over Chinese soldiers down to the battalion level. That control, however, did not appear to discriminate against the former nationalist troops on the battlefield, nor did they appear to resist that control. Guomindang soldiers were among the hundreds of thousands of Chinese soldiers who defeated American troops in the fall and winter of the first year of the war. Whatever their attitudes and loyalties may have been, political indoctrination and combat surveillance among the Chinese troops were strong and may explain the fact that Chinese soldiers who became POWs did so not through defection but through involuntary surrender.[20] When the war broke out there was considerable flux in the lives of Chinese soldiers, and the relatively relaxed environment of the early phase of China's "New Democracy" encouraged loyalty to the new order, even among former nationalist troops who had surrendered to the communists in the civil war. The sharp differences of the Chinese civil war appeared to surface in Korea only after the Chinese soldiers were captured and the Guomindang and pronationalist soldiers were given responsibility for managing the camps. Previous high morale throughout the winter gave way in the spring of 1951 when Chinese troops became overextended and experienced clear setbacks and defeats on the battlefield south of the thirty-eighth parallel. And when the POW camps became better organized, with the move to Kŏje-do in June 1951, and the American command discovered how the large number of former Guomindang troops could be used to advantage in embarrassing China on the Taiwan issue, the possibilities of using tattooing for political purposes became clear once again.

According to Jin, the tattooing began in July 1951 and was done willingly among the former Guomindang soldiers, who sincerely feared that repatriating to China might be difficult at a time when land reform and the campaign against counterrevolutionaries, which had begun in February, were in full swing. Indeed, when the tattooing began, the Chinese POWs were required to apply for the procedure with the support of two sponsors. Fear of returning to China and suffering discrimination or persecution for both political and cultural reasons was one incentive, but other powerful incentives were also employed. Those who were tattooed were better fed and assigned to lighter labor in the camps. Given the disorientation of POW life in general and the willingness of most POWs on all sides to accommodate in their effort merely to survive, many of those tattooed, Jin tells us, did so not only "willingly" but out of a firm determination to "oppose the communists and resist Russia"

(183). The turn in the story came in late summer and early fall, when it became clear that repatriation of the Chinese POWs in particular had already become a sticking point in the negotiations at Kaesong and, by October, at Panmunjom. In that setting American negotiators and other leaders all the way up to Truman had come to realize the propaganda value of large numbers of Chinese POWS preferring, and ultimately choosing, not to repatriate. In Jin's account, American officers in the compounds knew of the tattooing, although they did not participate in it. Rather, the procedure was performed by pro-Taiwan POWs who were currying favor with the Americans. Jin does not doubt the sincerity of many pro-Taiwan POWs who willingly asked to be tattooed. His story is focused rather on the "renegades" who forced others to be tattooed to gain favor with the Americans and also to rekindle the Chinese civil war.

Jin reflects on how fear of political persecution and fear of social ostracism combined to persuade the prisoners to be tattooed. The pro-Taiwan POW officers, along with all of the other Chinese POWs, especially those still loyal to China, "were of the same Chinese descent." Ancient Chinese culture had "cultivated its best and brightest in great numbers, but it had also produced the renegades who bore satisfaction in massacring, treading on, and betraying their own fellow countrymen." Separating the American officers from these renegades once again, Jin notes that "most U.S. officers, soldiers and officials deemed what the renegades did to be the meanest and dirtiest things" (82).[21]

The passive resistance of the procommunist POWs turned into active opposition and organization, which set the stage for the political and often violent struggles that characterized the POW camp life from October 1951 to their release in July 1953. In Jin's words, it was a time when "white terror reigned over the POW camps. Many POWs who had been forcibly tattooed cried through the night. Some POWs, withstanding great pain, tried to scrape the tattooed words from their arms by using razor blades the moment they returned to their tents. Others even hanged themselves. . . . There were quite a few POWs who committed suicide by swallowing broken pieces of glass or razor blades" (185).[22] In his story as told to Jin Daying, Zhang Da recalled his confrontation with Li Da'an, the pro-Taiwan POW in charge of compound 72, where Zhang stayed. Li asked Zhang, "Why haven't you been tattooed?" Zhang replied, "I want to return to my motherland." Li said, "If you go back to China, the Chinese Communist Party will either cast you into prison or kill you. The only way out for you is to get tattooed and go to Taiwan."

Zhang responded, "I would rather be put into jail or killed than to have those characters tattooed on my arm." Li and other officers then "tied me [Zhang] to a broken iron chair and connected it to electricity. I immediately fainted. After [cold water was poured] over me, I revived . . . and then [they poured] hot pepper water into my nose. After I fainted several times under this torture, they bound me to a pillar in the tent and tattooed my arm" (187–88). By November 1951, three thousand of the eight thousand procommunist POWs housed in compound 72 had, according to Jin, been tattooed, and by April of 1952, the number rose to six thousand. Those who refused to be tattooed were beaten up and deprived of food during the day and blankets at night, making survival in winter extremely difficult.

### General Ridgway's Visit to Kŏje-do

Jin devotes a long chapter to the visit of General Ridgway, accompanied by General Van Fleet, to the POW camps at Kŏje-do in November 1951. Since January of that year, prior to the large capture of Chinese POWs, Ridgway had expressed personal concern over the care and treatment of the North Korean and Chinese POWs and was instrumental in building the large encampment on Kŏje-do, where by the time of his visit an estimated 140,000 POWs were housed. In anticipation of Ridgway's visit, according to Jin, the pro-Taiwan POW leaders, supported by chaplain Wu Boli, had gathered a petition signed in blood by seven thousand POWs in compound 72. The petition read, "We would rather die than return to 'Red China' and are determined to carry through to the end the struggle of 'opposing the communists and resisting Russia.'" Among the signatures were those of the procommunist POWs, secured in the same manner as the forced tattooing. Jin suggests that upon seeing the tattoos of the Chinese POWs, Ridgway came to believe that the petition would be useful to Americans negotiating in Panmunjom with the Chinese. Ridgway departed from Kŏje-do "smiling, yet behind his smile the POWs of the Chinese People's Volunteers [the procommunists] were bleeding, groaning, and crying. What had been burned onto their bodies was life-long suffering and hatred" (190).

Ridgway's visit sharpened the political struggle and set into motion two later events that are among the most controversial episodes in the larger story of the Chinese POWs. The first, called Operation Scatter, was the polling of all POWs on both sides of the war to determine which of them would choose repatriation upon their release. The request was originally made by the Chinese and North Korean negotiators, who were confident that the numbers would work in their favor. The polling on Kŏje-do took place between April 5 and 15, 1952, with the result, according to Western figures, that only 70,000 out of a total of 170,000 POWs under UNC command, on Kŏje-do and elsewhere, would choose repatriation: 52,900 North Koreans; 5,100 Chinese; 7,200 civilian internees; and 3,800 South Koreans (200). When these numbers were reported at Panmunjom the North Korean and Chinese negotiators were angered and accused the American command of deriving the numbers through extortion. Even the American negotiators were surprised by the low percentage of prisoners choosing repatriation.

Jin acknowledges that the numbers of Chinese POWs preferring to go to Taiwan, as the result of Operation Scatter, were embarrassing to and infuriated the Chinese negotiators at Panmunjom. But his discussion zeros in on the "screening" process and the torture used previously in the tattooing and the signing of the petitions in blood. In his account pressure was put on the procommunist POWs not to sign, playing on the seventh point of battlefield discipline in the People's Liberation Army, which in Jin's account reads "I would rather die than be captured." The officers conducting the screening then explained, "Everyone knows the discipline of the Communist Party. Being a prisoner means death, and by returning to the Mainland you will only be the target of criticism and attack. You will not be able to clear yourself for the rest of your life." Jin then describes other forms of physical torture, such as cutting out pieces of flesh from the arms of young Chinese POWs, with the warning, "Leave your flesh if you want to go home." In 1986 Jin interviewed one of those who suffered this mutilation on his arm. He is Lin Mucong, who despite longtime family connections with the nationalist government admitted that his "journey to Kŏje-do" had begun with his decision the year before to join the Chinese army "because it was very fashionable." Under torture, Lin had blurted out that the Chinese communists were better than the Guomindang. In his interview thirty-four years later, he justified the outburst because his experience in the POW camp had "taught me a lot" and forced him to "recognize the differences between the communists and the Guomindang." Terrible as his experience was, including the humiliation as a returned POW, Lin could later laugh at himself: "Believe it or not, at that time, my mind was as simple as that" (200–3).[23]

By April 8, 1952, three days after Operation Scatter had begun, Jin reports that "ninety-nine POWs had been killed, over three hundred had suffered from flesh-cutting, and over three hundred and forty were seriously injured." Two narrow lanes led away from the exit of the screening tent, one to a gate for those not willing to repatriate and the other to a gate for those who were. Those passing through the former were given "A" cards, while those with "G" cards passing through the latter were forced to "dash through a line of swords and clubs." Some were "stabbed, some hurt in the waist, some stripped of their clothing, and some knocked down and carried" back to the other gate. In the week following the screening the POWs choosing repatriation began organizing on their own to protect themselves. But the American command, in Jin's account, dismissed their organization as merely rebellious and cut off their access to water and food. Some of those already in a weakened condition starved to death. At the end of his chapter on "screening," Jin describes the disappointment in the low figure, "only six thousand," who chose repatriation. Even the American representatives, he says, "were greatly surprised by this figure," which was to become "firm, permanent, and unchangeable" (220–26).

The second incident that traces back to General Ridgway's November 1951 visit demonstrates the tenacious and effective organizing of the pro-mainland Chinese POWs. This is the famous Dodd-Colson POW incident of May 7–11, 1952, in which Brigadier General Francis T. Dodd, then commander of the POW camps, paid a visit to Kŏje-do and upon entry into the enclosure was kidnapped by the Chinese POWs. Jin's lengthy account of the incident squares with much of the story as told in American historical accounts. Although he was clearly unprepared for and surprised by his kidnapping, Dodd was treated well. To secure his release, Brigadier General Charles F. Colson, second in command at Kŏje-do, had signed a statement "admitting cases of bloodshed in which many POWs have been killed or wounded by the United Nations [American] command . . . and assuring future humane treatment." He also agreed to halt the forcible screening and to recognize a delegation representing the North Korean and pro-mainland Chinese POWs' positions to the American authorities. Responding to their condition that he resolve the problem of voluntary repatriation at Panmunjom, Dodd said he did not have the "power to shape the decisions reached at the negotiations."

The world press seized upon Dodd's concession, extending unprecedented recognition of the authority and grievances of the POWs and creating a huge propaganda victory—an event that "shook the world"—for the Chinese and North Korean negotiators at Panmunjom. General Ridgway, who was about to depart Tokyo to assume command in Europe, was furious and ordered General Mark Clark, who was replacing him, to use all necessary force to recover control of the camps. Colson was replaced by Brigadier General Haydon L. Boatner, who put down what became known as the "Kŏje-do uprising." By June 10 in Jin's account, "several thousand armed soldiers, along with tanks and armored cars, massacred the POWs in compound 76. Flamethrowers burned down the tents, and the POWs retaliated and charged at the tanks with flaming gasoline bottles, shouting, 'Long live our motherland.'" Within a half hour, "more than one hundred and fifty POWs had been killed or wounded," and all of the North Korean and pro-mainland Chinese POW leaders were placed in a "special prison" as "war criminals" (240–47). Years later General Ridgway acknowledged the shame and harm this incident had brought, no less than any defeat in bloody battles, and both Generals Dodd and Colson were forced into early retirement for their yielding to the POW conditions. Sensitive to the impact of the Kŏje-do uprising on negotiations in Panmunjom, General Boatner was able to establish tighter control over the camps, gradually replacing the management of individual compounds by nationalist soldiers and pro-Taiwan POWs with American soldiers, whose numbers by then had significantly increased. Under Boatner's command there was no significant change in the number or proportion of Chinese POWs choosing to repatriate to the mainland or go to Taiwan.

Before ending his account of the Kŏje-do uprising Jin pointedly describes the story of a Chinese POW who wavered, first lining up with the pro-Taiwan POWs but then changing his mind and shouting, "I want to go back home." As he moved to the repatriate line, he was attacked by the squad leader, who tried to stab him with a knife. In Jin's account the "knife hit a metal piece, causing sparks to fly": an American soldier with a carbine had blocked its way. The squad leader shouted (presumably in English), "He is a communist bandit, a red element," upon which the American soldier pointed with his gun and said "Go back!" When the repatriate passed by, the "American soldier stood at attention and raised his right hand to his cap, with a military salute to another soldier" (252).

## The Last Year of Captivity

In July and August of 1952 all of the procommunist POWs were moved to Cheju island, Cheju-do, where most were to remain for more than a year before beginning their journey home. Encouraged by their success in the Dodd incident but respectful of Boatner's tight command, they channeled their patriotic fervor into improving the quality of camp life, which they now managed. This last year in captivity is a quiet and moving chapter in the interior history of the Chinese POWs. To celebrate the Chinese victory in the war against Japan, August 15, the POWs organized singing contests, art shows, theatrical performances, and sporting events. Although the singing was prohibited by the camp command, the prisoners were sufficiently secure in their organization and simply defied the prohibition. The U.S. Army study refers dozens of times to the singing of the Chinese POWS. Jin's account, too, repeatedly tells of their singing and includes many of their songs, whose lyrics in another time and place sound amply patriotic, but which in Jin's words "became a weapon for the empty-handed POWs." Some of the repatriates later told of singing songs "almost unceasingly." Camp life was a time when "we sang the most songs of our life." Some even sang songs when "they were falling down under fire from machine-guns and flame-throwers . . . [even] while their mouths bled." To prepare for the August 15 music celebration, gasoline barrels were "covered with rain cloth as drums," a "steel pipe became a bugle," and "empty cans covered with mice skins became *huqin* [two-stringed bowed instruments such as the *erhu* and *jinghu*]." Within a year, "more than 960 POWs had participated in musical performances, while more than three hundred had learned to play the *huqin*." Hundreds of programs were performed in this last year of captivity, including performances by POWs who were "maimed with broken arms and legs," some "crawling across the ground to perform." New songs were written and spread throughout the POW camps (265–69).

For the art exhibitions pictures were painted on "box paper and cement bag paper" retrieved from the American trashcans. Dyes were made from "leftover ash from cooking pans, lime, red clay, and grass." Most of the pictures were portrait paintings. One of them, titled *Such a Priest,* portrayed a priest wearing a mask and saying "amen" with a Bible in one hand, a "lethal weapon emerging from his black dress and his white gloves stained with fresh blood" in the other. Another painting, *Iron Soldiers,* showed the POWs "angrily rebuking the enemies while upholding justice during their interrogation." The paintings were first displayed within the camps and then hung on the wire enclosures facing the outside, thus enabling the American soldiers to view them and allowing reporters from various countries to take their pictures. Although the tension between the American soldiers and the POWs was never diffused and public announcements were made routinely to prohibit the exhibitions, they continued nonetheless. Jin describes a moment at one of the outdoor performances "with the stars, the moon, and the wire enclosures as their backdrop" when American soldiers watching outside the enclosures "shouted their praise: 'OK! OK!'" (270–71).

The literacy campaign also boosted POW morale. Among the six thousand repatriate Chinese POWs by the summer of 1952 were thirty-seven hundred who were illiterate or semiliterate. Most of them were workers and peasants' sons; others had been "blind men with open eyes" for generations. In the language of the "new China" they were hailed as "sons and daughters" of the motherland. The classroom was a tent with rows of students sitting on the ground, some blind, others disabled, and still others with wounded heads "encased in bandages." There were no textbooks, no platform, and no desks. A piece torn out of a raincoat was "draped over the tent wall to serve as a blackboard," and a "small brush stained with tooth powder water and bound by a rope was used as a piece of chalk." Pens were made from "tin cans[,] and ink was colored water produced by heating bits of torn colored cloth and the extracted dye from wild plants," while exercise books were "pieces of paper collected from the garbage cans in the U.S. Army barracks." The major courses taught were Chinese, mathematics, "general knowledge," geology, and history. Regular tests were given. When paper was not available to write Chinese characters, they used a "small stick to write words in the ground." Locked up and isolated from the outside world, the POWs were hungry for any news about China, which was then undergoing dramatic changes, not only in land reform, but also throughout Chinese society, such as the new marriage laws.

In the spring of 1953 one POW, who was repairing the road near the U.S. Army barracks, found a report by Fu Zuoyi (a former Nationalist general made minister of water and electricity in 1953) on the control of the Huai River. He carried it back to camp hidden in his trousers, and it was read eagerly under the light of the searchlights. The report was adopted as a textbook for one of the classes. In September 1953, when the POWs were yet to be released, a Xinhua News Agency reporter visiting the camps reported how a single copy of the *Liberation Daily* was retrieved out of a garbage can and smuggled into the compounds. Because "everyone wanted to look at it and touch it, it had passed through many hands" and "no longer resembled a newspaper." Years later one of the returned POWs, Jing Pu, could recall the "entire contents of the newspaper" and "recite several sentences from the articles." By June 1953, just one month before the signing of the armistice, all students were "awarded a medal comprised of a painting on a piece of iron in graduating ceremonies secretly held in the camps" (274–75).

## Repatriation and Humiliation

The second story—and here the shorter story—told in Jin's book is the terrible treatment of the Chinese POWs upon their repatriation to China. It is a story that validates the dire warnings, whatever their motives, by the pro-Taiwan POW camp managers, beginning in the spring of 1951, that the repatriates upon their return would not be treated as heroes but rather scorned by the motherland, in whose name they had sacrificed themselves. This part of the story exposes the double-edged sword of the Chinese revolution at midcentury: the patriotism that it could inspire and the retribution it could inflict.

The tragedy of Jin's story is tempered by the popularity of his book and its warm reception in Chinese reading circles. The simple telling of the POW story becomes a small act of redemption that extends the unfinished political rehabilitation that began in the early 1980s, when hundreds of thousands, perhaps millions, of Chinese people who had been wrongly accused of rightist thoughts and behavior—including many of the returned POWs—were officially restored to political favor. Given the political climate of the 1980s, when the book was written, Jin took considerable risks in exposing the story. At the same time, like the POWs themselves, he remains politically loyal and credits the policies of the Chinese Communist Party in the early 1980s with sparing the POWs from "going to their graves labeled POW" (384).

Between August 5 and September 6, 1953, the 5,640 Chinese POWs who had declared themselves repatriates at the time of the armistice left Cheju-do on an American ship bound for Inchon, and a few days later arrived in Panmunjom to cross the white line, marking their release from American captivity. It takes a bit of a stretch to imagine what must have been going through their minds as they crossed the line. Many had been gone from their homes and families for as long as three years, with little if any communication with them. They were terribly anxious about the radical political, social, and economic changes taking place in China during their absence. Given their early victories on the battlefield fol-

Pusan, Korea. Under the watchful eye of the military police these sick, wounded, and disabled communist POWs debark from an LST at the South Korean port en route to Panmunjom to be exchanged for Allied POWs in the big swap (Little Switch) now underway. *(April 21, 1953, National Archives)*

lowed by war's stalemate, they surely had mixed feelings about their role in the war. They were justifiably proud of their discipline and sacrifice, even if it meant the loss of dear comrades. After all, they were veterans of battles in which Chinese "volunteers" had defeated the mightiest army in the world. But in the face of the two-year stalemate, they had also become demoralized. Casualties were high, supply lines were thin, Mao's dictum that men—equipped so sparely and carrying so little—were more powerful than machines had proved wrong, and they had been captured. And then came the experience for more than two years in the POW camps. Whatever the mix of emotions, they showed defiance when crossing the lines, singing songs and throwing off the clothing provided by their American captors to walk into North Korea in their underwear.

This dramatic transfer was closely followed by the foreign press and is described in detail in the official U.S. Army history of the POWs.[24]

The fourteen thousand Chinese POWs headed for Taiwan left Cheju-do on September 13 and were placed under the command of the Neutral Nations Repatriate Commission, headed by officers and soldiers from India, and given the chance to reconsider their choice. Of these, after weeks of "explanation" by Chinese officers, only three hundred changed their minds and chose to repatriate to China.

Surprisingly, Jin dwells only briefly on these dramatic moments and chooses instead to pick up the story at the point where the POWs are put on trains heading back to China, this time crossing the Yalu River going the other way. He tells of a group of two hundred of the repatriates who, gathering in Changtu County in Liaoning Province, were transferred to the command of the Administrative Office in Charge of the Returned CPV POWs. Received by students with flowers and songs, they expected to rest a while, receive their job assignments, and then go home. But the tone changed "almost overnight" as "new instructions" arrived, warning of "rightist deviation" and ordering the POWs to go through a period of "study" to "make a clean breast of their behavior in the POW camps," to study the "revolutionary martyrs," and to explain why they had not "died for their country." The study lasted for several months and involved lengthy criticisms of how their "smoking enemy cigarettes" and giving "their true names and army unit designations" had betrayed "military secrets" to the enemy and made "traitorous" their behavior in camp. In Jin's account, the six thousand returnees, including the 760 injured POWs who had been released during "Little Switch" four months before the armistice, were degraded and made to feel "ugly" (387–90).

Jin then describes the ostracism and pain they suffered back home. They were labeled as "rightists" in various political campaigns for the next thirty years, most stridently in the Anti-Rightist Campaign in 1957 and throughout the period known as the Cultural Revolution, from 1966 through 1976 and Mao Zedong's death. "Many wives no longer regarded them as husbands, their children did not treat them as fathers, and their relatives felt ashamed." Painful as their reception was and linked as it was to the campaigns organized by the communist leadership, Jin observes that Chinese POWs released at the end of World War II were given similar treatment (397). The children of POWs were refused entry into the PLA. Two-thirds of the hundreds of letters of appeal that Jin was allowed to see in preparing for his book were written by former members of the Communist Party and Communist Youth League, now stripped of their membership. Because they suffered so much, one is touched by their deep—if naïve in Western eyes—patriotism and recurring wish not only to clear their names but "to rejoin the party." Their written appeals, begun already in 1954, were made to local party officials and even to the highest levels of authority, the Central Party Committee and the Central Military Committee. In March 1979 the Xinhua News Agency forwarded a letter to the desk of the General Political Department of the PLA and added a few words of its own endorsing the appeal. Prompted by this initiative and the gradually emerging political relaxation in China, leaders in the PLA itself began opening files going back a quarter century and conducting their own interviews with returned POWs in three provinces, Liaoning, Shanxi, and Sichuan. They discovered the POW stories of resistance to persecution and of tattooing. In their own defense, and at the same time out of their continuing patriotism, they had formed locally "secret revolutionary organizations." In September 1980 the Central Committee of the Chinese Communist Party gave permission to the PLA General Political Department to open the files and on a national scale to reexamine the appeals and begin to reverse the false accusations. Since then, many of the POWs have been restored to party membership and positions of military status and leadership generally throughout the country, some of them at high levels, including election as representatives in the National People's Congress. They are now "leading a new life in their old age" (410–14).

In concluding his book Jin Daying tells the story of Zhang Da, who as we recall had joined the CPV at the age of seventeen and, like many others, had strong family ties with the nationalist government. Having served as a major in the Guomindang army in the 1940s, his father was arrested in 1950 and sent to be reformed through labor. When the war broke out, Zhang was enrolled as a student in the Southwest People's Revolutionary University in Chengdu and became a member of the Communist Youth League. Zhang joined the Chinese volunteers in the fall of 1950 and was captured in the spring of 1951. He was forcibly tattooed by the pro-Taiwan POWs and over the next two years rose to leadership among the repatriate POWs. In one of his early interviews with Jin Daying—in September 1986—Zhang recalled a fellow POW who had been a friend of his father telling him, "You are a little kid. What good will the Chinese Communist Party do for you if you return to the Mainland?" Reflecting upon this early warning, three and a half decades later, Zhang could admit that he hadn't studied "Marxism and Leninism much," but it was sufficient to distinguish the "old China" which was corrupt and the "new China" which was "bright" and to "return with all my might to make a contribution"—that simple (417).

Upon arriving in his native town after the war, he was labeled a traitor. He sat once again for the university entrance exams and received high scores, but was denied acceptance for being "politically" unqualified. He then taught in a high school but was dismissed, again for political reasons. To earn a living over the next three decades, he worked as a boat tracker along the Min River in Sichuan Province, a water carrier in a chemical plant, a road builder in Liangshan County, and a maintenance worker repairing roads. Over twenty years his salary never exceeded thirty yuan a month, and he was dismissed from his job again and again for political reasons. During the Cultural Revolution he was accused of committing treason, and at one point the local government issued a warrant for his arrest. Despite his suffering, he never abandoned his wish to get a degree, and managed soon after the Cultural Revolution to complete a correspondence course from Sichuan Normal University (417–18).

## Rehabilitation

In August 1984 Zhang Zeshi, a fellow POW also from Sichuan Province and a leader among the POWs in Kŏje-do, persuaded Zhang to open a restaurant in Beijing. His first restaurant attempt, named Dong Po after the Song Dynasty poet Su Dongpo, also from Sichuan, was set up in a hotel operated by the Xuanwu District Construction Company in Beijing. He managed to secure a loan of fifty thousand yuan, or about eight thousand dollars at the time. But before he could open as scheduled in May 1985, he was deluged with letters maligning him for having an "unknown identity and serious problems in his personal record." The company withdrew its support for the restaurant. As Zhang tells the story, he held fast, inspired by his wish to do something "for his country" before "I meet Su Dongpo." To clear his name, he looked up his former commander in the Chinese army, Wei Jie, who wrote to the authorities, "I can prove that Zhang Da is not a traitor to the country . . . Zhang Da should have the right to work" (419–21). This time his name was cleared, and the restaurant was opened.

By 1999 the Dong Po Restaurant, located now at the north end of the National Library in Haidian District in western Beijing, had become a great success story. Hanging on the walls of the restaurant were paintings by prominent Chinese artists. In a brochure prepared by Zhang were the names, good wishes, and pictures of many famous writers—the elite of Beijing, including government leaders—who had heard Zhang's story, some of them through Jin's book, and had become regular patrons of the restaurant. His remarkable life of patriotic loyalty, followed by three decades of ostracism and political struggle, and eventual entrepreneurial success, is one part of China's larger story of political—and cultural—change. As he saw us off at the restaurant, he told us how much he was looking forward a few weeks later to joining other Chinese tourists on a trip to Korea, including a visit to Kŏje and Cheju Islands.[25]

Nearly a century and a half ago Walt Whitman wrote of serving for three years as a nurse to soldiers on both sides of the American Civil War. He reminded the reader that "the real war will never get in the books." The "interior history" of war itself, Whitman wrote, "not only never will be written, its practicality, minutiae of detail and passions, will never even be suggested."[26] Whitman's skepticism must thread the account of anyone aspiring to grasp the myriad human stories of war and becomes stronger when one attempts to tell these stories written not just in one language or from one broad cultural and historical perspective, but rather from three—Korean, Chinese, and English. Difficult, yes, but luring nonetheless, because we know that history is not only an account of what happened based on surviving evidence. History is also shaped by the interests, inclinations, and skills of those who write it. We constantly rewrite history, not only because we discover new sources of information, but because changing circumstances invite us to bring new questions to old documents. What we do with history is limited not only by what we can know about the past, but also by what we care to know. In the case of the Korean War and, too, the Asia Pacific and Vietnam Wars, new communication technologies make it easier to identify, collect, and ponder the many stories of war. The gradual ending of the Asian cold war also makes this kind of caring easier.[27]

This brief account of the Chinese POWs is a reminder of how complex the human stories of the Korean War are. Imagine how the fuller story of the Chinese POWs would look if someone like Jin Daying were to interview those who chose to go to Taiwan—many of whom are still alive today. Still harder to imagine are the stories of the much larger number of North Korean POWs who chose to repatriate, and of the millions of North Korean civilians whose lives were shattered by the war but whose voices are yet to be heard.

## Notes

1. My study of Yanjing was published as *Yenching University and Sino-Western Relations, 1916–1952* (Cambridge: Harvard University Press, 1976). During my first visit to Beijing in the summer of 1981 I met with a number of former Yanjing students, faculty, and children of faculty. During my year as American Co-Director of the Johns Hopkins Nanjing University Center for Chinese American Studies in 1990, I had more conversations with Chinese veterans of the Korean War, including some who were staff members of the center.

2. Jin's book was published first in serial form and then in 1987 as a book by Kunlun Press. In an interview with Philip West April 2, 1999, Daying (the pen name for Jin Daying) said his book had gone through twelve printings and sold more than a million copies. The quotations from Jin's book are from an English translation of the book by Li Zhihua who did the translation in partial fulfillment of his master's degree completed at The University of Montana, 1993. Unless otherwise noted all references to sources appearing in parentheses in the text are to the page numbers in Li's translation.

3. Conrad C. Crane, *American Airpower Strategy in Korea, 1950–1953* (Kansas University Press, 2000), 125.

4. Max Hastings, *The Korean War* (New York: Simon and Schuster, 1987), 305.

5. William Stueck, *The Korean War: An International History* (Princeton: Princeton University Press, 1995), 244–96.

6. As quoted from Truman's diary in William Stueck, *The Korean War*, 258.

7. Lynn Montross et al., *U.S. Marine Operations in Korea, 1950–1953: The East-Central Front*, vol. 4 (Washington, DC: Government Printing Office, 1962), 35. Alexander L. George, *The Chinese Communist Army in Action: The Korean War and Its Aftermath* (New York: University of Columbia Press, 1967), 37. For a similarly dispassionate analysis of the Chinese soldiers, based on his interviews with Chinese POWs in Taiwan in 1955, see Allen Whiting, *1955 World Politics* 7 (July 1955): 598.

8. These figures are taken from James L. Mattray, ed. and contr., *Historical Dictionary of the Korean War* (Westport, CT: Greenwood Press, 1991), 554, and in turn from W. G. Hermes, *Truce Tent and Fighting Front* (Washington, DC:, Center of Military History, Department of the Army, 1966).

9. The controversy over the behavior of the American POWs was brought to public attention in 1957 with the publication in the *New Yorker* of an article by Eugene Kincaid, "A Reporter at Large: The Study of Something New in History" (26 October 1957), followed by his book-length *In Every War but One* (New York: Norton, 1959). Kincaid's studies spearheaded a wider discussion on so-called give-up-itis among American soldiers in the first year of the war and the broader social decay of American culture. In 1963, Albert D. Biderman vigorously refuted Kincaid's conclusions in *The March to Calumny: The Story of the American POW's in the Korean War* (New York: Macmillan, 1963). In his book Biderman argued that if there was an increased measure of "misconduct" among the American POWs in the

Korean War, it was not that much different from the behavior of POWs in other wars generally and should be understood as the result of harsh treatment and indoctrination by the communists. Although opposite in their observations and conclusions about American POW behavior, the Kincaid-Biderman debate occurs within an ideological framework in which the enemy, especially the Chinese, is at once feared, blamed, and held in contempt.

10. The best known of these writers in the West is Ba Jin (1904–1998), whose *Yingxiong de gushi* (Stories of Heroes) was published in 1954 by the Foreign Languages Press, Beijing, with the title *Living Amongst Heroes*.

11. One useful standard history is Zhen Zonghong et al., eds., *Kang Mei yuan Chao zhanshi* (Military History of the Resist America–Aid Korea) (Beijing: Military Science Press, 1988). This history describes Chinese versions of the orders of battle and includes in the appendix comprehensive if not complete sets of statistics on military capabilities and on casualties (though only for the "enemy") and detailed maps focusing on the five Chinese campaigns, ending in the spring of 1991.

12. Xia Zhengnong, editor in chief, *Cihai* (Shanghai: Shanghai cishu chubanshe [Shanghai Dictionary Publishing House], 1980).

13. See Perry Link, Richard Madsen, and Paul G. Pickowicz, eds., *Unofficial China: Popular Culture and Thought in the People's Republic* (Boulder: Westview, 1989), 10.

14. On April 2, 1999, Jin arranged for me to visit Zhang Da at the Dong Po Restaurant adjacent to the National Library in Beijing. Zhang is the owner and manager of the restaurant and was willing to spend the afternoon and early evening recounting his life in the POW camps on Kŏje-do and the four and a half decades of his life as a repatriated POW.

15. Barton J. Bernstein, "The Struggle Over the Korean Armistice: Prisoners of Repatriation?" in *Child of Conflict: The Korean-American Relationship, 1943–1953*, ed. Bruce Cumings (Seattle: University of Washington Press, 1983), 261–306. Bernstein's study was largely completed by 1978 and was discussed widely in academic conferences on East Asia and the Korean War. Later histories of the Korean War such as the popular account by Jon Halliday and Bruce Cumings, *Korea: The Unknown War* (New York: Pantheon Books, 1988), also lend credibility to Jin Daying's perspective and purpose.

16. To cite some of the more prominent examples, John Toland's *In Mortal Combat: Korea 1950–1953* (New York: Morrow, 1991) includes a brief account of Zhang Da's capture as a POW and the taking as a hostage of General Francis Dodd, commander of the POW camps on Kŏje-do, by the Chinese and Korean POWs in May 1952. Toland is not unsympathetic to Jin's account, written much earlier, but his treatment of the POW issue is cursory at best. Russell Spurr's *Enter the Dragon: China's Undeclared War Against the U.S. in Korea, 1950–1951* (New York: Newmarket Press, 1988) was a fresh and credible look at the Korean War through Chinese eyes, both official and unofficial, but his account stops with spring 1951 and makes no mention of the POW issue. Bevin Alexander's *Korea, The First War We Lost* (New York: Hippocrene Books, 1986) is a relatively early American history of the war that incorporates Chinese perspectives. But even his sympathetic account is able to give only scant attention to the stories of the Chinese POWs. The account by Joseph C. Goulden, *Korea, The Untold Story of the War* (New York: McGraw-Hill, 1982) is the first of the 1980s' comprehensive histories of

the war to be published by a large commercial press. It is not unsympathetic to Chinese perspectives, but it devotes only 12 out of a total of 650 pages to the Chinese and North Korean charges of mistreatment in the POW camps. The largest tome of all is Clay Blair's 976-page *The Forgotten War: America in Korea 1950– 1953* (New York: Times Books, 1987). Its last chapter is titled "Red China Checked" and devotes ten pages to the POW issue. The POW issue is scattered throughout T. R. Fehrenbach's classic *This Kind of War: A Study in Unpreparedness* (New York: Macmillan, 1963, 660 pages). Because of its writing and publication at the height of the cold war, its slighting of the POW questions should not be surprising. The one popular history that approaches Bernstein's evenhandedness, devoting a whole chapter and then some to "Prisoners" (30 pages in the 344-page book), is Max Hastings's *The Korean War* (New York: Simon & Schuster, 1987).

17. William Lindsay White, *The Captives of Korea: An Unofficial White Paper on the Treatment of War Prisoners* (New York: Scribner, 1957), 176–77.

18. Biderman, *The March to Calumny*, 47.

19. Mattray, "UNC POW Administration," *Historical Dictionary*, 504.

20. George, *The Chinese Communist Army in Action*, 136–37.

21. Jin's observation is supported by Bernstein, "The Struggle Over the Korean Armistice," in which he quotes a number of American officials, including Frank Stelle of the State Department Policy Planning Staff, who wrote in January 1952 that the management of the compounds by the pro-Taiwan POWs was "violent and brutal . . . in effect a reign of terror." Bernstein also quotes Ambassador John Muccio, who referred to these POW trusties as "gestapos."

22. This "small scale war" in which "murders and atrocities had become commonplace" is confirmed by the U.S. Army's *Handling of Prisoners of War During the Korean War*, 26.

23. This naïveté may have been more widespread among the Chinese soldiers than conventional images of them as sacrificial, disciplined, and fearless fighters would lead us to believe, and suggests something in common with the simple views of American soldiers in the war. See Donald Knox, *The Korean War, An Oral History: Pusan to Chosin* (New York: Harcourt, Brace, Jovanovich, 1985), passim.

24. One excellent account of these dramatic moments in the war is shown in the ninth episode of the ten-hour documentary film *The Korean War*, produced by the Korea Broadcasting System, Seoul, 1989.

25. Interview with West and Jin, April 2, 1999.

26. Walter Lowenfels, *Walt Whitman's Civil War, Compiled and Edited from Published and Unpublished Sources* (New York: Knopf, 1960), 283.

27. For an overview of this approach to the three wars see Philip West, Steven Levine, and Jackie Hiltz, *America's Wars in Asia: A Cultural Approach to History and Memory* (Armonk, NY: M.E. Sharpe, 1998).

# 10

## In Search of Essences:
## Labeling the Korean War

## *William Stueck*

Historians invariably involve themselves in the business of oversimplification. They work with only a partial record of the past, which means that they can never know an awful lot about what happened. Even when they know a great deal, they must condense what they know into communicable form, that is, a book or article, which at best summarizes what they consider to be the most important aspects of their knowledge.

In summarizing, generalizing, and synthesizing, we historians constantly look for labels that will assist the reader in comprehending the essence of an event or events. Most prominently, we use labels in titles—of sections of chapters, chapters, essays, and ultimately books.

Labels in the titles of books probably represent the grossest oversimplifications in which historians engage. Many titles are purely topical in nature. Chen Jian's book *China's Road to the Korean War* is an example here, as is Robert Futrell's *The United States Air Force in Korea, 1950–1953;* so is my *The Korean War: An International History.*[1] Such titles are safe: so long as they accurately represent what the book is about, they rarely draw fire from reviewers. But numerous authors cannot resist the temptation to be argumentative or thematic in at least a portion of their titles, and it is here that the oversimplification becomes most striking. There is no way a single word or phrase can capture the complexity of an event like the Korean War.

Yet a label can identify at least an important dimension of the event being analyzed and, in some cases, place the author politically and/or historiographically. Here I intend to examine some of the labels historians have chosen for the Korean War—in titles and elsewhere—as a method of assessing the nature of that event and its place in history.

Korea is a very labeled war, and it is so in part because its significance is so ambiguous to so many people. Its placement in the American experience between World War II and Vietnam has made it less memorable to some, "the forgotten war," as Clay Blair entitled his massive volume.[2] This, in fact, has become the best-known label in the United States. Nonetheless, while describing the attitude of many Americans—certainly not Koreans—many years after the event, it does nothing to explain the event itself. It implies that there is something about the event that is worth remembering, but gives no hint of what it might be.

Another label clearly designed for an American audience is Bevin Alexander's, *The First War We Lost.*[3] Alexander tacitly concedes the inappropriateness of the title in his preface, where he argues that the United States actually won one war in Korea, that against North Korea, and lost another, that against China.[4] Indeed, more than half the volume is taken up with the war the United States clearly won! By his own standard, then, Alexander would have been more accurate had he used the title *The War We Won, The War We Lost.*

Even this label is grossly inadequate for anything but an account of strictly the American side of the war. Authors, of course, have the right to focus on any aspect of the war they please, but an account centering on the American experience plays down the role of parties that suffered far more death and destruction in the conflict than did the United States. In addition, in this case the unilateral approach blinds Alexander to the sense in which there existed a third war in Korea. The United States won the war to save the Republic of Korea from the initial North Korean attack, and it lost the war to unify the peninsula under a friendly government. But it also won the war to prevent the People's Republic of China from unifying Korea under the regime it desired or from achieving its goals of capturing Taiwan and gaining entry into the United Nations. Focusing on one side can all too easily cause a tunnel vision that ultimately produces misunderstanding of that side itself.

During the 1970s and 1980s, some American scholars, reacting against the prevailing tendency of their countrymen to focus on the U.S. role in the war and, in some cases, against the "cold war orthodoxy" that justified the United States' intervention in Korea, concentrated on the peninsular origins of the conflict. The most extreme practitioners of this genre settled upon the label "civil war" as "the proper appellation for the conflict."[5] This work brought needed attention to the fact that a civil war raged off and on in South Korea from the fall of 1946 to early 1950. Yet the label is severely limited, even misleading, as a characterization of what occurred in Korea from June 1950 to July 1953, or even as an instrument for grasping the origins of that conflict. The war included combatants representing twenty different governments. Fifty to sixty percent of the estimated casualties to military personnel were non-Korean. Virtually all of the weapons and ammunition employed came from outside the peninsula. A large portion of the civilian casualties and destruction of property resulted from UN—primarily U.S.—bombing of North Korea. To be sure, the incident at No Gun Ri in July 1950 in which American soldiers slaughtered dozens of Korean civilians is impossible to comprehend without referring to divisions among the Korean people. Yet Americans—outsiders—remain central to the story. Scholars who label Korea a civil war are really concerned about what they believe it should have been rather than what it was.

Even if we dwell entirely on origins, the most basic factor in the outbreak of war on June 25, 1950, was the division of the peninsula into occupation zones by the United States and the Soviet Union in August 1945. Koreans were hardly passive bystanders in the events that transpired in their country between then and June 1950. Deep fissures that existed in Korean society surfaced quickly after the liberation from Japan. Overlapping divisions between collaborators with the Japanese and resisters, police and civilians, landowners and peasants, leftists and rightists, and members of competing factions all contributed significantly to the division of the country into two hostile regimes in 1948.[6] Still, outsiders largely dictated the particular form that that division took, namely a communist regime in the North, a rightist regime in the South, separated by the thirty-eighth parallel boundary agreed upon by two great powers three years earlier without Korean input. Even the autumn uprisings of 1946 in South Korea, which are sometimes cited as the starting point of the civil war, were, according to new documentation from Russia, directed and financed by the Soviet occupiers in the North.[7]

In his massive two-volume study of the origins of the war, Bruce Cumings rightly points out that "no Korean recognized the thirty-eighth parallel as permanent."[8] Even so, Koreans, like the Soviets and the Americans, were far from agreed on the appropriate means for eliminating that boundary and unifying the country. Both leaders of the two indigenous regimes wanted to use force to achieve their purposes. Neither, however, could hope to achieve its goal without support from its great-power sponsor.

Cumings describes North Korea's decision to attack in June 1950 as "not made in a foreign office: it was made in a Korean mind that mingled cold calculation with a youthful, undaunted bravado. . . . In its indifference to the likely result . . . there was a solipsism and supercharged chauvinism that tells us that its authorship was local."[9] Although calculation and bravado were in plentiful supply in Pyongyang in 1950, in fact Kim Il-sung was far from solipsistic in the process by which he decided to launch his attack on the South. He had been handpicked to lead North Korea by the Soviets, who maintained a strong presence above the thirty-eighth parallel even after their troops withdrew at the end of 1948. As historian Kathryn Weathersby has shown, "North Korea was utterly dependent economically on the Soviet Union . . . [and] was simply unable to take any significant action without Soviet approval."[10] Kim consulted extensively with both Soviet and Chinese leaders about the proposed attack. Ultimately, Joseph Stalin and Mao Zedong gave the go-ahead and provided critical aid to ensure its success.[11] Soviet advisers worked closely with the North Koreans in drawing up invasion plans. According to one account, the initial draft plan was actually written in Russian, not Korean.[12] The North attacked the South rather than vice versa simply because the former was able to get outside support for its venture whereas the latter was not. Whatever the internal aspects of the Korean War, the essence of the event is best captured through an examination, first, of the evolving conflict—both on the peninsula and elsewhere—between the United States and the Soviet Union in the aftermath of the defeat of Germany and Japan in 1945; and, then, of the emerging situation in Northeast Asia with the communist victory on mainland China in 1949.

Cumings suggests that the Korean War can be readily compared to the Spanish civil war and the Vietnam War.[13] In the sense that all three possessed a revolutionary dimension he is certainly correct. Yet fundamental differences exist among the three. For one thing, the Spanish civil war was almost entirely domestic in origin. The Spain of the 1930s had not recently been freed of a colonial regime; it had not, even more recently, been occupied and divided by mutual agreement between two other great powers. The forces of the right did receive some aid and encouragement from Fascist Italy and then Nazi Germany, but its leaders had risen to their positions without foreign sponsorship. The left received virtually no outside assistance until the war was under way. Reading the standard works on the origins of the Spanish civil war is a far more insular experience than that of reading similar works on the Korean War, including Cumings's two volumes.[14]

One lesson that does emerge from examining the Spanish civil war is that, even when the sources of conflict are overwhelmingly internal, the international consequences of the conflict itself can, because of foreign involvement, be immediate and of considerable importance. Italian and German intervention in Spain clearly tipped the scales in favor of the forces intent on destroying the Republic and helped solidify the Axis alliance and demoralize the Western democracies. Similarly, whatever the weight of domestic factors in the origins of the Korean War, the result of a swift North Korean victory in 1950 could well have had momentous consequences far beyond the peninsula.[15]

The Vietnam War bears more obvious similarities to the Korean conflict than does the Spanish civil war. The Vietnam War did develop out of a struggle for independence and an effort from the outside to divide a country that had been united for over a century. In both Korea and Vietnam, the United States, while supporting social and economic reform, wound up backing forces hostile to them.

Still, sharp differences exist between the two cases. The United States played a critical role in liberating Korea from its colonial oppressor; in Vietnam, the United States for years supported France, which was attempting to reestablish its rule. In Korea, the United States supported the idea of UN–supervised national elections in an attempt to end the country's division; in Vietnam it resisted internationally supervised elections to achieve unity. The massive U.S. military intervention in Korea occurred at a time when the government in South Korea had at least temporarily defeated an insurgency from within and was under conventional attack from a regime created and armed by the Soviet Union. Such intervention occurred in Vietnam on behalf of a regime in the South faced with a lethal internal insurgency reinforced by a steady infiltration from without. The government promoting that infiltration was aided by the Soviet Union and China but possessed unimpeachable indigenous origins. The United States intervened in Korea with the enthusiastic backing of its allies and many neutrals; its intervention in Vietnam received mixed reviews from its allies and widespread opposition from neutrals. In South Vietnam the United States, either because of lack of interest or opposition by the government, did not see the implementation of an effective land reform until 1970, a full five years after it took over the fighting; in South Korea it implemented partial land reform prior to the end of the occupation, and then used the circumstances of war to pressure the government into finishing the job. By the end of 1951, redistribution was essentially completed.[16] The Korean contest was primarily a conventional military engagement with a civil component that only marginally influenced the outcome. In Vietnam, the civil dimension of the struggle largely determined the final result despite a gargantuan effort by the United States. A precise gauging of public opinion in South Korea and South Vietnam is not possible, but it is fair to say that a far larger portion of the people of the former accepted—and even approved of—the U.S. presence in their country from 1950 to 1953 than was the case in the latter during the late 1960s.

In attempting to educate his compatriots about what he labels "the unknown war," Cumings is so intent on producing a national guilt trip that he glosses over or denies the international aspects of the Korean conflict for the purposes of highlighting the internal, socioeconomic dimension, especially the problem of land distribution.[17] In reality, whether from the perspective of international legitimacy, practicality, or abstract morality, the American course in Korea, at least in terms of the portion designed to prevent North Korea's takeover of the peninsula, is far more defensible than that in Vietnam.

In entitling his book *Korea, the War Before Vietnam,* British historian Callum A. MacDonald draws on a connection made by Cumings and others, although his tone is not nearly so harsh on the United States.[18] MacDonald never explicitly addresses his intent in choosing the title, but his first chapter, "The Cold War and Counterrevolution," suggests that he sees a linkage between Korea and Vietnam as part of a larger struggle of the United States to contain revolution in the undeveloped world. Certainly there is a substantial grain of truth in this linkage, but to choose it as the key essence of the Korean War masks the rather fundamental differences between the two conflicts outlined above.

Another linkage between the two conflicts rests in the degree to which the first set the stage for the second. Surprisingly, MacDonald does not emphasize this connection. He even points out that "[U.S. President Dwight] Eisenhower preferred to concede North Vietnam to the communists in 1954, rather than risk another Korea." On the other hand, he notes the Korean War "helped shift American attention towards the Far

East, a tendency which accelerated in the following years," and it "froze the relationship between Washington and Beijing," thus making the containment of China a major objective of U.S. foreign policy. The Chinese reaction to the UN march to the Yalu in late 1950 also discouraged American leaders from sending ground forces into North Vietnam from 1965 onward.[19]

Scholar Yuen Foong Khong develops these points in far greater depth than MacDonald. Khong focuses on how U.S. decision makers used the analogy with Korea in making their choices on Vietnam during the early and mid-1960s. Through intense quantitative and qualitative analysis, he shows that the Korean War provided the single most important historical analogy for those in the John F. Kennedy and Lyndon B. Johnson administrations when defining and evaluating options on Vietnam. A generation later George Ball, the leading "dove" on the Johnson team, told him that "if we had not gone into Korea . . . it would have been very unlikely that we would have gotten into Vietnam." During the fall of 1964, Ball went to considerable lengths with his colleagues in trying to dispel the notion that the Korean situation in 1950 was comparable to the present circumstances in Vietnam, but to no avail.[20]

Despite the obvious connection between the Korean and Vietnam wars, it is crucial that, in labeling the former, we in no way imply that it is somehow less significant than the latter. Indeed, Khong's evidence suggests precisely the opposite: that, because Korea came first and was so influential in American decisions on Vietnam, it deserves a *more* prominent place in histories of the United States and the cold war. Yet, even if Korea is given first billing—and most readers probably do not interpret MacDonald's title as doing so—its overall significance is hardly captured merely through its linkage to Vietnam.

Korea's timing is critical to its broader importance. As the first major international military engagement after World War II and the dawning of the nuclear age, it proved instrumental in defining the parameters of conflict in the cold war era. Prior to the end of that era, political scientist John Mueller referred to the Korean War as "quite possibly the most important event since World War II." Before June 1950, the United States had pursued a policy that emphasized political and economic measures to contain the Soviet Union. The North Korean attack "demonstrated to the West that the danger of direct aggression was very real, and thus the military component of containment was vastly expanded." Mueller argues that, had the West not responded as it did in Korea, the Soviet

Union "might have been tempted to try step-by-step, Hitler-style probes leading ultimately to military action if it had felt that these would be reasonably cheap and free of risk." As it was, the Korean War was sufficiently destructive and dangerous in its course and outcome to discourage the Soviets from pursuing or sponsoring such military adventurism in the future. Thus Korea was a key "stabilizing event" in the cold war.[21]

Mueller also points out that Korea led American military leaders to think seriously about limited war.[22] From 1945 to 1950, they had planned only for war on a grand scale, but the U.S. intervention in Korea and then the Chinese entry into the fray led them to the conclusion that preparations for more limited conflicts were essential.

British writer David Rees, who in 1964 published what would stand for a generation as the standard English-language survey of the Korean War, used the concept of limited war and the trauma it caused in the United States as his organizing theme. Rees contended that "the Korean War was the first important war in American history that was not a crusade." The liberal tradition in the United States disassociated "power and policy." Peace was the natural state of things: war "an aberration . . . [that] can only be justified when fought as a crusade against tyrants in a mood of righteous indignation."[23] He would agree with George Kennan, the diplomat-historian, who during the early stages of the Korean War likened American democracy "to one of those prehistoric monsters with a body as long as this room and a brain the size of a pin." "He is slow to wrath," Kennan observed, "[Y]ou have to practically whack his tail off to make him aware that his interests are being disturbed; but, once he grasps this, he lays about him with such blind determination that he not only destroys his adversary but largely wrecks his native habitat."[24] Yet, despite intense pressure from General Douglas MacArthur and numerous others in the military, Congress, the press, and general public, the administrations of Harry S Truman and Dwight D. Eisenhower succeeded in limiting the war within the confines of Korea. In so doing, Rees concluded, they kept "the [Western] coalition intact, repelled the Communist aggression and strengthened Western defenses." Rees viewed this result as "the major Western political achievement since 1945."[25]

A generation later, armed with thousands of newly declassified documents from American and British archives, historian Rosemary Foot devoted an entire book to the question of why the United States limited the war. Her title, *The Wrong War,* grew out of a 1951 statement by General Omar Bradley, the chairman of the U.S. joint chiefs of staff, that to expand the war to China would put the United States "in the wrong war, at the wrong place, at the wrong time, and with the wrong enemy."[26] She found that the debate within the U.S. government on expanding the war was "much more extensive, rich, and complex than has hitherto been thought."[27] In the end, though, the United States resisted the temptation for reasons familiar to Rees: it feared the breakup of the Western alliance and the exhaustion of its resources against a secondary enemy.

Certainly the labels "limited war" and "wrong war" have descriptive force in characterizing the Korean conflict. Although Rees and Foot concern themselves primarily with American policy, the labels could apply to the Soviet Union as well. Stalin did approve the North Korean attack and gave his ally the means to carry it out, but he took care from the start to avert a direct clash with the United States. Soviet personnel on the ground stayed well behind the front lines and Soviet pilots engaged only in operations along the northern boundary of Korea. The communist side never launched air attacks on U.S. bases in Japan and South Korea, nor did it attempt a major air offensive against enemy ground forces. Our knowledge of interaction between the Soviets and the Chinese regarding the air war remains thin, but it is fair to assume that the former kept a close watch on the use of its planes in an effort to limit the conflict. If the Soviet Union possessed a conventional military advantage in Europe, its atomic stockpile and mobilization potential remained far inferior to that of the United States. Stalin did take some serious risks during his last years of a direct confrontation with the United States, but on balance he sought to avoid it.

Still, the labels "limited war" and "wrong war" do not address Mueller's contention that the Korean War was a critical stabilizing event in world politics during the era of the cold war. It is in this context that I want to suggest the label "the necessary war." The strongest objection to this label is that it can be easily misunderstood. The first time I advanced it, in a conference paper, a Korean-American in the audience took me to task, remarking that he had lost his parents in the war, that he resented my suggestion that the war was necessary. I hope I can do a better job of communicating what I mean by that label than I did on that occasion.

I use the word "necessary" in the tragic sense that the American theologian Reinhold Niebuhr understood it. While war raged on in Korea, Niebuhr wrote in *The Irony of American History* that "the tragic element in a human situation is constituted of conscious choices of evil for the sake of good. If men or nations do evil in a good cause; if they cover themselves with guilt in order to fulfill some high responsibility; or if they sacrifice some high value for the sake of a higher or equal one they make a tragic choice." The classic example of tragic choice on the contemporary scene was "the necessity [to American statesmen] of using the threat of atomic destruction as an instrument for the preservation of peace." This analysis grew out of Niebuhr's "Christian realism," his belief in the inherent sinfulness of humankind, especially when acting in groups.[28] Because "no group acts from purely unselfish or even mutual intent[,]" he argued in 1953, "politics is . . . bound to be a contest of power."[29] As political theorist Thomas W. Smith observed, this outlook led Niebuhr to the conclusion that "the balance of power, that archetypical tragic political construct . . . [was] an irreplaceable international strategy."[30]

In retrospect, there is reason to believe that the American policy planners who drafted the famous document NSC 68 during early 1950 were essentially correct in their belief that a dangerous threat existed to the balance of military power between the Soviet Union and the United States.[31] Scholars have justifiably criticized the paper for its repetitive and overwrought prose, for its implication that Moscow possessed a master plan, perhaps even a timetable, for world conquest. Yet its claim that the Soviets held a growing military advantage, especially in Europe, the key theater of the cold war, remains plausible in the face of new evidence from Soviet archives. David Holloway, author of a distinguished study of Soviet military strength and planning in the early cold war years, concludes that in 1948 Soviet armed forces in Europe were probably well below what Moscow "considered desirable for large-scale strategic offensive operations." "The Soviet posture was far from being unambiguously defensive, however," and between the summer of 1949 and spring of 1950 the Kremlin added eighty thousand men to its forces in Germany and stepped up training exercises there. It also commenced a reorganization and buildup of the armed forces of its Eastern European allies and incorporated them into the Soviet order of battle. East German Alert Police, now fifty thousand strong, received "Soviet military equipment, including tanks."[32] The United States was not inactive during this period. In the fall of 1949, it commenced a modest foreign arms aid program, which centered on its NATO allies, and an expansion of its capacity to produce atomic bombs. In January 1950, it announced the beginning of a crash program to develop a hydrogen bomb. Still, a

$13 billion ceiling remained on the defense budget and, even in the face of the alarming analysis in NSC 68, President Truman talked publicly about actually decreasing that spending during the upcoming fiscal year.[33]

The drafters of NSC 68 believed that the United States had four years to counter the Soviet conventional advantage. By 1954, they estimated, the Soviets would possess a substantial stockpile of nuclear weapons and a major capacity to deliver them to the United States. This would seriously undermine the American nuclear deterrent, thus increasing the likelihood of an all-out Soviet attack on Western Europe. Meanwhile, the primary danger was of a more limited Soviet attack to exploit a local advantage, which through miscalculation on both sides could eventually escalate into a direct confrontation of the superpowers.[34]

A half century later, we cannot say with confidence that these fears were unfounded. Although Stalin generally displayed caution in initiating military action across established boundaries, he was not shy about using his own or proxy forces, or the threat of such use, to probe an adversary's strength and intentions. He did so in Iran and Manchuria in 1946, in Greece from 1946 to 1948, against Turkey in 1946, Berlin in 1948, and South Korea in 1950. There is evidence that in 1949 and 1950 Stalin gave serious consideration to an invasion of Tito's Yugoslavia.[35]

In addition to what we know of the actions and plans of Stalin in the international arena, his behavior at home should not have inspired confidence among those seeking to gauge his potential for mischief abroad. Scholars have uniformly conceded that he was a mass murderer in his own domain, but some have denied the pertinence of this fact in estimating his intentions beyond Soviet borders.[36] This view needs to be challenged. The course of a ruler at home, particularly one with the near-absolute power enjoyed by Stalin, reveals what he will do when free from external restraint and thus can—indeed must—be considered by foreign observers when trying to anticipate his actions abroad in cases where the balance of power tips in his favor. If a good Niebuhrian must accept the inherent sinfulness of all humankind, one can also suspect, without straying from the fold, that some of us harbor a more hefty dose of evil than others. When we look at the combination of Stalin's actions on the Soviet periphery after World War II and his course inside the Soviet Union during his lengthy reign, we should have no difficulty summoning a modicum of sympathy for alarmists within the national security bureaucracy in Washington during the early months of 1950. Military historian Allan Millett wrote that "the United States cannot make major changes in its defense policy without an international crisis, for only such a crisis creates the domestic political consensus for change. . . . [The Korean War] provided the required crisis in 1950 to move the United States to a defense policy that would make the foreign policy of 'containment' viable."[37] It is possible that, had the Korean War not broken out when it did, some other crisis would have occurred, most likely in the Balkans over a Soviet bloc attack on Yugoslavia. Given the complex nationalities question there, the suitability of the terrain for and the expertise of Tito's forces in guerrilla warfare, and the proximity of Yugoslavia to the focal point of the cold war, a war in the Balkans would have been extraordinarily difficult to contain or to end. Unlike in Korea, the United States would not have intervened quickly with its own forces, but as the fighting continued it would have become more and more deeply engaged, with the prospect of a direct Soviet-American clash increasing by the day. In the absence of a crisis in Korea, an eruption in the Balkans might well have taken place. A Balkan crisis would have provided an adequate context for American rearmament, but it could also easily have escalated into something even more destructive than what actually did occur in Korea.

Or, absent the Korean crisis, Stalin might have refused to provide the Americans with a context for major rearmament and continued to build up his atomic capability and his conventional military advantage in Europe. For the middle and long term, such a scenario would have encouraged military probes by the Soviets beyond their sphere and heightened the risk of superpower confrontation. In its timing and its location on the periphery of the Soviet-American contest, therefore, the Korean War may have been necessary to prevent something even worse. William J. Williams, who has entitled a volume of essays he edited on Korea *A Revolutionary War,* emphasizes along with Millett the impact of the event on the development of the Western military alliance;[38] but in its broadest sense Korea did not transform the international system as did World War II. Rather, it solidified the loose bipolar system that had emerged with the total defeat of Germany and Japan in 1945.

Koreans can hardly be expected to take much consolation from this analysis. For the rest of the world, the war was limited, both geographically and in weapons employed, but for Koreans it was the most devastating they had ever experienced. Korea's losses in the number of people killed, wounded, and missing approached three million, a tenth of the entire population. Another ten million Koreans saw their families divided; five million became refugees. In property, North Korea put its losses at $1.7 billion, South Korea at $2 billion, the equivalent of its gross national product for 1949. North Korea lost some eighty-seven hundred industrial plants, South Korea twice that number. Each area saw six hundred thousand homes destroyed.[39] Adding to the tragedy was the fact that the country remained divided, with little prospect for change in the foreseeable future.

The most positive light we can put on the war from the Koreans' perspective is that, once over, it was unlikely to resume. The peninsula had become an armed camp, the world in miniature, but never again would the United States lower its guard there as it had in the year before June 1950. In 1951 it had held firm in negotiations with the other side for several months to secure a defensible armistice line. When the shooting stopped in July 1953, Washington quickly negotiated a security pact with Seoul and mobilized contributors to the UN war effort to join in a warning of an expanded war if the fighting resumed; it also maintained sizable forces in Korea and continued to train and arm the much-expanded Republic of Korea armed forces. Simultaneously, the United States made clear to its ally that any move northward would result in the withdrawal of support. For their part, the Soviets and the Chinese did nothing to encourage Kim Il-sung to repeat his adventure of the summer of 1950. As political scientist B. C. Koh observed, the war led the North Korean leader to downgrade "the use of military force . . . from a practical to a theoretical option."[40] Although neither side proved scrupulous in abiding by the limitations in the armistice agreements regarding increased armed capabilities, the balance of forces and clarity of purpose of the great powers on both sides kept the peace.

We must never lose sight of the pain and suffering the war produced, whether in Korea or worldwide. Less than four months before the fighting ended, U.S. President Eisenhower spoke movingly about the depressing future of the world if current trends continued. The worst prospect was atomic war, the horrors of which he found no need to describe. Even the best prospect was hardly pleasant to contemplate:

> [A] life of perpetual fear and tension; a burden of arms draining the wealth and the labor of all peoples; a wasting of strength that defies . . . any system to achieve true abundance and happiness for the peoples of this earth.[41]

If a fair portion of that fear and tension preexisted June 25, 1950, there can be no doubt that the Korean War greatly exacerbated their scope and depth. It also made more likely an American decision to engage in limited war at some point in the future.

Yet an atomic war did not occur, then or later, nor did a clash between the great powers on a scale remotely comparable to the two of the first half of the twentieth century. In contemplating the impact of the Korean War on "the long peace" between the superpowers in the aftermath of the holocausts of 1914–1918 and 1939–1945, we should consider the possibility that the sacrifices endured from 1950 to 1953, however tragic, were not entirely in vain.

## Notes

1. Chen Jian, *China's Road to the Korean War* (New York: Columbia University Press, 1994); Robert Futrell, *The United States Air Force in Korea, 1950–1953* (New York: Duell, Sloan & Pearce, 1961); William Stueck, *The Korean War: An International History* (Princeton: Princeton University Press, 1995).

2. Clay Blair, *The Forgotten War: America in Korea, 1950–1953* (New York: New York Times Books, 1987).

3. Bevin Alexander, *Korea, The First War We Lost* (New York: Hippocrene Books, 1986).

4. Ibid., ix.

5. Robert R. Simmons, *The Strained Alliance: Peking, P'yongyang, Moscow, and the Politics of the Korean Civil War* (New York: Free Press, 1975), xv. Although he does not use "civil war" in any of his titles, Bruce Cumings has done more to promote the theme than has any other author. See his *The Origins of the Korean War*, vol. 1, *Liberation and the Emergence of Separate Regimes 1945–1957*, and vol. 2, *The Roaring of the Cataract* (Princeton: Princeton University Press, 1981 and 1990).

6. See my "The United States, the Soviet Union, and the Division of Korea: A Comparative Analysis," *Journal of American-East Asian Relations* 4 (spring 1995): 1–27.

7. See Internet H-Diplo message of 18 May 1995 by Gyoo Kahng, then of Ohio University.

8. Cumings, *Origins*, 2: 770.

9. Ibid., 2: 771.

10. Kathryn Weathersby, "Korea, 1949–50: To Attack or Not to Attack? Stalin, Kim Il-sung, and the Prelude to War," *Bulletin of the Cold War International History Project* (spring 1995): 2.

11. Sergei Goncharov, John W. Lewis, and Xue Litai, *Uncertain Partners: Stalin, Mao, and the Korean War* (Stanford: Stanford University Press, 1993), chap. 5; Kathryn Weathersby, "New Findings on the Korean War," *Bulletin of the Cold War International History Project* (fall 1993): 1, 14–18. For up-to-date information on the Soviet side in the origins of the Korean War, see Weathersby, "'Should We Fear This?' Stalin and the Korean War," paper presented at the conference "Stalin and the Cold War," Yale University, September 1999. I wish to thank Dr. Weathersby for providing me with a copy of this paper.

12. Yu Sŏng-chŏl, "My Testimony," part 8, published initially in Korean in *Hanguk Ilbo*, 9 November 1990; translated into English and published in *Foreign Broadcast Information Service*, 27 December 1990.

13. Cumings, *Origins*, 2: 770.

14. See, for example, Gabriel Jackson, *The Spanish Republic and the Civil War 1931–1939* (Princeton: Princeton University Press, 1965).

15. Regarding the general analogy of Korea with the 1930s, historian Frank Ninkovich wrote recently that "the Spanish civil war resembled far more closely than Munich the problem faced by the West in Korea inasmuch as it was widely viewed as a test of the West's will to resist fascism. Even so, the parallel is far from exact. Despite a civil war whose contending factions were backed by ideologically hostile outside powers, there had been no occupation or territorial division, no collective security commitment by the League of Nations, and, from the American perspective, the Spanish civil war could not be evaluated in the kind of black-and-white terms used in Korea." See Ninkovich, *Modernity and Power: A History of the Domino Theory in the Twentieth Century* (Chicago: University of Chicago Press, 1994), 374 n. 55.

16. On land reform in South Korea, see Donald Stone MacDonald, *U.S.–Korean Relations from Liberation to Self-Reliance: The Twenty-Year Record* (Boulder, CO: Westview Press, 1992), 234–35. On the land reform issue in South Vietnam, see Frances Fitzgerald, *Fire in the Lake: The Vietnamese and the Americans in Vietnam* (Boston: Little, Brown, 1972), 120–25, 152–57.

17. Cumings and his coauthor Jon Halliday entitle their pictorial history of the war *Korea: The Unknown War* (New York: Pantheon Books, 1988).

18. Callum A. MacDonald, *Korea, the War Before Vietnam* (New York: Free Press, 1986).

19. Ibid., 263.

20. Yuen Foong Khong, *Analogies at War: Korea, Munich, Dien Bien Phu, and the Vietnam Decisions of 1965* (Princeton: Princeton University Press, 1992), chap. 5. For the Ball memorandum of 5 October 1964, see the *Atlantic Monthly*, July 1972, 35–49.

21. John Mueller, *Retreat from Doomsday: The Obsolescence of Major War* (New York: Basic Books, 1989), 118, 129–31.

22. Ibid., 129.

23. David Rees, *Korea: The Limited War* (New York: St. Martin's Press, 1964), xi.

24. George F. Kennan, *American Diplomacy, 1900–1950* (Chicago: University of Chicago Press, 1951), 59.

25. Rees, *Limited War*, 446.

26. Rosemary Foot, *The Wrong War: American Policy and the Dimensions of the Korean Conflict, 1950–1953* (Ithaca, NY: Cornell University Press, 1985), 23. For Bradley's statement, see U.S. Senate Committees on Armed Services and Foreign Relations, *Military Situation in the Far East*, 82nd Cong., 1st sess., 1951, 731–32.

27. Foot, *Wrong War*, 23.

28. See, for example, Reinhold Niebuhr, *The Irony of American History: Moral Man and Immoral Society* (New York: Scribner, 1932).

29. Reinhold Niebuhr, "Human Nature and Social Change," *Christian Century* 50 (1953): 363.

30. Thomas W. Smith, "The Uses of Tragedy: Reinhold Niebuhr's Theory of History and International Ethics," *Ethics in International Affairs* 9 (1995): 179.

31. The document is published in U.S. Department of State, *Foreign Relations of the United States, 1950*, vol. 1 (Washington, DC: Government Printing Office, 1976), 235–92.

32. David Holloway, *Stalin and the Bomb: The Soviet Union and Atomic Energy 1939–1956* (New Haven: Yale University Press, 1994), 232, 240–41.

33. *Public Papers of the Presidents of the United States: Harry S Truman, 1950* (Washington, DC: Government Printing Office, 19??), 286.

34. See, for example, U.S. Department of State, *Foreign Relations of the United States, 1950*, vol. 1 (Washington, DC: Government Printing Office, 1976), 145–46, 293. After the outbreak of war in Korea, the U.S. Central Intelligence Agency upped their likelihood that the Soviet Union would "'deliberately provoke' a general war in the near future." See Marc Trochtenberg, "Melvyn Leffler and the Origins of the Cold War," *Orbis* (summer 1995): 452–53.

35. Bela Kiraly, "The Aborted Soviet Military Plans Against Tito's Yugoslavia," in *At the Brink of War and Peace: The Tito-Stalin Split in Historic Perspective*, ed. Wayne S. Vucinich (New York: Brooklyn College Press, 1982), 273–88. Regarding the general caution of Stalin when considering overt military action across established boundaries, recently available documentation indicates that in April he approved of Kim Il-sung's idea to begin fighting on the Ongjin Peninsula, an isolated area on the west coast of Korea. The area had been the site of numerous skirmishes between North and South Korean troops, many of which were initiated by the South. Kim could claim that the South had attacked first; then he could launch a well-prepared counterattack along the entire thirty-eighth parallel, making plausible the assertion that the South had initiated hostilities. On the eve of the June attack, however, Stalin approved a shift in this strategy to make the outbreak of hostilities on the Ongjin Peninsula virtually simultaneous with the offensive elsewhere. This was because Kim had received information from intelligence sources that South Korea had received wind of the impending attack, thus making haste critical in executing the main attack. Still, hostilities did begin in Ongjin slightly before those in the other areas and the North Koreans did claim their offensive to be a counterattack. See Weathersby, "'Should We Fear This?'" 13, 17–18.

36. See, for example, Daniel Yergin, *Shattered Peace: The Origins of the Cold War and the National Security State* (Boston: Houghton Mifflin, 1977).

37. Allan R. Millett, "The Right War: The Korean Conflict and the Revolution in United States Defense Policy, 1945–1955," paper presented at the Third International Conference on the Korean War, Seoul, 20 June 1991, 1–2, as quoted in William J. Williams, ed., *A Revolutionary War: Korea and the Transformation of the Postwar World* (Chicago: Imprint Publications, 1993), 1.

38. Ibid.

39. B. C. Koh, "The War's Impact on the Korean Peninsula," in *A Revolutionary War*, ed. Williams, 246.

40. Ibid., 254.

41. *Public Papers of the President of the United States: Dwight D. Eisenhower, 1953* (Washington, DC: Government Printing Office, 1966), 179–88.

# 11

## Imagining a Different Korea: What If . . .

*Chae-jin Lee, Donald Oberdorfer,*
*Byong-chu Koh, and William Stueck*
*Edited by Philip West*

As the chapters in this volume amply show, the process and art of re-membering lead to diverging and conflicting interpretations of war. They remind us that there are many different kinds of remembering. The mean-ings of war that we glean from history books can be very different from those gleaned from art and poetry. And because the exercise of remem-bering is tied so closely to the human feelings of sorrow, suffering, hor-ror, and regret, remembering creates an urgency in asking the question "Why?" Isn't there some way that war and all its suffering could have been avoided? The questions of the war's origins and the events leading up to the war hold particular urgency for Korean people, whose suffer-ing dwarfs that of any other people involved. Why, after the Japanese surrender in 1945, was Korea divided in the first place? Could the war have been fought differently? Could it have ended differently, perhaps with less bitterness and divisiveness on the Korean peninsula? And there is the terribly human question—however much we may aspire to delay judgment—of who is responsible, and who is to blame.

In his *What If?: The World's Foremost Historians Imagine What Might Have Been* (New York: Putnam, 1999) Robert Cowley reminds us that history indeed is "properly the literature of what did happen." But, he adds, "[T]hat should not diminish the importance of the counterfactual." The "what if" exercise examines and questions long-held assumptions that we bring, as writers, teachers, and students, to the study of war.

Entertaining "what-if" questions reminds us of the decisive impact that decisions of individual people can have on how wars are started, fought, and ended. Think, for example, of the many turns in the war affected by decisions made at particular moments by Kim Il-sung or Syngman Rhee, Truman or Stalin or Mao, MacArthur or Peng Dehuai. And then ask how their attitudes and assumptions about other peoples and about friends and enemies affected those decisions, made at times in split seconds. Engaging in the exercise of counterfactuals can sensitize us to the dangers of fraudulent or biased hindsight inherent in committing ourselves to explanations of war, even those made by the most careful scholars, that can distort or misrepresent the way war really happened. Much as we like to think otherwise, Cowley writes, "Outcomes are no more certain in history than they are in our own lives. If nothing else, the diverging tracks in the undergrowth of history celebrate the infinity of human options. The road not taken belongs on the map" (pp. 1–2).

In the counterfactual exercise that follows we have solicited the views of four experts, whose books on Korea and the Korean War have been highly reviewed in both the United States and Korea. For Chae-jin Lee, it is *The Korean War: 40 Year Perspectives* (Keck Strategic Studies, 1990); for William Stueck, it is *The Korean War: An International History* (Princeton University Press, 1995); for Byong-chu Koh, it is *The Foreign Policy Systems of North and South Korea* (1984); and for Donald Oberdorfer, it is *The Two Koreas: A Contemporary History* (Basic Books, 1997). Theirs are the voices of scholarship—political science, history, and journalism. Their responses to the counterfactual questions remind us how difficult it is to know enough and to be fair and evenhanded in writing about the Korean War. War by nature is a fight contested by all sides, and the fighting stories are told and retold for years and decades. The counterfactuals may give some rest to the enduring questions of right and wrong and who is to blame. But the discussion does not end. The comfort in finding explanations does not always last. Even the experts may never agree on the answers. In some mysterious calculus, the urgency of these questions seems to match our inability to agree on the answers and may explain the universal and enduring human fascination for the stories of war.

*How might the Korean peninsula look today had the United States occupied all of Korea, as it did Japan? Similarly, how might the peninsula look today had it been occupied by the Soviet Union?*

## Chae-jin Lee

If the United States had occupied all of Korea at the end of the Second World War, the Korean peninsula might have been placed under U.S. tutelage (direct rule) for a relatively long period of time (perhaps ten to fifteen years); afterward, the United States might have preferred to make the peninsula an independent, united, and neutral state as a buffer zone—more like Switzerland than Japan. The success or failure of this policy might have depended upon Korea's internal political development as much as its external environment. If, however, the Soviet Union had occupied all of Korea, the Soviet Union might have sponsored and sustained a pro-Moscow government on the peninsula. However, as the Sino-Soviet conflict developed, Korea might have become a Titoist state by asserting a degree of independence from both Moscow and Beijing.

## Donald Oberdorfer

If the Korean peninsula had been unified at the end of World War II rather than divided at the thirty-eighth parallel, the situation within the peninsula would have been more settled and less tense than it has been in the past half century. There would have been no Korean War and no painful division of an ancient nation.

Had the United States occupied the entire peninsula, a U.S.–dominated state would have bordered on both China and the Soviet Union. This would have been uncomfortable for all three major powers. Very likely there would have been a highly militarized border between Korea and the two communist powers, at least until the 1980s. When the détente era began to take hold in the 1970s, Koreans would probably have been more eager than the United States to forge cordial relations with its big-power neighbors, and possibly more successful at it. Domestically, Korea would probably have been on a more predictable, less tortuous path toward political maturity than was the case, especially because the Korean military would have been less dominant. Park Chung Hee's coup and lengthy authoritarian rule would not have set back Korean democracy. On the other hand, his powerful leadership in economic development would also not have taken place, so Korea would have had more measured—but perhaps more soundly based—economic growth.

Had the entire peninsula been occupied by the Soviet Union in 1945, the line of international tension and potential East-West conflict would have been drawn through the Sea of Japan or, as the Koreans term it, the East Sea, with a Soviet-dominated Korea on one side and a U.S.–oriented Japan on the other. Because the Soviet pressure on Japan would have been much more tangible, Japanese remilitarization would have been more likely, raising great fears among Koreans. Soviet dominance in Korea would, over time, have led to tense relations with China, because the Yalu River and other boundaries would have been, in effect, an extension of the Sino-Soviet border. Domestically, Korea would probably have resembled East Germany, with a very strong Moscow influence, because of its vulnerability to Chinese and USSR influences. Korea's political development as well as its economic development would have been retarded, at least until the Gorbachev era began in the mid-1980s.

### Byong-chu Koh

Had the United States occupied all of Korea following Japan's surrender in 1945, the Korean peninsula would have remained unified territorially, if not ideologically. The tragedy of the Korean War would have been obviated. Korea would have experienced occupation by the U.S. forces, and American military rule would have ensued. The latter, however, would most probably have come to an end within three to five years. There would not have been any compelling reason for the United States to request UN assistance in setting up a government in Korea. Elections for a constituent parliament (national assembly) could have been organized and supervised by the U.S. occupation forces.

What type of government would have emerged under these circumstances? Syngman Rhee (Yi Sŭng-man) would have faced many rivals in the political arena—such as Kim Ku, Kim Kyu-sik, Cho Man-sik, and Yŏ Un-hyŏng. Any one of these leaders would have been elected president by the constituent national assembly. One cannot rule out the possibility that the latter would have opted for a parliamentary system of government.

Regardless of what the national assembly might have done, the path to democracy would have been rocky. The absence of any experience with democracy and the fragmentation of the political scene would have hampered a smooth transition. And one cannot be sure that the government that would have emerged would have had the vision and capability to pursue socioeconomic reform and accelerated development. Eventually, however, democracy would have become consolidated, and economic growth would have occurred. There is a good chance, then, that Korea would have joined the ranks of stable democracies with solid economic foundations.

Had the Soviet Union, not the United States, occupied all of Korea in 1945, Korea would most probably have become a Soviet satellite like most of the Central European countries and Mongolia. The only positive aspect of this scenario is that the fratricidal civil war would not have erupted. Both politically and economically, however, Korea would be incomparably worse off than it is today. This is likely to be the case notwithstanding the harsh reality that today's Korea is no paradise. But instead of having only half the peninsula and a third of its population suffering in an Orwellian political system that is incapable of feeding its citizens, the whole peninsula and all of its inhabitants would be enduring the unendurable and tottering on the brink of a famine.

It is possible, of course, that Korea would have managed to jettison the shackles of Leninism and command economy alike in the wake of the collapse of socialism in and the disintegration of the Soviet Union, as the latter's former satellites in Eastern Europe have done. For even a Kim Il-sung would have found a unified peninsula harder to govern and the denizens of the southern half less malleable than their brethren in the northern half. Even if that had been the case, however, the political and economic conditions in Korea would be closer to those in Romania or Slovakia than to those of Poland, Hungary, or the Czech Republic, let alone those of South Korea today.

## William Stueck

The first question is more difficult to answer than the second, because the Soviet Union was in a much better position to stir up trouble in Korea under an American occupation than the Americans were under a Soviet occupation. The Soviets could have made the U.S. position difficult by supplying subversive elements within Korea who had spent the twenties, thirties, and early forties in Manchuria or the Soviet Union. It is unlikely that the United States would have done much from Japan to undermine the Soviets had they occupied the entire peninsula.

There is an excellent chance that, in the latter case, the Soviets would have chosen the young Kim Il-sung as the leader of an independent Korea and that he would have survived in power until he died in the mid-1990s. Although he would have possessed the advantage from the start of better-balanced economic resources, there is an excellent chance that Kim would have left Korea largely as he left North Korea—increasingly an economic basket case that would only get worse under his chosen successor. It is also possible that China would have intervened right up to the present to prevent the collapse of the regime, although the absence of an alternative (the Republic of Korea) closely allied to the United States might have made a difference here.

Under the scenario of an American occupation, Korea would clearly have faced serious problems at the beginning. Yet the American occupation would not have faced problems as severe as it did in relation to economic dislocation and refugees. It is also quite possible that Syngman Rhee would not have emerged as the top political leader as he did in the South. It is a good guess that the process of occupation and movement toward independence would not have been pretty but, in the end, would have resulted in an anticommunist government closely tied to the United States. With many bumps along the way, my surmise is that Korea in the present would be as or more prosperous economically and as democratic politically as South Korea is today. However, for this to be the result, an anticommunist government would have had to weather the storm that undoubtedly would have resulted from the communist victory on mainland China. It is by no means certain that the United States would have been as protective of a united Korea faced with serious internal turmoil as it was of a South Korea under conventional military attack from a Soviet- and Chinese-supported North Korea.

*How might your interpretation of the American role in post–World War II Korea be different, had the U.S. military been less involved than it was in the suppression of the rebellions in the South in 1948 and 1949?*

### Byong-chu Koh

The American role in post–World War II Korea had both positive and negative aspects. Of the latter, support for the conservative forces, failure to take effective measures to address the glaring inequities in socioeconomic conditions, and suppression of rebellions in the South stand out. All of these factors, of course, were interrelated. Had American policy been half as enlightened as that in occupied Japan, things might have turned out much better for all concerned. Had Americans on the scene had wisdom and foresight, they could have prevented or stopped the atrocities committed by the South Koreans against their brethren.

## William Stueck

It's hard to imagine informed Americans not regretting the U.S. role in the suppression of the rebellions in South Korea during 1948 and 1949. There was the mitigating factor—on the mainland at least—of those rebellions being supported by the North Koreans and the Soviets, although the degree of support remains in question. But there is no question that the sources of the rebellions were, to a considerable extent, the outgrowth of local conditions and that those conditions were partly the result of U.S. policies.

South Korea is the one occupation after World War II over which Americans have little reason to be proud. In the end, and with hindsight, we can say that it *may* have saved Koreans from something even worse, but it must be admitted that much that went on during the occupation was a result of narrow-mindedness, ignorance, and extraordinary insensitivity. It fits in rather well with a fair portion of U.S. foreign policy in the Third World.

*How good might the chances have been for a unified Korea to emerge, had the outside powers not been involved on the peninsula in the five years following the Japanese surrender?*

## Chae-jin Lee

If the outside powers had not been directly involved in postwar Korea, there might have been a prolonged period of chaotic and violent situations in Korea, which could have brought about civil strife among the contending forces and might have led to Korea's eventual unification by military means or negotiated compromises. (The unification by the Silla Dynasty and the establishment of the Koryo Dynasty may suggest a way to consider a possible scenario. Nicaragua, Zaire, and other contemporary cases may be useful, too.)

## Donald Oberdorfer

I think the chances for a united Korea would have been better but a unified outcome still not certain. The border skirmishes between the South and North in the late 1940s would have escalated to more intense struggles. Over time these might have brought about conquest of one side by the other or, on the other hand, a more serious effort by both sides to negotiate unification or, more likely, a confederation arrangement leading to eventual unification. However, once the peninsula was divided as it was, it was probably unrealistic to believe that the outside powers would stay out.

## Byong-chu Koh

If one can assume that the Japanese colonial authorities could have peacefully evacuated all Japanese, both civilian and military, from the peninsula, the chances of territorial division would have diminished measurably or even evaporated altogether. Given the Korean people's lack of any firsthand exposure to democracy and given their notorious propensity to engage in factional disputes, the political arena would undoubtedly have verged on chaos. On the other hand, leaders of the various groups—the returnees from China, those from the United States, nationalists, communists, and others—might eventually have succeeded in reaching a modus vivendi. Formation of a unified government by the Koreans themselves, in other words, was not beyond the realm of feasibility.

## William Stueck

It is hard to imagine outside powers not being involved on the peninsula after World War II, given the Japanese presence there during the war and the location of the country. If events had played out that way, however, Korea in all likelihood would have been unified within a decade. The chances of that unity emerging without substantial civil conflict are, nonetheless, small.

*In retrospect, how would you assess President Truman's policy in Korea? Are there points along the way when Truman might have acted differently and thereby softened the war's tragic results?*

## Chae-jin Lee

In retrospect, it might have been better for all parties concerned if Truman had (1) stopped at the thirty-eighth parallel in October 1950, (2) let only South Korean troops cross the parallel, (3) stopped at the Pyongyang-Wonsan line to seek a negotiated ceasefire, or (4) heeded China's warnings seriously and accommodated some of its demands and interests prior to its intervention in the war.

## Donald Oberdorfer

For Truman, like most other great power leaders most of the time, Korea was a low-priority area until crisis erupted. Had Truman decided that Korea was an area of important interest to the United States and clearly communicated this to Moscow, there would have been no Korean War, because Stalin was anxious not to confront the United States militarily. Truman's actions in June 1950 in sending U.S. troops to reverse the North Korean invasion was sensible and proper, but an earlier show of interest and strength would have made it unnecessary. As for the conduct of the war itself, Truman might have fired MacArthur earlier. If Ridgway or another U.S. commander had refrained from approaching the Chinese border and restrained the South Koreans from doing so, Chinese intervention would have been less likely.

## Byong-chu Koh

I believe that President Truman's decision to intervene in the Korean War was exceedingly beneficial to the Korean people. Had it not been for the U.S. intervention, Korea would have become a communist country under Kim Il-sung. Nor is it conceivable that Korea, albeit only half of it, would emerge as a powerhouse in global trade and achieve a relatively smooth transition to democracy. If Truman had not opted for an all-out victory and had stopped the UN forces at the thirty-eighth parallel in the fall of 1950, however, the war could have ended much sooner, and vast numbers of lives on all sides would have been saved. Because the territorial gain for the South at the end of the three-year conflict was marginal, such a decision would have been most welcome.

## William Stueck

Clearly Truman erred in withdrawing the last U.S. troops from Korea in June 1949. It is not at all beyond the realm of possibility that relative peace could have been maintained on the peninsula indefinitely had the United States made a concerted effort at deterrence.

Truman also erred in crossing the thirty-eighth parallel in October 1950. Had he not done so, the war could have ended at that time, although the Syngman Rhee regime and many Koreans in the South would have been outraged at the loss of opportunity to reunify the peninsula.

Finally, Truman's decision to stand firm on the issue of Chinese POWs in February 1952 probably prolonged the war for over a year. I find this decision more defensible than the first two, but I still doubt that it was worth the death and destruction in Korea from the spring of 1952 into the summer of 1953 to save some fifteen thousand Chinese prisoners from an unpleasant life back in China.

That said, Truman certainly erred in permitting a slowdown of UN military operations on the ground after the agreement on the armistice line in November 1951. This enabled the communists to dig in over the next several months, which put them in a strong position to resist U.S. demands on the POW issue. Higher casualties on both sides in the short term *probably* would have saved lives in the long term.

*What do you think were the major barriers that prolonged the war after the military stalemate had been reached in the summer of 1951? Relatedly, how important is the handling of the POW issue, on all sides, in shaping the outcomes and contested interpretations of the war since 1953?*

## Chae-jin Lee

The major barriers that prolonged the war after July 1951 were a series of disputes and disagreements over the POW issue and a line of military demarcation. If the United States had honored a provision (Article 118) of the 1947 Geneva Convention which mandated the repatriation of all POWs without delay after active hostilities ceased, refrained from insisting on the principle of voluntary repatriation, and accepted the status quo antebellum (namely, the restoration of the thirty-eighth parallel), a cease-fire agreement might have been concluded much earlier; it could have significantly reduced the number of casualties and the loss of resources on all sides.

## Donald Oberdorfer

We know now from the Soviet and Chinese archives that the major barrier to the settlement of the war from mid-1951 was one man—Joseph

Stalin—who insisted that the war continue even after the battered North Koreans were ready to quit and after major elements of the Chinese party and state were also ready to end it. In the summer of 1951, Stalin rebuffed those on the communist side who wanted to negotiate an armistice, and after that, he never wavered. Only two weeks after Stalin's death in March 1953, the Soviet government reversed Stalin's position and began to search for a peaceful solution. The handling of the POW issue postponed the final result, but was secondary to the fundamental decision on the part of Stalin.

## Byong-chu Koh

The perception by both sides that a victory was still within their grasp may have been one factor in the equation. The communist side, in particular, lacked a real incentive to push for an early termination of the hostilities through negotiation. The POW issue was an important one, and I believe that the UN side made a right decision when it rejected the communist side's demand for their unconditional repatriation. Syngman Rhee's unilateral decision to release "anticommunist" POWs under South Korean custody in the spring of 1953 was reckless, nearly torpedoing the armistice agreement that was close to being wrapped up. From his perspective and, perhaps, from the standpoint of South Korea's national interests as well, however, Rhee's action was not only understandable but, ultimately, productive. Substantial "payoffs" Seoul received from Washington, not the least of which was the U.S.–ROK mutual defense treaty, might not have materialized had it not been for Rhee's intransigence.

## William Stueck

Second question first. I'm not sure that there exists an "uncontested" interpretation of the war. As to "outcomes," I'm not sure what you mean.

Nearly five months were taken up agreeing on an armistice line. American insistence on a defensible line, namely the battle line rather than the thirty-eighth parallel, was definitely worth the effort, because it enhanced deterrence later on. Four more months were taken up resolving such issues as the rebuilding of airfields, the buildup of troops, supplies and weapons, and inspection. These agreements did not hold up long in the postarmistice period. The remainder of the delay was over the POW issue.

The above relates to specifics. The difficulty in working out specifics, however, related to a larger hostility and distrust on both sides, which was rooted in history and an ideological struggle that gave added symbolic significance to every concession made by each side. The issue of the fate of Chinese POWs, for example, related directly to the ongoing civil war between the nationalists and communists and to the larger ideological struggle between liberal democracy and authoritarian communism.

# Contributors

**Max Desfor**, longtime correspondent (forty-five years) with the Associated Press and later with *US News & World Report*; Pulitzer Award for photograph of Korean refugees fleeing over the destroyed Taedong River Bridge in December 1950; other Asian assignments included the Battle of Saipan, the Olympics in Japan, and the Nixon trip to China.

**William D. Ehrhart,** coeditor with Philip K. Jason, *Retrieving Bones: Stories and Poems of the Korean War* (1999); author, *Ordinary Lives: Platoon 1005 and the Vietnam War* (1999), *Beautiful Wreckage: New and Selected Poems* (1999); *To Those Who Have Gone Home Tired* (1984); U.S. Marine Corps, 1966–1969, Sergeant, Purple Heart.

**Donald Gregg**, President and Chairman of the Board, The Korea Society, New York, since 1993, upon completing forty-three years in U.S. government service; National Security Advisor to President George Bush, 1982; American Ambassador to South Korea, 1989–1992; Central Intelligence Agency assignments in Japan, Burma, Vietnam, and Korea.

**Steven I. Levine**, Mansfield Professor of Asia Pacific Studies, The University of Montana; author, *Anvil of Victory: The Communist Revolution in Manchuria, 1945–1948* (1987); coeditor, with James Hsiung, *China's Bitter Victory: The War With Japan, 1937–1945* (1992); coeditor, with Philip West, *America's Wars in Asia: A Cultural Approach to History and Memory* (1998).

**Lary L. May**, Professor of American Studies and History at The University of Minnesota; cochair with Elaine Tyler May, Program Committee, American Studies Association, 1990; *Recasting America: Culture and Politics in the Age of the Cold War* (1989); *The Big Tomorrow: Hollywood and the Politics of the American Way* (2000).

**Roe Jae-ryung**, lecturer in Art History, Kyungwon University, Seoul; Curator, National Museum of Contemporary Art, Seoul, 1989–1995; Rockefeller Fellow, Humanities Program, New York, 1993–1994; guest editor, *Art and Asia Pacific*, 1996; work in progress, book on contemporary Korean art.

**William Stueck**, Professor of History, University of Georgia; author, *The Wedemeyer Mission: American Politics and Foreign Policy During the Cold War* (1984); *The Road to Confrontation: American Policy Toward China and Korea, 1947–1950* (1987); *The Korean War, An International History* (1995).

**Suh Ji-moon,** Professor of English, Korea University, Seoul; editor and translator of Korean literature into English, *The Rainy Spell and Other Korean Stories* (revised and expanded, 1997), *The Descendants of Cain* (1997), and *The Golden Phoenix: Seven Contemporary Korean Short Stories* (1998); selected commentary and essays for Korean newspapers (published in Korean).

**Philip West,** Director of the Maureen and Mike Mansfield Center, The University of Montana; author, *Yenching University and Sino-Western Relations, 1916–1952* (nominated by Harvard University Press for a Pulitzer Award in 1976); coeditor with Frans A. Am Alting von Geusau, *The Pacific Rim and the Western World* (1987); coeditor with Steven I. Levine, *America's Wars in Asia: A Cultural Approach to History and Memory* (1998).

# Index